Louis Proal

Political Crime

Louis Proal

Political Crime

ISBN/EAN: 9783743407794

Manufactured in Europe, USA, Canada, Australia, Japa

Cover: Foto ©Suzi / pixelio.de

Manufactured and distributed by brebook publishing software (www.brebook.com)

Louis Proal

Political Crime

POLITICAL CRIME

BY

LOUIS PROAL

WITH AN INTRODUCTION
BY Prof. FRANKLIN H. GIDDINGS
OF COLUMBIA UNIVERSITY

NEW YORK
D. APPLETON AND COMPANY
1898

COPYRIGHT, 1898,
BY D. APPLETON AND COMPANY.

INTRODUCTION.

Monsieur Louis Proal, a judge of the Court of Appeal at Aix, is a recognised authority on the theory of crime and punishment. His first important work, "Le Crime et La Peine," published at Paris in 1892, was crowned by the Institute. Offering an interpretation of increasing crime different from that which had been forced upon public attention by criminal anthropologists, it insisted upon the reality of moral responsibility and the duty of the state to punish the evil-doer. It was marked throughout by a sincere ethical spirit as well as by scientific carefulness, and was a much-needed corrective of the more extreme "anthropological" views of the Italian school. In 1895 appeared the work here translated, "La Criminalité Politique."

The term "political crime" has two meanings. Perhaps the more familiar one is that of crimes against governments, such as treason, insurrection, and rebellion. The phrase is used in this sense by the Italian writers Lombroso and Laschi in their work "Il delitto politico e le rivoluzioni in rapporto al diritto, all antropologia criminale ed alla scienza di governo" (Political Crime and Revolutions). The other meaning is that of crimes perpetrated by governments for alleged reasons of state, and by politicians for alleged reasons of expediency or for political advantage. It is this latter sort of political crime that M. Proal chiefly deals with in the present volume. Beginning with the history of Machiavellism, he takes up in order assassination, anarchy, political hatreds, political hypocrisy, political spoliation, the corruption of politicians, electoral corruption, the corruption of law and justice by politics, and the corruption of manners. All of these topics he considers at length and with much detail of historical fact. The teachings of political leaders, churchmen, and moralists in regard to them he subjects to a critical examination; and he tries to analyze the general opinion or sentiment of society upon them as it has been historically manifested at different times and places. The book may therefore be described as a first attempt conceived in the modern scientific spirit, to establish as a true induction the ancient conviction that "righteousness exalteth a nation."

The American edition of this book appears at an opportune moment. Both the scholar and "the plain man" are giving to the critical examination of actual politics an amount of time and effort comparable only to the time and effort that were bestowed upon political theories a century ago. This is true not only in Europe, where liberal government is yet on trial, but also in the United States, where an unprecedented campaign has recently been fought through to a remarkable triumph on the single question whether common honesty shall be the cornerstone of our financial policy. Everywhere men are acknowledging the duty so impressively emphasized by President Cleveland at the Princeton University sesquicentennial ceremonies, of that attention to politics which has in the past been regarded too much as a privilege. Moreover, this awakening is quite as distinctly ethical as intellectual. The present age has cared for science rather than for conscience, and in politics it has valued intellectual clearness more than devotion to principle. There are multiplying signs that conscience is again asserting its authority, and that the masses of the people intend, in the near future, to demand integrity no less than clearness and strength in the management of political affairs. The more thoughtful of our people are quite prepared to take to heart the admonition of Rabelais with which M. Proal so effectively concludes his argument, that science without conscience is the ruin of the soul, and that politics without morality are the ruin of society.

Most of the historical facts and illustrations that M. Proal has marshalled he has very naturally drawn from European chronicles. American history furnishes others that, if less sensational, horrible, or dramatic, are not less impressive. We have no long record of assassinations instigated by monarchs, like the murder of William of Orange by the will of Philip of Spain, or of infamous wars waged for trivial dynastic reasons, for ambition, for glory, or even for revenge; and yet, even of unjustifiable war our hands are not stainless. While conscientious and competent historians will continue to differ about the necessity of the Mexican War, there can be no such difference as to a long series of aggressions upon our native Indian tribes. When that noble-minded and gifted woman of letters, Mrs. Helen Hunt Jackson, turned aside from her original literary aims to tell the story of our Indian wars in the West, she brought together a mass of historical materials which fully justified the title of her book, "A Century of Dishonour."

The United States has been comparatively free, too, from crimes of theft or embezzlement by public officials. The stealings of the Tweed ring in New York city, and of Bardsley in Philadelphia, startled the people quite as much because of their unusual character as because of their enormity. Such crimes happily have been most infrequent in our State and national governments.

It has been in various forms of aggression, intimidation, and venal corruption that American political crime and immorality have most frequently been manifested. The "spoils system," whose first infamous advocate and sponsor in American politics was Aaron Burr, has consisted of a series of acts a very large proportion of which have been not merely political immoralities, but political crimes at positive law, and punishable as such by penalties of fine or imprisonment. Many of the acts of carpet-bag governments during the period of reconstruction were political crimes of the most high-handed description. Yet worse were the crimes of ballot-box stuffing and of intimidation at the polls which so frequently occurred in South Carolina, Mississippi, and other Southern States in 1875 and 1876. Whether or not the alleged "counting out" of Mr. Tilden, in the electoral canvass of 1876, was "the great fraud" which for years a prominent New York newspaper continued to call it, no historian will ever be able to deny that many specific official acts of that famous campaign and subsequent contest were technically and morally criminal. The people of New York have not yet fully forgotten, and we may hope they never will forget, the outrages perpetrated upon innocent individuals by the magistrates' courts and a black-mailing police, which were disclosed by the Lexow investigation.

Even more numerous than acts of wanton aggression have been acts of venal corruption. It is unpleasant to recall the " Crédit mobilier " scandal, the " story of Erie," the Indiana " blocks of five," the extensive bribery of the Massachusetts Legislature in the interests of West End rapid transit, and the crime of the Broadway franchise in New York city. Yet it is very necessary that from time to time we should recall these things, and soberly ask ourselves whether we are gradually diminishing their frequency, or permitting them to multiply until they shall threaten to destroy the reality of popular government.

To review these incidents of our history as we read M. Proal's argument, is necessarily sobering, but not by any means necessarily discouraging. And here I can not do better than conclude this introduction by repeating what I said in a review of M. Proal's volume when it first appeared in France.

Two unpleasant conclusions must be accepted as the starting points of our endeavours to make things better. The first is, that the active politician, the world over, continues to believe in the maxim that in politics, if not in individual conduct, the end justifies the means. The second is that, although the practical consequences of this maxim are invariably disastrous, they are often so involved or so long delayed that a presentation of the facts is more likely to confuse than to enlighten the average voter. The great value of M. Proal's work lies, first, in the success with which he has overcome this difficulty by extending his survey over a long period of time and by carefully attending to his perspective, and, secondly, in the skill with which he has exposed the essential sophistry of some of the more plausible disguises under which the maxim conceals itself. One of these is the dictum that the public safety, rather than reason, honour, or principle, is the supreme law; as if the very question of what the public safety requires could be answered if men forget principle and sneer at reason. Another is the contention that deceit is legitimate in party warfare, and lying in diplomacy. Among the strongest pages of M. Proal's volume are those which expose the imbecility, not to mention the peril, of diplomatic lying. Yet another sophism is the belief that stealing, defamation of character, and other iniquities are justifiable if they are in the order of "manifest destiny," or are contributory to a "cause." The defence which the "practical" man always sets up for his evil maxim is that in a finite world ethical rules after all are, like truth, purely relative. Accepting this idea without analyzing it, the practical man soon begins to sneer at "absolute" morality and at ideals, and to talk ponderously about the horrors that men of ideals and absolute standards, like Rousseau and Danton, have brought upon mankind. The plain truth of the matter, however, is that it is exactly this type of the practical man who is of all men the most abstract in his thinking, and whose ethics, such as he has, are of the most absolute sort. The doctrine that the end justifies the means is absolutism unqualified. It ignores the relativity of ends. The man who really understands that morality is relative, and who feels it as well, always remembers the relativity of the end in view not less than the relativity of the means that may be employed to its attainment, and he insists that the first comparison instituted shall be one between the ethical value of the end sought and that of the means chosen. Moreover, such a man will guard himself against an overvaluation of the desired end which would insidiously lead him to underrate the importance of choosing unquestionable means; and he will hold himself ready to make sacrifices or to endure suffering before adopting means that he would under other circumstances pronounce evil. Finally, it is only such a man who can really appreciate the great truth, which Burke so clearly and fully demonstrated, that in politics ends and means must be not only ethically but also historically right, as natural incidents in the normal and continuous evolution of a people.

FRANKLIN H. GIDDINGS.

COLUMBIA UNIVERSITY, *April, 1898.*

PREFACE.

The art of governing, that noble and important art, has been disfigured by a great number of false maxims, which have made of it the art of lying and deceiving, the art of proscribing and despoiling, under a cloak of legality. It is these sophisms that I propose to combat.

Side by side with the politicians who have governed in the national interest there are others who have only sought in the exercise of authority the satisfaction of their passions. It is these passions that I wish to study.

Humanity has had for its governors slaughterers, fanatics, robbers, false coiners, bankrupts, madmen, men who have been corrupt, and men who have sown corruption. Immense is the responsibility of these men, who, endowed with authority that they might enlighten and moralise the peoples over whom they were set, have depraved and degraded them by bad laws and a bad example. There are no greater malefactors than the political malefactors who foment divisions and hatreds by their ambition, cupidity, and rivalries. Ordinary evil-doers who are judged by the courts are only guilty of killing or robbing some few individuals; the number of their victims is restricted. Political malefactors, on the contrary, count their victims by the thousand; they corrupt and ruin entire nations.

Civilisation has accomplished improvements in every direction except in that of politics, which continue a field for the display of deceit, intrigue, and contempt for right and liberty. Contemporary society, which is so proud of its industrial progress and scientific discoveries, has less reason to plume itself when it takes stock of its political and financial customs. It may be able to show marvellous machines at exhibitions, but that great political machine, called the Government, is still very imperfect, and those who have charge of it are not always among the wisest or the most enlightened. "With us," as Littré remarked, "everything prospers with the exception of our political organisation, which, blundering, bad or senseless, robs us periodically of all our advantages."

In relating the crimes committed by political systems, based on craft and violence, my object has been to prove by facts that a loyal and honest policy is the only great policy; that politics, where they part company with morality, are demeaned to begin with, and degenerate as well into a matter of adventures and shifts; and finally, as Tacitus has said, that "there are no better instruments of good government than good men." *Vir bonus, discendi peritus* was Ciceros' definitio of orator. May not a statesman, if he is a true one, be defined as *Vir probusagendi peritus?*

The political question, just as the social question, is above all a moral question. The true aim of politics should be to render men more enlightened, more moral, more united, and happier. The best policy is, in consequence, that which accomplishes a little good, lessens unmerited suffering, appeases hatreds, encourages merit and labour, and develops the moral sense of the people. Political quarrels that turn upon questions of words or persons, merely agitate the country without being the cause of any progress. It is not ministerial combinations, ordinances decrees, or ill-considered, changeable, and multifarious laws that bring about the progress of society, but the sterling sentiments, the great thoughts, that come straight from the heart ; the good example set by those in authority. It is for this reason, that without going so far as to say with Plato, that States can only be governed by philosophers, I believe that power can only be wielded worthily by those who have some inkling of philosophy, and who possess principles inspired by some form of religious belief. A sincere spiritualism is the salt that keeps societies from corruption. Unfortunately this salt has, of late years, lost much of its efficacy in Europe.

I am aware that the passions will always play their part in politics. Still it is permissible to hope that politics may become more moral.

Human reason has brought about the disappearance of slavery and serfdom, of the privileges and omnipotence of kings. Why should it not succeed in introducing into politics a little more moderation and loyalty; a little more justice and humanity?

CONTENTS.

CHAPTER I.

MACHIAVELISM 1

Machiavelli not the inventor of Machiavelism—Demoralising effect of political power—The early years of tyrants show that it is power which demoralises them—Men in power are unscrupulous—Immorality of political maxims—The theory of two moralities—This theory held by the ancients—Cicero on political justice—Politics in the Middle Ages was the art of deceit and assassination—In modern times politics are not regulated by justice, but by reasons of State—Diplomacy a school of deceit—Machiavelli on the duties of ambassadors—Montaigne and the sixteenth century moralists on political deceit—Political assassinations: St. Bartholomew—Christian moralists and Machiavelism—Views of Bossuet, Fénelon, Massillon,—Machiavelism in the eighteenth century—Machiavelism and the French Revolution — Political doctrines of Mirabeau — Political doctrines of the principal Revolutionists: Danton — The Reign of Terror a practical application of Machiavelism—Robespierre a disciple of Machiavelli—Marat—Politics of Napoleon—Political crime is not justified by its results—Examples of this fact—The political blunders of Louis XIV. and Napoleon were also moral errors—A moral policy is the most successful policy.

CHAPTER II.

POLITICAL ASSASSINATION AND TYRANNICIDE 23

The bloodthirstiness of political passion—Political assassins—Murder of children on political grounds—Reasons of State urged to justify every possible crime—The massacre of prisoners during the French Revolution—Greek ideas regarding political assassination—Roman ideas regarding political assassination—Ideas of the Middle Ages regarding political assassination—Protestant and Catholic ideas regarding political assassination—The French Protestants and political assassination—Milton on tyrannicide—Catherine of Russia on tyrannicide—Views of the Jacobins and Emigrants—Political assassination in the nineteenth century—The assassination of tyrants does not destroy tyranny—The doctrine of regicide.

CHAPTER III.

ANARCHISM 49

Anarchism adopts the doctrine of tyrannicide—Resemblance between the Anarchists and Terrorists—the Nihilists—Kropotkine—Proudhon—The Ishmaelites — Anarchists and Capitalists — Jacobin and Anarchist theories—Babeuf's doctrine of Anarchy—Diderot and Rousseau on Equality—Social Equality is the aim of modern Anarchism—Proudhon the father of Anarchism—Anarchist views on property—Property and Crime—"Robbery is Restitution"—Equality and Liberty—Revolutions reveal the black side of human nature—Saint Simon on Capitalists—The social theories of Lammenais—Elisée Reclus on Equality—Anarchist programme—Anarchists and Militarism—Lammenais on Crime—Jonathan Swift on political corruption—Sentimentalism at the root of attacks on the Social system — Louis Blanc — Kropotkine's sentimentalism—Sentimentalism of the French Revolutionists—The Anarchist substitutes himself for the State—Anarchist view of human rights—Vanity and Fanaticism among Anarchists—The apologists of revolutionary crimes make Anarchists—Thiers on the Revolutionary Tribunal—The victims of books—Duties of the historian—The effects of the Revolution on France—Philosophical Materialism and Anarchism — Vaillant — Ravachol — Effects of philosophical materialism—The doctrine that society is responsible for all social miseries—Anarchists assert that they are the victims of society—Marat's hatred of society—The chief end of life according to Anarchism—The Christian view of wealth—Patriotism and Anarchism

—The aim of Anarchism and Socialism is to divide wealth—Revolutionary ideas and materialist theories—Nietzche's teaching—Christian morality and Anarchism—The classes who despise morality—The young Anarchists—Instruction without morals—The Anarchist Henry—Science cannot assure happiness—Intellectual poisons—Political Anarchy is the consequence of moral Anarchy—Views of Auguste Comte—Venal politicians and the unworthy rich are largely responsible for the growth of Anarchism.

CHAPTER IV.
POLITICAL HATREDS 105

The range of human hatred—War has been the normal condition of the human race—Causes of war—In international relations might is right—Man hates whatever differs from himself—Race hatreds—Statesmen inflame international animosities — Republicanism and war—Class animosities—Conflicts of classes in history—Contemporary class hatreds—Party hatreds—The fate of moderate men—Political calumny—Temporary reconciliation of political parties Political executions—Political persecutions— The mob in politics—Political riots—Political excesses of the mob—Political vengeance—Political reaction—Political apathy—Political ferocity.

CHAPTER V.
POLITICAL HYPOCRISY 132

Devices of the political hypocrite—Religion used as a cloak for political hypocrisy—Political ambition—Personal greed of politicians—The dissimulation of politicians—Politicians conceal their ambition under the cloak of hypocrisy—Cromwell's hypocrisy—Mendacities of politicians—Political persecutors—Demagogues always speak in the name of the people—Timidity of moderate politicians—The influence of fear in politics—Cowardice of the Convention—Politicians follow the crowd—Politicians as flatterers of the people—Gullibility of the people—Washington on the "Friends of the People"—The politician and the courtier—Abuse of the word Liberty—The Satanic principle—The desire for true liberty is rare—The misleading character of party names—The falsehood of official statements—Charlatanism of political parties—Criminals in revolutionary times—Goethe on the apostles of liberty.

CHAPTER VI.

Political Spoliation 173

Wars made for purposes of robbery—Enslavement of the vanquished — Labour degrading, but pillage honourable — The Romans converted war into an instrument of pillage—Militarism a means of getting rich — The feudal system was the exploitation of the conquered — Pillaging expeditions — The English in Ireland—Armies and plunder—The right of shipwreck —The old régime a form of spoliation—Confiscation and Civil wars—Material interests and revolutions— The Roman Republic fell from economic causes— The Reformation partly a movement to despoil the Church—Confiscations of Louis XIV.—Rapacity of courtiers—Spoliation during the French Revolution —A revolution means a transference of property— Civil wars and pillage—Politicians in alliance with financiers—Politics and finance in ancient Rome—The difficulty of convicting politicians of peculation— Politicians and financiers corrupt the Press—Deputies sell their votes to financiers—Progress in spite of corruption—Socialist charges against the middle class—Social equality.

CHAPTER VII.

Corruption amongst Politicians . . . 206

(I.) Political corruption in Rome—Corruption may prevail under any form of Government—Bribery in Rome—Venality of demagogues—Responsibility does not necessarily moralise politicians—Peculation in Rome—Corruption of judges among the Romans— Political corruption in Athens—Alcibiades—Pericles— Aristophanes on Demagogues.—(II.) Political corruption in England — Lord Bacon — Corruption among members of parliament—Louis XIV. as a corrupter of foreign politicians—Corruption in England after the Revolution—Walpole's methods of corruption—Corruption as practised by George III.—Purchase of seats in Parliament.—(III.) Political corruption in France —Richelieu's Views—Peculation under Louis XIV. —Louis XIV. on the necessity for watching government officials—La Bruyère on the financiers of the 18th century—The nobility and the financiers— Peculation in the 18th century—Political corruption under Louis XV.—Corruption during the Revolutionary period—Political morality under the Empire—Venality of Talleyrand—Political morality during the Restoration—Political corruption under the July monarchy—Deputies as directors of public companies—Heine on corruption in France.—(IV.) The causes of political corruption—Levity of life among politicians—Instances from ancient Rome—Influence of women in politics—Love of luxury and display among politicians—Simplicity of life the best safeguard against political corruption.

CHAPTER VIII.

ELECTORAL CORRUPTION 259

Corruption under universal suffrage—How votes are purchased—A wirepuller's manual—Cicero on the way to win votes—Political condottieri—Corruption of electorate by rich candidates—Electoral returns—Demagogues in political assemblies—Aristotle and Montesquieu on democracy—Democracy and merit—Political apathy of honest citizens—Evils of political indifference—Cato on public duty—La Bruyère on public life.

CHAPTER IX.

THE CORRUPTION OF LAW AND JUSTICE BY POLITICS . 279

The law as an instrument of injustice—English penal laws against Irish Catholics—Laws are made to favour the party in power—Exceptional laws are political laws—Lawyers find plausible reasons for bad laws—It is independent thinkers and not lawyers who improve law—Political assemblies often pass unjust laws—Laws are often passed under the influence of political passion—Characteristics of men in masses—In assemblies the violent often intimidate the moderate—Crude legislation and useful reforms—The corruption of justice by politics—Judicial murders—The calumniation of political opponents—Servility of judges to governments—Servility in the old English courts of justice—Juries and justice—French magistrates under the old régime—Governments dislike an independent magistracy—Independence of character essential to a good judge—Dangers of special commissions—The French Revolutionary Tribunal—Military men as judges—The police in politics—Judges should not be politicians.

CHAPTER X.

THE CORRUPTION OF PUBLIC MORALS BY POLITICS . 312

The character of the government affects the character of the nation—Evil results of frequent changes of government—Politicians of the Talleyrand and Fouché type—Fortunes made in politics—Political upstarts—Political ambition—Place hunters—Bureaucracies in democracy—Aristocracy in the nineteenth century—The two ruling passions among men are the desire for honour and wealth—Thiers on political corruption—The administrative services in France—The relation between moral and political corruption—Bentham on the French character—Comparison between France and Rome—A nation must not always be judged by the character of its politicians.

CHAPTER XI.

CONCLUSION 340

Politics are not above the moral law—Machiavelli's doctrines are immoral rather than profound—An immoral policy is unworthy of modern society—The moral standard of politicians is determined by public opinion—Moral beliefs are the only remedy for political corruption—Modern society is suffering from moral disease—The principles of international politics—The true field of international rivalry—International arbitration—Politics without morality mean the ruin of society.

CHAPTER I.

MACHIAVELISM.

> Machiavelli not the inventor of Machiavelism—Demoralising effect of political power—The early years of tyrants show that it is power which demoralises them—Men in power are unscrupulous—Immorality of political maxims—The theory of two moralities—This theory held by the ancients—Cicero on political justice—Politics in the Middle Ages was the art of deceit and assassination—In modern times politics not regulated by justice, but by reasons of State—Diplomacy a school of deceit—Machiavelli on the duties of ambassadors—Montaigne and the sixteenth century moralists on political deceit—Political assassinations: St. Bartholomew—Christian moralists and Machiavelism—Views of Bossuet, Fénelon, Massillon—Machiavelism in the eighteenth century—Machiavelism and the French Revolution—Political doctrines of Mirabeau—Political doctrines of the principal Revolutionists: Danton—The Reign of Terror a practical application of Machiavelism—Robespierre a disciple of Machiavelli—Marat—Politics of Napoleon—Political crime is not justified by its results—Examples of this fact—The political blunders of Louis XIV. and Napoleon were also moral errors—A moral policy is the most successful policy.

Machiavelism does not date from Machiavelli. It was not he who invented it, and all he did was to relate what he saw being done by the politicians of his time. His only crime—and it is a grave one—is to have explained without blaming it a policy based on violence and trickery, and to have shown how cruelty and craftiness may be turned to account to acquire and keep authority.

Politics did not await the advent of Machiavelli to become shifty, violent, and sanguinary. Statesmen did not need the lessons of the Italian writer to teach them to lie, to proscribe their adversaries, and to confiscate their belongings. The desire to rule and the exercise of authority teach fraud and violence.[1]

It is difficult to wield power with equity and moderation. Tacitus, when he wishes to explain the cruelties of Tiberius, writes that he had been led away and transformed by his tenure of power: "*Vi dominationis convulsus et mutatus.*" Power is an agent of corruption. Sylla in his youth, says Plutarch, was of a good disposition, "liking to laugh, inclined to pity to the point of weeping easily, and yet, in the end, he too, having grown cruel, spoke ill of and condemned great accession of power and honours on the ground of their being the cause of men's habits not remaining as they were in the beginning, but undergoing a change resulting for some in madness and making others vain, cruel, and inhuman." *Honores mutant mores*, runs a Latin proverb. It is so rare for power not to corrupt that Tacitus writes of Vespasian at the opening of his career, that he was the only man who, passing from private to public life, had become more virtuous.[2]

---

[1] Ut nemo doceat fraudis et sceleris vias, Regnum docebit.—(Seneca.)

[2] Tacitus, "Historiæ," l. I., § 50. See also Aristotle, "Politics," III., ch. xi., § 4. Cicero, "De Amicitia," § 15.

The earlier years of Nero, of Charles IX., and of a great number of other princes, did not foreshadow the crimes they were to commit. The Chancellor de l'Hôpital, astonished at the change that had come over the character of Charles IX., wrote to one of his friends: "I have attained to old age, and I regret my long life because I have seen a generous character deformed, a king develop into a tyrant. Nobody would have made me,—the witness of his early years,—believe this."

Intoxicated by flattery, and blinded by pride, princes, whose power is great, end by losing their heads. The rules of morality seem to them to apply no longer to their case. Napoleon, on his death bed, looking back on his career, declared: " Power affects the intelligence of men."

In order to attain their aims, the men who exercise authority are in general but little scrupulous in the choice of means. They are fond of saying that the end justifies the means, and that when morality is opposed to a useful measure, one must be prepared to sacrifice it for State reasons and in the interest of the public safety. Politics warp the conscience. It is politics that is responsible for the putting in practice of those baleful maxims: "Might is stronger than right;" "The end justifies the means;" "The safety of the people is the supreme law." There is no crime that politics has not sought to justify on the score of State reasons. There is little that is reasonable about these reasons of State. They have served as a pretext for wreaking revenge, for proscribing the innocent, for laying hands on the possessions of others, and for pursuing self-aggrandisement in defiance of all justice. Politicians use this expression as a cloak for every iniquity. It is in the name of State reasons that Socrates was condemned to drink hemlock, that the Christians were persecuted by the Roman Emperors, and that the Protestants were massacred by Charles IX. and banished by Louis XIV. It was on the pretext of the interest of the State that Nero obtained the justification of the murder of his mother, etc., etc.

The Machiavelian theory is already to be found in the "Phœnissæ" of Euripides where these words of Eteocles occur: "If it be needful to resort to injustice to attain to power, let us have recourse thereto; but under all other circumstances let us be honest." This is the theory of two moralities, one for private, and one for political life. Men who in private life are respectful of justice, allow themselves every license in politics. Thucydides relates that the Athenians were wont to say of the Lacedæmonians: "Amongst themselves and in their national institutions they observe in general the dictates of virtue, but in the case of their foreign relations it is different. Where these are concerned, they regard what is agreeable as honest, and what is useful as just, more openly than other people with whom we are acquainted."[1]

[1] Thucydides, l. V., § 105.

The politics of the Athenians did not differ greatly from that of the Lacedæmonians. The Roman Senate also put in practice a Machiavellian policy when it invoked the interest and the safety of the Republic.

Injustice is cloaked as a rule in politics by lying pretexts. Occasionally, however, ambitious men who are free from scruples make a barefaced avowal of their contempt for justice. For example, a deputation hailing from Corinth stated: "Nobody has ever refused out of considerations of justice to utilize an opportunity of achieving aggrandisement by force."

Among the ancients, Cicero refuted the false maxim that it is impossible to govern in accordance with justice, and that the interest of the State authorises the employment of every expedient. He blamed the statesmen who advocated unjust measures, alleging that "the interest of the State is a paramount consideration." "Not only," adds Cicero, "is it false to say that men cannot be governed without violating justice, but the truth is, in fact, this: it is by absolute justice, and by justice alone, that it is possible to govern States." Cicero developed his contention by setting forth in a series of noble reflections the relations between what is upright and what is useful.[1]

While philosophy was demonstrating that justice is the most solid foundation for human societies, politics, under the Roman Emperors

[1] "De Officiis," l. III., § 21, 32.

and during the Middle Ages, continued its work of oppression, corruption, and injustice. The Italian princes in particular made of politics the art of deceiving, assassinating, and poisoning. Christianity was in perpetual conflict with Machiavelism, but could not succeed in effecting its extirpation. In Spain, England, Germany, and France, among the most civilised nations, politics were regulated by reasons of State. It was for State reasons that Ferdinand and Isabella expelled the Jews from Spain, and that the Kings of England committed so many acts contrary to justice. The English, essentially a utilitarian people, are given to confounding what is useful with what is just, and their statesmen have often proposed unjust measures because they were demanded in their opinion by the safety of the State.[1]

The best French kings, with the exception of Saint Louis, and the greatest French Ministers, Richelieu and Mazarin, gave their adhesion to the doctrine that proclaims the all-importance of reasons of State. Henry IV. himself advised Queen Elizabeth to order the carrying out of the sentence of death pronounced against Mary Stuart.

[1] This confusion between what is useful and what is upright may be traced in the speeches of the most illustrious English statesmen. When Canning, for example, in 1821, was combatting the exclusion of the Catholics from Parliament, he admitted that their exclusion would be just if it were necessary, and to prove that it was not just he maintained that it was unnecessary. Recalling the unjust laws promulgated against the Catholics under James I., Canning adds: "Unjust as these stipulations were, the safety of the State rendered them necessary."

In private life the man who resorts to deceit is despised; in politics equivocation, cunning, and every means of dissembling the truth, form part of the science of the diplomatist. Diplomacy furnishes pretexts for every sort of aggression, and veils ambition and greed under high-sounding words. Politics in ancient times, the politics of the Greeks, the Carthaginians and the Romans were not characterised by good faith. The Punic faith, *fides punica*, has remained a by-word. Deception and audacity were the principal means by which the Romans achieved their aggrandisement. Among modern nations politics have just as little been a school of good faith and equity. When Mazarin desired to employ Marshal de Faber in a negotiation of dubious sincerity, the latter begged to be relieved of the task in these terms: "Allow me, Sire, to refuse to deceive the Duke of Savoy, and the more so in that the matter at issue is of slight importance. It is of common knowledge that I am an honourable man. In consequence keep my honesty in reserve for an occasion when the salvation of France is at stake."

During the 15th and 16th centuries underhand dealing in politics carried with it no stigma, but was considered a proof of ability deserving of praise. Brantôme qualifies as "good tricks" the stratagems of Louis XI., to which Comines refers as "fine lies." When, in 1494, the Ambassadors from Milan swore to Comines that their Duke had no hand in the league formed against France,

Sanuto, a Venetian, declared they had acted "as men skilled in the affairs of State ought to act, assuring their enemies that their intention is to act in one way and acting afterwards in a way entirely contrary." Machiavelli maintained that an Ambassador should be capable of lying[1] and of breaking his word, while to enable him the better to deceive he should earn a reputation for uprightness. His contemporaries were not revolted by these immoral maxims.

The false maxim that the end justifies the means was allowed by the majority of the moralists of the 16th century, and in particular by Montaigne and Charron. In the Essays of Montaigne a strong repulsion is noticeable for the cruel and treacherous acts which were of so frequent occurrence during the religious and political struggles of his time.[2] And yet Montaigne writes that "the weakness of our case often drives us to the necessity of employing reprehensible means to a worthy end."[3]

[1] Plato in this matter is of the same opinion as Machiavelli: "It seems to me that our magistrates will often be obliged to have recourse to lying and deceit in the interest of their fellow-citizens, and we have declared elsewhere that a lie is useful when it is employed as a remedy—and rightly so."—*Res Publica V*. Priezac, a king's councillor, in a discourse upon the "Politics" of Aristotle, published in 1652, declared that craft, where politics are concerned, is blameless because it is useful. "Seeing," he wrote, "that painting is never so esteemed as when it deceives the eye by its lights and shades, . . . who can account it strange that in politics, the mistress, that is, of the arts and sciences, it should be allowable to make use of sophisms to a nobler and more spacious end?"

[2] Montaigne, Bk. I., ch. xxx.

[3] Ibid., Bk. I., l. ii., ch. xxxiii.

Charron is of the same opinion. "One is often constrained," he says, "to resort to and employ reprehensible means to avoid or escape from a greater evil or to achieve a good end. And to such a degree is this the case that it is sometimes necessary to hold legitimate and to authorise things that not only are not good but are positively bad."[1]

In his treatise on wisdom this moralist authorises dissimulation and violence when they are useful to the State. "Dissimulation," he writes, "which is a vice in private persons, is most necessary to princes, who, without it, would be incapable of reigning or of exercising command to advantage. .... The simple and open, whose thoughts, as it is said, can be read on their faces, are in no sort fitted for this profession of commanding."[2]

Further, according to Charron, "the prudent and wise prince should not only be capable of governing in accordance with the law, but of imposing his authority upon the laws themselves if necessity demand it." "Finally," he says, "so as to be just in great matters, it is sometimes necessary to be less just in small matters; so as to do the right when great interests are con-

---

[1] Charron, "De la Sagesse," Bk. I., § 86.

[2] Ibid., Bk. III., § 7. This idea that a prince should be capable of lying is still widely entertained even to-day. An illustrious historian of high character, M. Mignet, talking with one of my friends of the events in Italy that followed the Treaty of Villafranca, said of Napoleon III., whom he did not like: "I admit, however, that this prince has two important qualities—he knows when to stop and how to lie."

cerned, it is allowable to do wrong on occasions
of lesser import."[1]

Necessity is an excuse for everything: "It is
impossible that good princes should not commit
some injustice." These acts of injustice are
excusable if they are useful to the State. Princes
should resign themselves to perpetrate them,
"regretfully and with sighs."

Gabriel Naudé, the librarian of Mazarin, in his
volume entitled "A Politic View of Coups d'Etat"
goes still further than Charron in his contempt
for justice in politics and in the theory of the two
moralities. "Common justice," he says, "is
exacting, and in consequence a source of inconvenience in the conduct of affairs. It is therefore needful to adapt it to the necessities of politics. In the interest of the State a prince should
resign himself to measures that strict justice
would condemn, and should be content to follow
the example of his compeers. He writes: "The
justice, virtue, and probity of a sovereign have
a somewhat different carriage than when private
individuals are concerned; they have an ampler
and a freer gait." The sovereign, no doubt, should
make an effort not to separate the useful from the
honourable, but where this union is impossible,
it suffices that he should deviate from the right
as little as may be. Naudé defines *coups d'état*
as "bold and exceptional acts which princes
are constrained to commit in difficult and desperate cases without regard to equity, or even respect

[1] Charron, "De la Sagesse," Bk. III., § 10.

for any shape or form of justice, but risking the interest of the individual for the public good." Princes, Naudé declares, should only resort to *coups d'etat* in extreme cases; they are powerful remedies which ought to be reserved for grave diseases. However, when a *coup d'état* is necessary, action should be prompt; a well-combined *coup d'état* should strike like lightning before the thunder is heard.

According to Naudé, assassination is allowable when the prince acts for the public good, or for his own, which is inseparable from the former. Naudé approves of the Saint Bartholomew massacres and finds them deserving of praise. He justifies this effusion of blood by saying that it did not equal that at Coutras or Montcontour, that Charles IX. made fewer victims than other kings, that Cæsar caused the death of "one million one hundred and ninety-two thousand men in his foreign wars, Pompey that of a still greater number, while Quintus Fabius, in the colonies, dispatched one hundred thousand Gauls into the other world, and Caius Marius two hundred thousand Cimbrians. . . . Whoever considers these bloody tragedies . . . will have sufficient cause to be taken aback at so many barbarities, and to esteem further, that that of Saint Bartholomew was not among the greatest, although it was among the most just and necessary." Naudé has only one fault to find with the massacres of Saint Bartholomew, and it is that they were incomplete and were only accomplished by halves. If "all the heretics had been included in the slaughter, there would remain nobody to blame it, at least in France." In coming to Paris, Coligny and his friends were guilty of such grave imprudence "that it would have been an equal fault on our part to have let them escape." In other words, when a political adversary gives you a chance of dispatching him, it would be a fault not to take his life. According to this reasoning, when Luther betook himself to Augsburg, Charles V. ought to have had him assassinated for the good of humanity. By this murder he would have prevented the wars of religion. Morality forbids murder, but politics permit it when it is called for by the good of the State: such in a word is the doctrine of Mazarin's librarian.

The Memoirs of Cardinal de Retz may also be considered as a course of political immorality. The Cardinal openly enforces all the principles of Machiavelism in this work, whereas in his sermons he condemns them.

The immoral theory of the paramount importance of reasons of State has been put in practice by all Governments, by monarchies as well as by republics. No Government put it in practice with more cruelty than the Council of Ten in Venice, which got rid of all its political adversaries by poison or drowning. "We act more than we talk," wrote a Venetian ambassador in Rome, in a despatch dated 27th April, 1566. "We do not have recourse to fire and sword, but we see to it that those who deserve their fate are secretly done to death." The Venetians were in the habit of saying: "We are Venetians in the first place and Christians in the second."

The Christian moralists who wrote upon politics in the 17th and 18th centuries, Bossuet, Fénelon, Massillon, Condillac or Mably, combatted Machiavelism, and endeavoured, but in vain, to assure the triumph of principles inspired by a political morality. Bossuet in his "Politique tirée de l'Ecriture Sainte," and Fénelon in "Télémaque" and his "Instructions pour la Conscience d'un Roi," taught the Dauphin and the Duke of Burgundy to dispense with violence and bad faith, to avoid false cunning, and not to separate politics from justice. "Télémaque" sets forth a system of Christian politics. The politics of Bossuet are drawn from the Bible, those of Fénelon from the New Testament. Christendom, in the opinion of the Bishop of Cambrai, is a vast family, a sort of universal republic, and each nation is a member of this vast family. Fénelon is desirous that war, if it be inevitable, should always be conducted with good faith and without cruelty: those who are at enmity are none the less men and brothers. He instructed the Duke of Burgundy not to confound his personal pretensions, his wish for glory, and his ambitions with State necessities and State needs. He taught him that politics did not relieve him of the duty of being just, sincere and compassionate, and did not raise him above the ordinary laws of justice and humanity.

Massillon and Condillac continued during the

18th century the work of Bossuet and Fénelon, by impressing, the former upon Louis XV., the latter upon the Duke of Parma, the union that exists between politics and morality. In his "Etudes de l'Histoire" Condillac combatted the false maxims that dishonour politics, "a medley of pettinesses, ruses, subtilties, and absurdities, which, he says, "people would have you admire," and which he calls political charlatanism.

But while the Christian moralists and some philosophers such as Holbach,[1] Barbeyrac, and Mably were refuting Machiavelism, the Regent, Dubois, Louis XV., Frederic II., and Catherine of Russia were continuing in the 18th century a policy bereft of principle and morality. The Minister Terray thought to justify bankruptcy by saying: "Necessity justifies everything." In France, as was the case with the other European nations, politics remained Machiavelian and resorted to every expedient to insure success;—to ruse, to deceit, to intrigues with the feminine favourites of sovereigns and ministers, to secret

[1] Holbach combatted Machiavelism in a book entitled "Système Social," that is not without merit, but is little known. This book is a development of the conception that politics by right should be the application of morality to the government of States. Barbeyrac attempted to unmask that political hypocrisy which under the cloak of religion, and the public good, resorts to illegality and violence. The illusions, he said, ought to be dissipated in the name of which dust is thrown in people's eyes by the use of certain high-sounding expressions and big words which have no meaning (" De la Liberté de Conscience"). Mably in his "Entretiens de Phocion" set himself the task of proving that politics cannot compass the welfare of society except so far as they do not deviate from the strictest rules of morality.

agents and to corruption. "The interest of the State as guiding principle and goal, and intrigue as the means, such," M. Sorel rightly says, "was the beginning and end of politics in the 18th century."[1] The notion that the interest of the State is the supreme law in politics found general acceptance. It is even to be noted in the writings of the Abbé de Saint Pierre, who asserted that a sovereign is not bound to keep his word: "The law that declares that the pledged word must not be broken is a law subordinate to that other law: *Salus populi suprema lex* " ("Les Rêves d'un Homme de Bien," p. 50). The diplomacy of the time was unscrupulous. The philosophers admired and overwhelmed with flattery Frederick II. and Catherine of Russia, who were the disciples of Machiavelli. The King of Prussia, who in his youth had refuted "The Prince," set to work as soon as he had assumed power to put in practice the immoral maxims of the Italian author. He did not hesitate to write in the preface to his "History of My Time" that a sovereign should break his word and disregard treaties when he considered that to do so was useful. He forgot that he had himself stigmatised such perfidy in the following verses:

When politics, resorting to sophisms,
Draws its inspiration from the treacherous doctrine of Machiavelli,
The spectacle afforded is that of rogues, deceivers, and liars,
Of ministers tricked and of ministers who are tricksters;
These false maxims did away with probity,
And the art of governing was a school for crimes.

---

[1] Sorel, "L'Europe et la Révolution Française," Vol. I., p. 89.

When the French Revolution was brought about in the name of the great principles of justice and humanity, it seemed reasonable to hope that politics would cease to be conducted on immoral lines. Sieyès, in his famous pamphlet, "Qu'est-ce que le Tiers Etat?" (ch. v.), protested against those "who hold just and natural methods of little account in social concerns, and who only esteem those artificial expedients which, more or less iniquitous, and more or less shifty, establish, everywhere, the reputation of statesmen and great politicians." Unfortunately these optimistic expectations were not destined to be realised; the Revolution severed itself from morality and was accomplished by dint of a series of *coups d'etat*. Some years previously, Montesquieu had said in "L'Esprit des Lois": "A beginning has been made in the matter of curing ourselves of Machiavelism, and this cure will be proceeded with day by day. . . . What were called formerly *coups d'état* would to-day, apart from the horror that attaches to them, be mere acts of imprudence."[1] Events gave the lie to this optimism in cruel fashion. The Revolution begun in the name of justice was carried through by force. How many dates, such as 15th October, 2nd September, 20th June, 10th August, 21st January, 1793, 31st May, 2nd June, 1793, March and April, 1794, 9th Thermidor, 13th Vendemaire, 18th Fructidor, and 18th Brumaire, how many dates, we say, recall the triumph of force.

[1] "Esprit des Lois," Bk. XXI., ch. xvi.

The Revolution was nothing else but a series of *coups d'état:* 20th June, 10th August, *coups d'état* against the monarchy ; 31st May, 2nd June, *coups d'état* against the Girondins ; 2nd April, 1794, *coup d'état* against Danton ; 9th Thermidor, *coup d'état* against Robespierre ; 18th Fructidor, *coup d'état* against the moderate Republicans and the Royalists ; 18th Brumaire, *coup d'état* against the Directory. During the Terror, people were massacred and guillotined in Paris, drowned at Nantes, and shot at Lyons and Toulon. Under the Directory the victims were transported, and on the occasion of the 18th Brumaire they were exiled. These massacres, drownings, shootings, and transportations became a system of government at the time that the political programme was based on the three great principles of Liberty, Equality, and Fra ternity.

Almost all the politicians of the Revolution, from Mirabeau to Bonaparte, practised Machiavelism. Mirabeau was inspired by Machiavelli when he said: "Petty morality is fatal to the highest morality." In the memoir he drew up for the use of the Court, he gave the king Machiavelian advice; he recommended him to ruin the authority of the Assembly by a series of dishonest manœuvres, to lay traps for that body, to put obstacles in its path, to egg it on to usurp all authority. "This procedure," he said, "will disorganise the kingdom more and more, and will add to the anarchy, but for this very reason it will pave the way for a crisis, and the evils from which the kingdom suffers enduring and growing more acute, there will soon be nothing left for it but to have recourse to the royal authority."[1] This policy, which Mirabeau counselled Louis XVI. to adopt, was immoral, because it consisted in augmenting the evil, in the very problematical hope of thereby producing good.[2]

Mirabeau also urged the Court to conciliate the party leaders by any means. "If flattering their ambition," he said, "is insufficient to win them over, it is by other means—and I make no exception of any kind—that a greater measure of success must be scored." It was on the pressing recommendation of Mirabeau that Mdme. Montmorin distributed seven millions amongst the popular party.

The policy of the other principal actors in the Revolution was a mere servile imitation of the immoral policy of the old régime. It was a policy of expedients, of ruse, and of violence, a policy that had recourse to force, to rioting, and to *coups d'état*. In its turn it resorted to arbitrary arrests, massacres, the inquisition, the proscription of suspected persons, and confiscation. It sought its inspiration in the doctrine of the interest of the State, it borrowed the principles of absolute governments, such as the all-importance of the goal and contempt for the individual, and it outdid the violence of Henry VIII., Philip II., and the Duke of Alba.

---

[1] "Les Mirabeau," by Louis de Lomenie, Vol. V., p. 230.

[2] Rivarol, in his "Lettres à Necker," which date from the same period, counselled an identical policy.

The Athenian Assembly refused to listen to the reading of a law of which Aristides had said that it was useful but unjust. The Legislative Assembly and the Convention were not burdened with such scruples; they voted a number of laws because they thought them useful but while knowing them to be unjust. Michelet, who is so indulgent for the men of the Revolution, admits "that on coming to the head of affairs they made no difficulty about accepting the very false doctrine that there are two moralities, one private, the other public, and that the first in case of need may be overlooked by the second. This was the theory of all the politicians of the period. They imagined that in this respect they were the descendants of Brutus, whereas their real ancestor was Machiavelli.[1] In their eyes the end justifies the means. They esteemed every measure allowable that was directed against the "aristocrats." "You have a serious failing," a revolutionary declared to Garat; "it is that you will not lend yourself to a bad action, although it be demanded by the public' good." Basire maintained from the tribune that all means are acceptable when employed against the enemies of the nation. Leclerc exclaimed: "A Machiavelism for the use of the people must be founded." Danton allowed that he would not stop short at crime when he judged it necessary. He provoked the September massacres with a view according to his own expression, to put a

Michelet, "Histoire de la Révolution Française," Vol. VI., p. 9.

river of blood between the Parisians and the Emigrants.[1] When the Paris Commune, after the September massacres, urged the provinces to follow the example of Paris, Danton, at the time Minister of Justice, let this abominable incitement to massacre be dispatched with his ministerial seal appended to it.[2]

The Terror was an application of the false doctrines of Machiavelli. The Italian author had said: "When a State undergoes a revolution, whether it be that a republic becomes a tyranny, or that a tyranny is replaced by a republic, it is necessary that a terrible example should strike fear into the hearts of the enemies of the new order of things."[3]

Machiavelli had added that it was fitting to be prompt and audacious in the extermination of political adversaries.[4] The word audacity was for ever on the lips of the Terrorists. On the occasion of the September massacres, Danton exclaimed: "Be bold! be bold! always be bold!" The motto of Saint Just was the same as that of Danton. "To dare," he said, "constitutes the whole secret of revolutions." The men of the Terror dared greatly.

Robespierre, in his speeches, combatted

[1] The participation of Danton in the September massacres has been contested, but it has, nevertheless, been proved by MM. Wallon, Taine, Mortimer-Ternaux, and Louis Blanc. Michelet himself admits it in spite of his admiration for the political genius of Danton.

[2] E. Quinet, "La Révolution," Vol. I., p. 351.

[3] Machiavelli, "Discourses upon Livy," Bk. III., ch. viii.

[4] Machiavelli, "Il Principe," ch. viii.

Machiavelism, but resorted to it in his acts. "The art of governing," he declared, "has, up till now, been the art of deceiving, and corrupting men. It ought to be nothing else than the art of enlightening them and making them better." And yet his behaviour was always that of a disciple of Machiavelli. He invoked the interest of the State as an excuse for suppressing his enemies, and he considered that proscriptions were necessary to establish liberty, equality, and fraternity.

Machiavelli had said: "In every case where a measure has to be debated on which the safety of the State depends entirely, one must not be stopped by any consideration of justice or of injustice, of humanity or of cruelty, of glory or of ignominy."[1] The Terrorists repeated the same idea when they cried: "Let our memory perish so long as the country is saved!" Marat wrote in the *Ami du Peuple* for February 28th, 1791: "The safety of the people is at stake. Before this supreme law all other laws should be as naught. To save the country all means are good, all means are just, all means are meritorious." As did Marat, very many Jacobins thought to justify the proscriptions on the ground of the greatness of the end in view and of the safety of the republic.

It will be seen from these comparisons between sundry passages from Machiavelli and the doctrines of the Terrorists that these statesmen who gave out that they were inaugurating a new policy were merely copying and even exaggerating the

[1] Machiavelli, "Discourses upon Livy," Bk. III., ch. xli.

old policy of despotic Governments. They had no comprehension of the new principles introduced by the French Revolution. They lacked the sentiment of liberty, equality, and fraternity. Instead of being pioneers in the field of politics, all they did was to copy the old Machiavelian policy. They employed in defending the cause of the people the criminal means that had been resorted to before them by the defenders of an absolute monarchy.

The Directory kept up the Machiavelian traditions. It only retained the reins of power by craft and force, and by violating on the 18th Fructidor the rights of the representation of the nation.

The 18th Fructidor, which was the work of three audacious Directors and of Augereau, an unscrupulous soldier, speedily brought about another *coup d'état*, the 18th Brumaire, accomplished by another general, whose moral sense was not on a par with his genius. This *coup d'état*, the execution of the Duc d'Enghien, the abduction of the Pope, and the Bayonne ambuscade, make it impossible to admit that the policy of Napoleon I. was always loyal and just. The name of "Great" may be allotted Napoleon I., since history, taking count of intellectual rather than of moral greatness, gives the name of "Great" to all conquerors, to Alexander, Cæsar, Louis XIV., and Frederick II., but he cannot be called either the wise or the just, since he did not hesitate to violate justice on the plea of serving the interest of the State. "The interest of the State," he declared, "has taken the place in modern times of the fatalism of the ancients. Corneille is the only one of the French tragic authors who has appreciated this truth. Had he lived in my time I should have made him my Prime Minister."[1]

To conclude this chapter I would wish to examine whether the advantages of an immoral policy are as great as is thought. It appears to me that the advantages of a Machiavelian policy are exaggerated because, as a rule, only the immediate advantages are taken into consideration, and the remoter consequences are neglected. Human life being very short, a man may profit by a crime and die before he has been punished. The life of nations being much longer, a political crime, after resulting in momentary advantages, is always expiated in the end. The triumph of cunning and force is often transitory, and if a lengthy period be examined, one is struck in a general way by the fact that failure attends an immoral policy. A politician face to face with a serious difficulty, thinks recourse to an unjust expedient of immediate utility the simplest mode of escape from it, but the future is not slow to teach him the drawbacks of injustice.

Cunning and injustice do not always result in advantage, but have more than once cost those who resorted to them dearly. The examples of

---

[1] It is a fact that the theory of the interest of the State is to be found in Corneille. His development of the hateful doctrine is not, however, the expression of his own thoughts, but is contained in words which he puts in the mouth of Photin, the Minister of Ptolemy.

political perfidy and cruelty which Machiavelli cites as specimens of adroitness turn to his confusion, for the princes whose elaborate treachery he admires did not long enjoy the fruit of their crimes. His hero, Cæsar Borgia, did not bask in the smiles of fortune. Machiavelli himself, in spite of his genius, was an unsuccessful man, a man who, absorbed by the desire to make his way, achieved nothing.

Political, like other crimes, are not committed with impunity. The disciples of Machiavelli who, out of political considerations, have caused the death of innocent persons, have often come themselves to a tragic end. Those who have proscribed others are themselves proscribed in turn. The Girondins, who were responsible for the events of the 21st January, were the victims of the 31st May. The Dantonists, who accused the Girondins of moderation, were themselves proscribed as moderates. Robespierre and his friends, who sent so many victims to the guillotine, were guillotined in their turn. The principal Jacobins to whose initiative was due the establishment of the revolutionary tribunal perished the victims of that tribunal. The members of the Long Parliament, who had Charles I. executed and who proscribed a great many of their colleagues, were themselves driven ignominiously from their seats by Cromwell, who said to them as he expelled them: "As for you, you are a drunkard, and you a debaucher, and you an adulterer, and you a thief."

The faults that endanger the prosperity of a

nation often have their origin in the failure to recognise what is just. The great political mistakes of Louis XIV. and Napoleon I. were at the same time mistakes from a moral point of view. Louis XIV. thought to strengthen the State when he revoked the Edict of Nantes: in point of fact, he weakened it. When the wife of the First Consul, on learning the abduction of the Duc d'Enghien, implored her husband with tears not to spill his blood, Bonaparte replied to her: "You are a woman. My policy is beyond your comprehension. Your part is to keep silent."[1]

He fancied that he would derive great advantages from this iniquitous act, whereas the real outcome of this violation of justice was to arouse the indignation of all good men in France and throughout Europe, and to cause him to lose the support of Prussia, of which he stood in need at the time, a circumstance that was favourable to the aims of England. The man who exclaimed on being told of the execution of the Duc d'Enghien, "It is worse than a crime; it is a blunder," gave utterance to an immoral remark, since a crime seemed to him less serious than a political mistake; but he was not wrong in describing the act as a mistake. The sensitive woman had had a better intuition of the truth than the politician of genius. The intelligence, acting alone, is apt to make mistakes. Even in politics the feelings may dictate a reasonable course, which would never be suggested by reasons of State, and attain

[1] Thiers, "Histoire du Consulat et de l'Empire," Bk. XVIII

to a lucidity that would not result from calculation. Politics severed from the emotions are deprived of a fruitful source of inspiration.

Napoleon I., when he took away the crown of Spain from Charles IV. and his son Ferdinand, attempted to excuse his violence and trickery on the score of political necessity. "From a certain point of view," he said, "what I am doing is not right, but politics have their exigencies and are inevitably rigorous. . . Politics, politics," he said, "ought to direct all the actions of such a man as myself."[1]

He thought to excuse this political crime by the greatness of the end he had in view, which was the regeneration of Spain. He failed, however, to attain this end, and his attempt upon the independence of the Spanish nation was productive of results disastrous to himself.

How false is the Machiavelian maxim that the end justifies the means will be seen from these examples. It is not even certain in politics that an advantageous end may be gained by reprehensible means. Napoleon by his attack upon the independence of Spain no more attained the end he had in view than Louis XIV. by the revocation of the Edict of Nantes achieved the religious unity at which he aimed.

Genius comes under the law that ordains the punishment, sooner or later, of political as of other crimes. Had Napoleon, instead of seizing upon the power by force, awaited till he was

[1] Thiers, "Histoire du Consulat et de l'Empire," Bk. XXX.

legally intrusted with it, he would have accomplished the great acts that have made his name illustrious, while the check that would have been imposed upon his ambition would have preserved him from the follies that proved his perdition and involved France in his ruin. The greatest genius of modern times having erred in his political calculations, it is permissible to hold that the surest policy is a moral policy.

The stumbling block of the cause of the French Revolution has been Machiavelism. The unrest with which the country has been afflicted for a hundred years past, which is not yet at an end, has resulted from the fact that the men entrusted with the application of the new political principles have ignored morality. It is not these principles themselves that have caused the trouble but the culpable means by which they have been put in practice. The employment of force, organised rebellion, proscriptions, the revolutionary tribunal and the scaffold have delayed the realisation of political liberty and the union of all Frenchmen.

CHAPTER II.

POLITICAL ASSASSINATION AND TYRANNICIDE.

The bloodthirstiness of political passion—Political assassins—Murder of children on political grounds—Reasons of State urged to justify every possible crime—The massacre of prisoners during the French Revolution—Greek ideas regarding political assassination—Roman ideas regarding political assassination—Ideas of the Middle Ages regarding political assassination—Protestant and Catholic ideas regarding political assassination—The French Protestants and political assassination—Milton on tyrannicide—Catherine of Russia on tyrannicide—Views of the Jacobins and Emigrants—Political assassination in the nineteenth century—The assassination of tyrants does not destroy tyranny—The doctrine of regicide.

When studying the history of proscriptions, one is appalled at the acts of cruelty it offers. Bossuet was indeed in the right when he wrote: "There is nothing more brutal or sanguinary than man"—especially when he is animated by political passion. Turn about, the patricians have proscribed the plebeians, the plebeians have proscribed the patricians, kings have decimated the people, and the people have slaughtered kings. Political passions have bathed the earth in blood; kings, emperors, aristocracies, democracies, republics, all governments have resorted to murder out of political considerations, these from love of power, those from hatred of royalty and aristocracy, in one case from fear, in another from fanaticism.

Pagan emperors had thousands of men done to death because they were Christians; later on Christian princes persecuted those of their subjects who were Jews; Catholic kings have slaughtered Protestants, Protestant princes have slaughtered Catholics.

Famous kings and illustrious emperors have not hesitated to be guilty of murder: Alexander slew Clitus and Parmenion; Titus caused Coccina to be killed as he was leaving a banquet to which he had invited him; Charles V. had Rincon slain and Philip II. the Prince of Orange; Charles IX. was responsible for the murder of Coligny; Henry III. for that of the Duke of Guise; Ferdinand II. for that of Wallenstein, etc., etc. The Roman emperors[1] and the Italian princes, when disputing the power between them, had recourse to assassins. Venice offered rewards to those who should murder its adversaries. During the wars of religion the kings and the party leaders had assassins in their pay. During the Fronde Cardinal de Retz caused the proposition to be made to the Queen that Condi should be assassinated. The Duc d'Orleans came to the Parliament to ask that the sum

---

[1] Tacitus, "Historiœ," Bk. I., § 75. "Then Otho and Vitellius dispatched assassins."

destined to recompense whoever should take the life of Mazarin should be made up to 150,000 livres. A few years previously an attempt had been made to assassinate Richelieu. The Cardinal de Retz relates in his Memoirs that he had himself formed the project of killing Cardinal Richelieu during the ceremony of the baptism of the Queen's daughter. He is not afraid to write: "I decided on the crime, which seemed to me sanctioned by great examples, and justified and honoured by great perils." The scheme came to nothing, owing to the ceremony not taking place. Retz adds: "This enterprise would have covered us with glory if it had been successful."

During the 16th, 17th, and 18th centuries the spectacle is offered of queens and empresses committing murders, or allowing them to be committed. Mary Stuart let Darnley be slain; Christina of Sweden had Monaldesky assassinated; Catherine of Russia did away with her husband. When Charles II. sent assassins in pursuit of Sidney and other English patriots, it was his sister, Queen Henrietta, the sister-in-law of Louis XIV., who was charged with giving the orders and with paying the murderers their wages.

There are cases of a political murder having been rewarded by a patent of nobility. Philip II. ennobled the murderer of the Prince of Orange.

It is due to politics that the slaughter of the children after the murder of the parents was long accepted as a maxim of government. "One must be mad," said a Greek proverb, "to let the children live after having slain the father."[1] Philip, King of Macedon, was in the habit of quoting this horrible maxim, and of putting it in practice. According to Dionysius of Halicarnassus,[2] the Greeks invariably put to death the children of tyrants. The Romans were at first less cruel. When Cassius was sentenced to death for having aspired to be a tyrant, the question was debated whether his children should suffer the same fate; they were not condemned to any penalty.[3] However, under the Roman emperors the slaughtering of children became a governmental practice. Mucius, for instance, put to death the son of Vitellius, with a view, as he said, to stamp out the seeds of war.

It is commonly known that under the Frank kings, vengeance was wreaked on the son as well as on the father, and that the desire to get rid of pretenders to the crown was often the cause of the slaughter of children. The two sons of Clovis, Childebert and Clother, slew two of the children of their brother, Clodomir. The Italian princes continued this barbarous practice. Cæsar Borgia caused the extermination of the entire stock of the noblemen whom he had despoiled.[4] After recalling this cruel proceeding, Machiavelli adds, that not only does he see nothing to blame in the conduct of the Duc de Valentinois, but that in his opinion this personage might be

---

[1] Aristotle, Rhetoric, Bk. I., ch. xx.
[2] Dionysii, Halicarn, "Antiquitates Romanæ," Bk. VIII.
[3] Montesquieu, "Esprit des Lois," Bk. XXII., ch. xviii.
[4] Machiavelli, "Il Principe," Part I., ch. viii.

offered as an example. When Louis XI. had the Duc de Nemours beheaded in 1477, he did not kill his children, but he subjected them to a still more atrocious torment: he had them placed under the scaffold, so that they were bathed in their father's blood. He then handed over the eldest son of the duke to one of the judges who had received a portion of the condemned man's inheritance; it was not long before the child died.

During the Terror, when all the atrocities of the Machiavelian policy of the 16th century were revised, there were wholesale drownings of children. In 1793 the Nantes revolutionary committee caused three hundred Vendean children to be drowned, alleging that "from the viper the viper is bred."[1]

In Belgium recently, at the time of the glass workers' strike, a rioter was heard to cry: "Shoot down the capitalists; do not spare the children, who are seedling capitalists."

The thirst for power excites such violent passions in the human soul that fathers have been seen to put their children to death, children to slay their father and their mother, and brothers to kill each other. Clother put to death his son Cramme; Nero, his mother, Agrippina. "The wife of Tarquin the Younger, the daughter of Servius, consumed by this passion (the passion of reigning), and trampling upon all filial tenderness, excited

[1] Michelet, "Histoire de la Révolution Française," Vol. VIII. p. 323.

her husband to rob her father of both his throne and his life, to such a point did she attach greater price to being queen than to being daughter of a king.[1]

On the score of the interest of the State, of the safety of the commonwealth, politics have caused the perpetration of every possible crime. The considerations in question have occasionally been invoked by fanatics, who thought to save the people by political crimes; but they have as often been advanced by the ambitious, by political informers, and by courtiers. When Marcellus, in the intention of being agreeable to Nero, asked the Senate to order the execution of Thraseas, he made out that the safety of the State was at stake.[2]

The massacres of prisoners that have taken place on various occasions in French history, and have been sometimes attributed to explosion of popular fury, have been desired and brought about in reality by designing politicians. The September massacres were debated and advocated by several sections. Danton desired them, Robespierre accepted them. Danton admitted to Louis Philippe, who was serving at the time in the army of Dumouriez, that he had wished for the massacres,[3] as he was of the opinion that he could only govern by inspiring fear. The General Council of the Commune was informed of the massacre,

---

[1] Machiavelli, "Discourses upon Livy," Bk. III., ch. v.
[2] Tacitus, "Annales," Bk. XVI., § 28.
[3] Wallon, "Journal des Savants," March, 1894, p. 133.

and did not interfere. For three days the slaughter proceeded of the prisoners at the Carmes, the Abbaye, the Conciergerie, and the Force. "There might be ground for surprise," says M. Mignet, "that a crime so stupendous and spread over so long a period should have been conceived, carried out, and permitted were it not known to what lengths politics or party fanaticism will go, and what people will submit to under the influence of fear."[1] At the prison of the Force members of the Commune, bearing their insignia of office, were present to give the massacres an air of legality. Marat glorified these execrable crimes and advised their imitation. The authors of the September massacres were unquestionably paid assassins, for several of them put in a claim for the salary due to them, and some of the receipts they gave are to-day in existence.

When the Orleans prisoners were transferred to Paris, the band of assassins that had got together hastened out to Versailles to slaughter them. "In the twinkling of an eye," relates M. Thiers, "the rumour spread that fresh massacres were about to be perpetrated. The President of the Criminal Tribunal hurried to Paris to warn the minister Danton of the danger the prisoners ran. 'These men are very guilty,' was the only reply he obtained to his representations. 'That may be so,' insisted President Alquin, 'but they must be judged according to the law.' 'Do you not understand,' retorted Danton, in a terrible voice,

[1] Mignet, "Histoire de la Révolution Française," ch. viii.

'that I should already have answered you in a different manner had I been able? What are these prisoners to you? Go back to your duties and cease to concern yourself with them.'"[1]

When on the 5th Floréal, 1795, seventy or eighty prisoners, alleged to be Terrorists, were massacred at Lyons, the massacre was inspired by the societies known as the Soleil and the Jehu.

When the men of Burgundy conquered the Armagnacs, who were in possession of Paris, the prisoners were massacred without the Duke of Burgundy making any effort to stay the slaughter. In twenty-four hours 1,600 prisoners were done to death. A few days later, at the instigation of the University, the massacres of prisoners began again: the Duke of Burgundy did not intervene.

After the perpetration of political massacres it may often be observed that the parties take the assassins under their protection. In the arrest of certain of the authors of the September massacres, the party of the mountain contrived that their trial should not be proceeded with. The Girondins themselves showed leniency to the Avignon murderers. In 1792 the Legislative Assembly proclaimed an amnesty in favour of those who had committed crimes arising out of the Revolution, and in particular in favour of Jourdan, known as "Cut-head," the chief of the Avignon assassins. How often since 1871 have we seen Deputies demand amnesty in favour of

[1] Thiers, Vol. III., p. 135

the incendiaries of the Commune and of the murderers of Watrin.

Tyrannicide.

Politics pervert the conscience to such a degree that from ancient times down to the present day the assassination of a tyrant has been presented as a lawful and even a glorious act. Amongst the Greeks it was a duty to slay a tyrant. The teaching of the moralists was to this effect. Plutarch, in his treatise on Destiny, cites the murder of a tyrant as an act of civic virtue. Timoleon, when he acquired the conviction that his brother was arriving at the establishment of a tyranny, made it his duty to put him to death. A monument was erected in honour of Æmodius and Aristogiton, who had designed to murder Hippias. And yet it was not the love of liberty that had induced Aristogiton to act as he did. Having remarked that Æmodius, for whom he entertained a profound affection, was also beloved by Hipparchus, he conceived a violent hatred against the latter, "and fearing lest his rival should resort to force, he thereupon decided to leave no stone unturned to destroy the tyranny."[1]

The Romans also excused and admired tyrannicide. Plutarch relates that Cato, at the age of fourteen, had wished to kill Scylla. Cicero did not blame the murder of Cæsar,[2] and he

---

[1] Thucydides, Bk. VI., § 54.   [2] "De Officiis," Bk. II., § 7.

expressed admiration for the assassination of Tiberius Gracchus. In the eyes of Brutus and Cassius the murder of Cæsar was merely a noble action. The murders of tyrants were so numerous in ancient times that Juvenal could say with reason: " Few tyrants die a natural death."

The belief that it is allowable to kill a tyrant for the good of the State was still prevalent in the Middle Ages, notably at the time of the assassination of the Marshals of Champagne and Normandy, and later at the epoch of the struggle between the Armagnacs and the Burgundians. Etienne Marcel, after the murder of the Marshals of Champagne and Normandy, invoking the right to slay tyrants, addressed these words to the populace from a window of the town hall: "What has been done is for the good and profit of the kingdom." The people made answer: "We admit the act and it has our support." The following day Etienne Marcel assembled the citizens and deputies of the towns, who were present in Paris, and obtained their approbation of the murder just committed. When the Duke of Orleans was killed by the Duke of Burgundy, a doctor of the Sorbonne, the monk Jean Petit, took pains to prove in a long harangue that the Duke of Orleans had been slain in the interest of God, because the Duke of Orleans was the enemy of God; in the interest of the King, because the Duke of Orleans was a traitorous vassal; and in the interest of the Commonwealth, because the Duke of Orleans was a tyrant. "He who slew him," he said, "watching him cunningly and craftily to save the life of the King . . did not commit a crime." The popularity of John the Fearless was not lessened by the murder of the Duke of Orleans.

In the 16th century the right to kill a tyrant was taught by theologians, Protestants, pastors, and jurists. Althurius, a German jurist and a Protestant, who wrote a book on politics, defined the doctrine of tyrannicide. George Buchanan, in his book *de jure regni*, classed the tyrant among ferocious beasts, and wrote that he should be treated as such. Bodin, in his book *de la République* (Bk. II., ch. xiv.), maintained that it is justifiable to kill a tyrant even after the tyranny has been ratified by the people, "for," he says, "what tyrants extort from the people deprived of their power cannot be called consent." La Bœtie approved the murder of Hipparchus.

At the period of the wars of religion, both Catholics and Protestants proclaimed the right to kill a tyrant. Jacques Clement prepared himself by religious observances for the assassination of Henri III. He imagined that he saw an angel appear to him in a dream and say: "I am the messenger of Almighty God, and am come to assure you that you ought to put to death the tyrant of France; think, then, of your state and make you ready, just as the martyr's crown is ready for you." Although tyrannicide had been condemned by the Council of Constance, the murderer of Henri III. was honoured as a saint by numerous fanatics. Cardinal de Retz relates in his memoirs that even in his time he had seen an officer wearing a gorget, "on which was engraved the portrait of the Jacobin who slew Henri III. It was in silver gilt, and bore the inscription: St. Jacques Clément." When Jean Chastel, who made an attempt upon the life of Henry IV., was questioned upon the motive of his crime, he answered that "he had heard it said on several occasions that it must be accounted a true maxim that it was rightful to kill the King, and that those who spoke thus called him a tyrant. Asked if this talk of killing the King was not common with the Jesuits, he said he had heard them say that it was possible to kill the King; that he was outside the Church, and that he was not to be obeyed or held to be king until he had been recognized by the Pope." Put to the torture and urged, when called upon to make his apology, to say that he repented of his crime and asked pardon of God, Chastel answered "that he cried to God for mercy for the sins he had committed in the course of his life, and in particular to forgive him for that he had failed in his endeavour to rid the world of the worst enemy of the Church to-day on the earth."

The Huguenots, for their part, regarded the leaders of the Catholic party as tyrants, and considered that the Old Testament contained a glorification of tyrannicide (Judith, Joel). The Duke of Guise escaped from several attempts to assassinate him before he was murdered by Poltrot de

Meré.[1] Poltrot resorted to prayer to prepare himself for the murder of the Duke of Guise. Théodore de Bèze relates that he prayed God "most ardently that He would graciously change his intention, if what he purported doing were not agreeable to Him, or else that He would endow him with firmness and force enough to kill the tyrant. . . . ." Coligny and Théodore de Bèze have been accused of having egged on Poltrot to commit this murder.

It is certain that they did not blame the assassination and that they considered it justifiable. Théodore de Bèze declared that Poltrot's act was a just judgment of God. Coligny asserted that Poltrot and other Huguenots had apprised him of their homicidal projects, and that while he had not encouraged them to proceed to their execution he had not deterred them. Poltrot, when under examination accused Coligny several times of having encouraged his project, and he persisted in this accusation until the hour of his execution. He said that it was in concert with the admiral that he betook himself to the camp of the Duke of Guise, under the pretext of making his submission; that when starting on his enterprise he "went so far as to say to him that it would be easy to kill the Lord of Guise; that the admiral did not utter a word to dissuade him, but that, on the contrary, although he was aware of his

---

[1] An account of one of these attempts at assassination is to be found in Montaigne (Bk. I., ch. xxiii.), who had been told of it by Amyot.

design, he gave him twenty crowns on one occasion and a hundred crowns on another."[1] It is also certain that the Protestant ministers pictured the Duke of Guise as an implacable persecutor of the Protestants, and gave public expression to the wish that God would deliver the world of him. It was these utterances that aroused the desire in Poltrot to serve as an instrument of Providence in the interest of the Reformation, a desire that he manifested on several occasions, and in particular at the siege of Rouen at which the King of Navarre was killed. The death of this prince being under discussion, Poltrot exclaimed, "It is not enough; a still greater victim must be sacrificed," and when he was asked who this victim was, he answered, "The great Guise;" at the same time uplifting his right arm he said: "Behold the arm that will strike the blow and will put an end to our trouble!" D'Aubigné relates that everybody in the Protestant party knew and hoped that Poltrot would commit the murder. When it had been perpetrated "the joy found expression even in the guise of services in the churches, and in such universal delight that one saw plainly that everybody, far from abhorring the act — an idea that occurred to nobody—would rather have considered it an honour to have accomplished it."[2]

At the time of the English revolution tyrannicide

[1] Bossuet, "Histoire des Variations," Bk. X., § 54.
[2] Bossuet, "Cinquième Avertissement aux Protestants."

was declared legitimate by numerous political writers, and in particular by Milton.

It was an Empress of Russia who, in the 18th century, defended the legitimacy of tyrannicide with the greatest boldness. When Catherine caused her husband Peter III. to be murdered, in excuse of her crime she published a manifesto that would not be disowned by theorists of regicide and anarchism. She maintained that Peter III. was the enemy of the nation and of religion, and that the courageous men who had rid Russia of him were to be congratulated.

During the Revolution the Jacobins asserted their right to kill a tyrant. The right was also upheld by the Emigrants, who hired assassins to dispatch the First Consul. An Emigrant of the name of Pelletier, in a newspaper that he issued in London, alleged that an usurper had not the right to live, and that it was justifiable to kill him. The First Consul caused him to be prosecuted, and Pelletier was judged by the English courts and condemned. Georges Cadoudal's attempt upon the life of Bonaparte was admired by the fanatical Royalists, and the Revolutionists who did not participate in this crime regretted that it had not been committed by their party, so glorious did it appear to them. The Chancellor Pasquier relates in his recently published memoirs (Vol. II.) that the plan to assassinate Napoleon devised by Maubreuil, seems to have been countenanced by the Coalition and by Talleyrand.

Under the Restoration, under Louis Philippe,

and under Napoleon III., there were numerous attempts upon the lives of the sovereigns and of the princes of the Royal family. Six attempts were made by fanatics upon the life of Louis Philippe. The Dukes of Aumale and of Nemours were the object of a seventh attempt. The most abominable of all was that of Fieschi, who to reach the King killed and wounded forty-two persons.[1]

Hatred of society, vanity, the reading of revolutionary publications, and especially of the works of Saint Just,[2] and the incitements of the newspapers, which were perpetually calumniating Louis Philippe, were the principal causes of these attempts. Alibaud maintained before the Court of Peers "that regicide is the right of the man who can only obtain justice by his own hand, and that he was as much in the right in what he had done against Louis Philippe as was Brutus in slaying Cæsar." Quenisset, one of the authors of the attempt upon the Dukes of Aumale and Nemours, admitted that he had been educated in the doctrine of regicide by the secret societies. "He had been moulded," he said, so as to make of him a man of action.[3]

It was the society known as the "Working Men

---

[1] The infernal machine that Georges Cadoudal had exploded in front of the carriage of the First Consul had also caused the death of a great number of persons.

[2] The works of Saint Just were found at the dwellings of Pepin and Alibaud.

[3] It being easier to "mould" the young than men of mature age, it is especially to the young that the leading spirits of secret societies turn their attention in their efforts to proselytise.

Partisans of Equality" that incited Darmès to regicide. In the case of this latter, the hatred of the middle class went side by side with the hatred of royalty. Darmès referred to the bourgeoisie in the same terms as are employed by the Anarchists of to-day. "The middle class," he said, "is solely composed of those who were freed in 1789, and who, after robbing the nobility, their masters, have become the enemies of the masses, whom they are oppressing in their turn." [1]

In the case of the regicides of this period, as in that of the present-day Anarchists, political fanaticism was often brought to a pitch by vanity. Fieschi admitted that the desire for celebrity had been the principal motive of his attempt. Henri, the last of the fanatics who attempted the life of Louis Philippe, declared that, disgusted with existence, he had committed the attempt in order that his death might attract wide attention. Pride, too, was one of the principal motives of the crime of Louvel, who compared himself to Charlotte Corday, and sought to derive glory from his exploit. Vaillant declared, after his crime, that by this notable act he had placed himself among the ranks of the benefactors of modern society, and that his name was henceforth immortal.

Attempts on the life of the sovereign were also very numerous under the Second Empire. Mazzini never ceased to advocate the assassination

---

[1] "La Répression Pénale," by Bérenger. "Sciences et Travaux de l'Académie des Sciences, Morales, et Politiques," August and September, 1855.

of the Emperor, and to dispatch Sectaries to Paris to effect it. Felix Pyat, at the time a refugee in London, exclaimed: "What need is there to discuss any longer the legitimacy of regicide? To do so would be superfluous in the country of Charles I. The sons of the men who guillotined a Capet have nothing new to say on this subject to the descendants of the executioners of a Stuart."

The European revolutionary committee, which held its sittings in London, endeavoured, on several occasions, in 1853 and in 1855, to bring about the assassination of Napoleon III. by Italian Sectaries. The attempt that was made on the 14th January, 1858, by Orsini and his accomplices, resulted in the wounding of 156 persons, of whom eight succumbed, and yet Orsini, in the course of his cross-examination, pretended that his principles did not admit of assassination, and Pieri maintained that he was not so overweening as to constitute himself the judge of kings.

Orsini's counsel, Jules Favre, pronounced an eloquent condemnation of tyrannicide. "My beliefs," he said, "have not as symbol assassination and the dagger. I abhor violence, and I condemn force when it is not employed in the service of the right. Were a nation unhappy enough to fall into the hands of a despot, it would not be a dagger that would break its chains. The hours of a despot are measured by God, who counts them. He has in store for them catastrophes more inevitable than the infernal machines of conspirators." Jules Favre was right: the death of the tyrant does not do away with the tyranny. When a country is ripe for servitude, the tyrant who is slain is soon replaced by another; the murder of Cæsar did not re-establish liberty in Rome. Under the Roman Empire a great number of princes were put to death, but they were replaced by others who were no better.

What would become of States if it were admitted that a citizen is entitled to decide that a prince is a tyrant, and that he has the right to kill him on his own private authority, without a trial, for the good of the State and of religion, or for the salvation of the people? What, to repeat, would they become "unless it be a slaughter-house, and the perpetual and ever blood-stained theatre of civil wars"?[1] A Catholic writer, who after the trial of Jean Chastel issued an apology for his crime, remarked that there was no difference between Protestants and Catholics, "except in respect to the determining who is a tyrant and who is not." In the eyes of the Protestants the Duke of Guise was a tyrant; in the eyes of the Catholics the tyrant was Coligny or Henry III., or even Henry IV. The most easy-going kings, Louis XVI. or Louis Philippe, for example, have been held to be tyrants by demagogues. Why should not the members of a Parliament be considered tyrants? The truth is, that what Bossuet said of the principle set up by Jurien is applicable to tyrannicide. "His principle is just as much an attack on any other

[1] Bossuet, "Cinquième Avertissement aux Protestants."

public authority, sovereign or subordinate, whatever be its name, and in whatever form it be exercised. For what is lawful against kings will, in consequence, be lawful against a Senate, against the entire body of magistrates, against States, against a Parliament, when these institutions or persons shall make laws that are contrary or are held to be contrary to religion and the safety of the subject."

The regicide affirms that his action is justified by the end he has in view, which is the saving of his country. The reply may be made him that the murder of a defenceless man is not a certain means of saving his country, and further, that the lawfulness of the end in view does not justify the employment of reprehensible expedients. The duty of saving one's country does not do away with the duty respecting human life. To save one's country, one has the right to sacrifice one's life, but not the right of disposing of the lives of others. The interest of the country does not authorise assassination. Were it sufficient that a Catholic should declare a Protestant leader to be a tyrant or that a demagogue should accuse a sovereign of tyranny for them to have the right to slay, it would be necessary to say with Bossuet, that society would become a slaughter-house.

It is no more allowable to kill a tyrant to save one's country than to burn a heretic with a view to being agreeable to God. Did the end justify the means, there would be no such thing as duty, and every description of crime would be permissible.

Good intentions do not justify a criminal action. Murder is still crime, even when it is held to be expedient. To slay a man unjudged, whether king or bourgeois, whom one has set down as a tyrant, on one's own private authority, is to be a tyrant oneself.

CHAPTER III.

ANARCHISM.

Anarchism adopts the doctrine of tyrannicide—Resemblance between the Anarchists and Terrorists—The Nihilists—Kropotkine—Proudhon—The Ishmaelites—Anarchists and Capitalists—Jacobin and Anarchist theories—Babeuf's doctrine of Anarchy—Diderot and Rousseau on Equality—Social Equality is the aim of modern Anarchism—Proudhon the father of Anarchism—Anarchist views on property—Property and Crime—"Robbery is Restitution"—Equality and Liberty—Revolutions reveal the black side of human nature—Saint Simon on Capitalists—The social theories of Lamennais—Elisée Reclus on Equality—Anarchist programme—Anarchists and Militarism—Lamennais on Crime—Jonathan Swift on political corruption—Sentimentalism at the root of attacks on Social system—Louis Blanc—Kropotkine's sentimentalism—Sentimentalism of the French Revolutionists—The Anarchist substitutes himself for the State—Anarchist view of human rights—Vanity and Fanaticism among Anarchists—The apologists of revolutionary crimes make Anarchists—Thiers on the Revolutionary Tribunal—The victims of books—Duties of the historian—The effects of the Revolution on France—Philosophical Materialism and Anarchism—Vaillant—Ravachol—Effects of philosophical materialism—The doctrine that society is responsible for all social miseries—Anarchists assert that they are the victims of society—Marat's hatred of society—The chief end of life according to Anarchism—The Christian view of wealth—Patriotism and Anarchism—The aim of Anarchism and Socialism is to divide wealth—Revolutionary ideas and materialist theories—Nietzche's teaching—Christian morality and Anarchism—The classes who despise morality—The young Anarchists—Instruction without morals—The Anarchist Henry—Science cannot assure happiness—Intellectual poisons—Political Anarchy is the consequence of moral Anarchy—Views of Auguste Comte—Venal politicians and the unworthy rich are largely responsible for the growth of Anarchism.

The disappearance of the monarchical system of government does not put an end to attempts upon the person of the Chief of the State. The spirit of revolt manifests itself under a republic, as well as under a monarchy; against the presidents of republics and legislative assemblies, as well as against sovereigns.

Anarchism is merely an adaptation of tyrannicide, a consequence of the false maxim that a political crime may find its excuse in the end in view; that it is lawful to kill in order to secure the triumph of a cause. "Death to the tyrant!" cry the regicides. "Death to the well-to-do classes!" re-echo the Anarchists. The theory of the latter is the same as that of the Leaguers and the Terrorists, who declared: "The end justifies the means, and assassination is excusable when it is resorted to to assure the triumph of religion or the safety of the country."

A journalist recently intimated to the Anarchist M. his astonishment at finding that he admired the crime committed by Vaillant. "I fancied," was the Anarchist's answer, "that the bourgeois republicans admired regicide, that of 1793 for example, by which they profited. Very well: the proletarian Vaillant committed an act of regicide when he directed his bomb against the 'kings of the republic.'"

In order to justify his outrage, Vaillant maintained that his attitude towards the well-to-do class was that of a man who acts in self-defence. "Are we not defending ourselves," he said, "when we strike out in response to the blows that are dealt us from above?"[1] Here we have the sophism by which the regicide thought to

[1] "Gazette des Tribunaux," 11th January, 1894.

excuse his crime. The citizen, he argued, has the same rights against a tyrant as against an enemy: he acts in self-defence. The author of the apology for Jean Chastel invoked this right, "and the more so," as he explained, "because the tyrant is unjustly at war with the entire people, in general and individually, while the community, on the contrary, is justly at war with him, and in consequence may attempt against his person whatever is allowed by the rules of war against a real enemy."[1]

The Terrorists, like the Anarchists of to-day, prided themselves on their crimes. They boasted of the priests they had drowned and of the aristocrats they had shot down. Neither Saint Just, Robespierre, Couthon, Collot d'Herbois, nor Billaud-Varennes experienced any remorse. They believed that the drownings, shootings, and massacres in which they had had a hand, were justified by the end they had had in view. They held that these blood-lettings[2] purified the social organism.

The Anarchists who throw bombs to terrorise society, plead the end they have in view in excuse of their abominable outrages. They are not

[1] Bayle's Dictionary. V. Chastel. Grotius admitted this right of war against a tyrant. (Bk. I., ch. iv., § 17.) He invokes the authority of Tertullian, who declared that every man is by birth a soldier, with a mission to combat criminals guilty of high treason or public enemies.

[2] The Spanish "*sans-chemises*," like the *sans-culottes*, maintain that "a good blood-letting, short but abundant," is needful. ' The rotten branches must be cut away from the social tree in order to allow it to develop."

ashamed of their exploits, because they aim at realising the welfare of humanity by the aid of dynamite, just as the Jacobins served themselves with the scaffold to effect the same purpose.

After Robespierre had put to death the Girondins and Dantonists, he exclaimed: "Now that we have got rid of the conspirators, there are no longer any obstacles to prevent us assuring the happiness of the people." He imagined that he had laboured for the welfare of the people by cutting off the heads of the moderate republicans. What difference is there between his doctrine and that of the Anarchists who, for their part, wish to destroy the capitalist class so as to do away with the obstacle which stands in the way of the welfare of the people?

The Anarchists wish to frighten the capitalists, just as the Terrorists wished to frighten the aristocrats. "We wish to spread terror so as to reign," an Anarchist remarked recently. The Russian Nihilists called themselves "Terrorists." They laid claim to this name when brought to trial, and declared that their object was to terrorise the Government. In this they were successful, since for several years Russia was terrorised by a series of the most audacious outrages. In a programme of the Russian Nihilists, seized at Kœnigsburg, the following passage was to be read: "As to the assassination of certain persons, we should be guided solely by considerations of the comparative profit that would ensue. . . . Death should strike them unexpectedly, should perturb the Government, and should spread abroad a tragic terror." The aims of the French Anarchists are identical: they would terrorise the Government, the magistracy, and juries. The bomb that was exploded in the restaurant Véry had a further object than the killing of the courageous citizens who denounced Ravachol; it was meant to terrorise the jury who were to try him.

Like the Terrorists of 1793, the Anarchists have adopted the motto of Danton: "Be bold! be bold! always be bold!" Danton is their model. "Brave men," says Kropotkine, "are aware that to be successful it is necessary to be daring."[1]

Let there be no pity, no hesitation, no half-measures; the danger is still there where Danton detected it, when he cried to France: "Audacity, audacity, and still audacity! What is wanted above all is intellectual audacity, which will not fail to bring in its train, and that at once, the faculty of willing with audacity."[2] This theory of Danton's, which was also the theory of Machiavelli, has always been that of the revolutionaries. It is the maxim that Proudhon put forward in 1848. "Recall," he exclaimed, "the words of Danton on the morrow of the 10th August, when France, in rebellion, demanded of its citizens a counsel that might save the country. 'It is needful,' cried Danton with an exterminatory gesture, 'it is needful to

[1] "Paroles d'un Révolté," p. 285.
[2] Kropotkine, "La Conquête du Pain," p. 97.

strike terror into the hearts of the aristocrats.'"[1] Similarly, when committing their monstrous outrages, the Anarchists declare: "The capitalists must be terrified." They know that they are in a minority, but they count upon the cowardice of honest folk, upon the audacity of their adherents and upon the contagiousness of example. "It is by *action*," writes Kropotkine, "that minorities succeed in awaking that sentiment of independence and that fever of audacity in the absence of which it is impossible that a revolution should be accomplished." Audacity must be awakened by setting an example: the spirit of sacrifice is contagious. "By dint of incidents that force themselves upon the general attention, the new idea filters into men's minds and wins proselytes. An act may do more in a few days to spread the doctrine than thousands of pamphlets. Above all it awakes the spirit of revolt, it breeds audacity. . . There have been audacious acts that have sufficed to put the entire governmental machine out of gear for several days and that have shaken the colossus. The masses perceive that the monster is not so terrible as they imagined, . . they foresee the victory, their audacity grows." "Moreover," adds the theorist of Anarchism, "when the passions of the populace are at fever heat, repression is powerless to damp the energy of those in revolt; it produces the contrary effect: calls forth fresh acts of revolt, . . . and step by step these

[1] Proudhon. "Avertissement aux Propriétaires," p. 10.

acts spread from class to class, become general, and attain their full development."[1]

This theory of the virtues of audacity, before it was inculcated by the Anarchists and the Jacobins, had been enunciated and put into practice by the sect of the Ishmaelites who flourished in Asia in the 11th century and were the terror of that continent for four hundred years. "To believe in nothing and to venture everything" was the main dogma of this sect, which taught that all actions are a matter of indifference, and alleged that to regenerate the world recourse to murder was necessary. This sect of assassins even founded a kingdom, "which held its own for four centuries, in hostility, not merely with the nations that surrounded it, but with all humanity." Hassan-ben-Sabah, who was the chief of these assassins, "was no mere vulgar brigand, but a theologian, a philosopher and a writer."[2]

"The safety of the people," declared Danton, on another occasion, when forcing a vote from the revolutionary tribunal, "demands extreme means and terrible measures." The Terrorists of 1793 said, when they ordered the guillotining of the Girondins: "The Republic is in danger; to save it the Gironde must perish." The Anarchists repeat the same sophism when they affirm: "Society is diseased; to heal it the capitalist class must disappear." For the Jacobins, the killing of an

[1] "Paroles d'un Révolté," pp. 284-287.
[2] Philarète Chasles, "Voyages d'un Critique (Orient)," pp. 310-312.

aristocrat, the guillotining of a Girondin, the drowning of a priest, were steps towards the salvation of the people, the preliminaries of the reign of fraternity. To assure the welfare of humanity, Marat, in his journal, proposed daily the cutting off now of 50,000, now of 270,000 heads. The Anarchists, in their turn, would bring about the welfare of humanity by the extermination of the capitalist class. "It is the capitalist class," they say, "that stands in the way of the happiness of the people; in consequence let it be done away with."

The Terrorists of '93 were in the habit of saying: "Among the aristocrats none are innocent." To-day the Anarchists declare: "There are none innocent among the capitalists." In the declaration that the Anarchist Emile Henry read in the court of assizes the following passage occurs: "For a moment, the accusation that had been made against Ravachol crossed my mind: what of the innocent victims? However, the problem did not long embarrass me. The building in which the offices of the Carmaux Company were situated was exclusively inhabited by members of the capitalist class. *In consequence, there would be no innocent victims.*"

The political methods of the Anarchist theorists are the same as those of the Jacobins of 1793, but it is only right to recognise that the ideas of the two parties with regard to property and government are different. The Anarchists wish to destroy these institutions, whereas the Jacobins desired their maintenance. Still, in 1793, the hatred of the rich and the thirst for pleasures had already inspired certain of the Jacobins with theories that bordered on Anarchism. Chaumette remarked: "We have got rid of the nobility and the Capets, but we have still an aristocracy to overthrow: that of the rich." Tallien demanded absolute equality, and termed the possessors of property "public robbers." Before Proudhon, Brissot had written in his "Recherchés Philosophiques sur la Propriété et sur le Vol": "The robber is the rich man; exclusive property is a robbery."[1] It is a question, too, whether such men as Marat and Saint Just may not be considered Anarchists: Marat, who incited the masses to massacre and pillage, and Saint Just, who demanded the confiscation of the property of conspirators, and who said: "Our only enemies are the rich and the vicious; we must needs make a new city."

The hatred of the rich, the scorning to serve in the army, the ardent longing for absolute equality, the thirst for material satisfaction, the belief that the end justifies the means, and that it is lawful to risk for the welfare of society in the massacre of those in authority—all these revolutionary passions and all these sophisms, which make up the doctrine of Anarchism, are to be found in the theories of Babeuf, who, under the Directory, had declared against society a war to

---

[1] Already in ancient times the Athenian demagogues had maintained that property is a robbery.

the knife. The Sectarian followers of Babeuf had taken the name of the "Society of Equals."[1] Like Kropotkine at the present day, they aimed at founding a republic of equals. Their profession of faith, drawn up by Sylvain Marchal, author of the "Dictionnaire des Athées," contained the following passages: " . . . We desire a real equality or death, . . . and we will have this real equality at no matter what cost. Woe to those who stand between us and it ! . . . The people have made short work of kings and priests. They will treat in the same way the new tyrants, the new hypocrites, who have taken the places of the old. . . . What we want is not merely that there should be mention of equality among the Rights of Man, . . . we want it in our midst, beneath the roofs of our houses. . . . The sole purpose of our sacred enterprise is to put an end to civil dissensions and public misery. . . . Let those who are for justice and the common welfare organise themselves with equality as their cry. The hour has come to found the republic of the equals. . . . The day of restitution has dawned. . . . Let there be an end to the revolting distinctions between rich and poor, the great and the humble, masters and servants, those who govern and those who are governed. For the future, let the only differences between men be those of age and sex. Since all have the same faculties and the

---

[1] Babeuf when writing to his accomplices addressed them: "My dear equal."

same needs, let them henceforth be educated alike and fed alike."

Babeuf, too, like the contemporary Anarchists, had endeavoured to deprive the soldiers of their love of country, and of their sentiments of duty and obedience. "Your blood is spilled," he said to them, "in useless and disastrous conflicts. In the meantime, your mothers and wives are allowed to die of hunger; the people are lean from privations. . . . You are treated like automatons that may be disposed of at will; you will be sold like the vile herd that its master sends to the pasture or the slaughter-house."

Babeuf and his accomplices wished to secure the triumph of their doctrine by the extermination of the governing class. They were resolved to put to death "all civil or military agents, all functionaries and magistrates. . . . All opposition will be overcome at once by force. Those who resist will be exterminated." The standard of the insurrection was to bear the words: Liberty, Equality, the Common Welfare.

During their trial, Babeuf and his accomplices endeavoured to intimidate the jury. Their attitude was insolent and overweening, and they insulted their judges. Babeuf, when he had been condemned to death, compared himself to Jesus Christ, asserted that he died a martyr to a noble cause, and consoled himself by the thought that upright and compassionate men would say of him: "He was supremely virtuous." He had adopted the same overweening tone in the letters he had addressed to the Directory, while the case against him was in preparation. He proposed to treat with the Government on a footing of equality, and delivered himself of the following utterance: "My scaffold will figure gloriously side by side with that of Barneveld and of Sidney. On the morrow of my execution altars will be raised in my honour."

The writings of Mably and Diderot, and in particular the discourse of J. J. Rousseau upon "inequality," were the sources whence Babeuf and his fellow-Anarchists had drawn their fanatical ideas. Germain, one of the band, confessed this in these terms: "I strengthened my courage against the oppressors of humanity by reading Mably, Rousseau, and Diderot." The truth is that Mably, in his "Traité de la Législation," attempted to prove that nature intended the fortune and social status of citizens to be equal, that it teaches men to hold their possessions in common, and that where equality is absent, there are oppressors and oppressed. This theory is precisely that of the present-day Anarchists, whose object is not moral and political equality, but social equality and equality in respect to well-being and material satisfactions. "We ought," writes Elisée Reclus, "to be able to assure to every one the complete satisfaction of his wants and desires."[1]

Since society, as at present constituted, tole-

---

[1] The preface by Elisée Reclus to Kropotkine's "Conquête du Pain," p. vii.

rates inequality, extreme opulence, and extreme destitution, it must be destroyed and replaced by a new order of things, which will insure for everyone his share of happiness. The Anarchists even mean eating and drinking just like the capitalists.[1] When they are confronted with the objection that the capitalist pays for what he consumes, they answer that he pays with money he has stolen.

Proudhon, whom Kropotkine styles "the immortal father of Anarchism," has been the continuator in our time of Babeuf. He too demands equality in respect to social functions and fortune. As he says himself, his love of equality amounted to an intoxication: "Owners of property, enriched by the sweat of our brows . . . the enthusiasm that possesses us, the enthusiasm for equality is unknown to you;" it is an intoxication more potent than life, more thrilling than love."[2] It is Proudhon who has endowed revolutionary socialism and anarchism with the two mottoes: "Property is robbery" and "Catholicism is the foe." Convinced that social and religious in-

---

[1] Léauthier, before committing his crime, ordered in a well-known restaurant an excellent luncheon, which he washed down with champagne and did not pay for. When it was remarked to him that people do not drink champagne when they are unable to pay for it, he retorted: "The well-to-do drink it all the same." Recently, at the Aix assizes, we judged another Anarchist who had ordered a dinner, costing some six shillings, and including a bottle of champagne. When asked why, being without money, he had drunk champagne, he replied: "I drank champagne so that there might be so much the less for those who drink too much of it."

[2] Proudhon, "Avertissement aux Propriétaires," p. 98.

stitutions are a mistake, Proudhon suggested "anarchy," the doing away, that is, with religion and courts of justice. "Begin," he cried, "by sending back to Heaven the Eternal Father. His presence amongst us hangs by a single thread, the budget. Cut the cord; you will know what the Revolution should put in the place of God. .... The Revolution can come to no terms with the Divinity .... there lies the enemy."[1]

I am not aware whether the contemporary Anarchists are still in the habit of reading Mably, but I have had occasion to judge, at the Bouches-du-Rhône assizes, an individual accused of theft, who had made J. J. Rousseau's discourse on inequality his habitual reading. This discourse is, indeed, a compendium of Anarchism.

It is with a view to establishing social equality that the Anarchists desire to put an end to individual property, to expropriate the capitalists, to burn everything in the shape of bonds or financial scrip, and to make an *auto-da-fé* of all the laws that guarantee the rights of property. Property in their eyes is as humiliating an institution as slavery or serfdom, and they regard the suppression of individual property, the restitution to the community of the totality of wealth, as the only means of doing away with social distinctions. Kropotkine, addressing himself to the working classes, says: "Lay hands on the belongings of

---

[1] "Idée Générale de la Revolution au XIX⁰ Siècle," pp. 286, 292, 294, 301.

the rich, instal yourselves in their palaces and private dwellings, and make a bonfire of the piles of bricks and worm-eaten wood that served you as hovels in the past. Private property is a robbery accomplished at the expense of the fortune of the community; . . . all products, the sum total of the savings and appurtenances of humanity, are the outcome of the mutual labour of all, and have but one proprietor—humanity."[1]

The suppression of property, the Anarchists add, will have the further advantage of bringing about the almost entire disappearance of criminality. "As for what are called 'crimes'—outrages upon the person—it is known that two-thirds and often three-quarters of these 'crimes' are inspired by the desire of obtaining possession of wealth belonging to another. This vast category of so-called 'crimes' will be abolished the day that private property has ceased to exist."[2] Diderot, before Kropotkine, had made this discovery. "I think," he said, "that it will not be contested that if private property did not exist, there would be an end to the existence of all its pernicious consequences." In other words, the only reason why there are thieves is because there are owners of property: do away with property and you do away with robbery. By a similar reasoning it might be said that adultery is only committed because marriage exists, and, therefore, that to do away with adultery, marriage

[1] "Paroles d'un Révolté," p. 312.   [2] Ibid., p 241.

should be abolished. Diderot, like the Anarchists, desired that property should be held in common in order to realise social equality. Babeuf spoke of him as "our principal forerunner, *our* Diderot."

Property being a robbery, according to the Anarchists, they are led logically to the corollary: robbery is only a *restitution*. I have had to try for theft an Anarchist, who said to me: "I am not a thief, but the author of a restitution." It is not merely in the course of the last few years that people of this persuasion have been met with. At the Seine assizes, in 1847, there was tried a band of ten criminals, who proposed, by means of pillage and incendiarism, to force the well-to-do to make restitution. They belonged to an association known as the "Materialist Communists." Perverted by the reading of revolutionary and socialist newspapers, they had formed the project of destroying society with a view to suppressing property. Pamphlets and songs were found in their possession similar to those that are found to-day in the possession of the Anarchists.

It should not cause astonishment that the wild desire for absolute equality in the matter of material satisfactions should result in so firm a hatred against owners of property, masters, and capitalists. Already, during the Revolution, the spectacle was afforded of the principle of equality, ill understood, breeding hatred of distinctions of every sort, hatred of wealth, hatred of the nobility, hatred of education, hatred of virtue, and hatred of politeness. By dint of developing the principle of equality to extremes, the revolutionary spirit caused people to address each other in the second person singular, and abolished the use of conventional expressions of politeness. The judges of Marie Antoinette addressed her in the second person singular, and called her the "woman Capet." The Jacobins did away with the expressions "Monsieur" and "Madame," and replaced them by that of citizen. The Constituent Assembly not only forbade the use of titles of nobility, but decreed penalties against those who should dress their servants in livery. (Decree of the 21st October, 1791.) The Convention ordered the confiscation, within a week, of all parks, gardens, enclosures, houses, and buildings where armorial bearings were exhibited. (Decree of the 1st August, 1793.) Equality, ill understood, becomes the enemy of liberty, talent, and virtue, and gives birth to a desire to reduce to the same level whatever surpasses the average. Everything excites jealousy: intellectual superiority, moral worth, knowledge, even physical advantages. During the Revolution, Fourcroy, the chemist, who was a member of the Convention, was reproached with devoting too much time to science. Fourcroy, alarmed, excused himself by saying: "I have only been seen three times in the university buildings, and my presence on these occasions was due to my desire to propagate revolutionary principles." Men of worth are often persecuted solely because people are

annoyed at hearing their virtues extolled. The
Roman soldiers clamoured for the punishment of
Celsus, because " his integrity and worth irritated them as if they had been crimes. . . .
Even glory and virtue are looked askance at,
since they seem, when too near at hand, to
imply the condemnation of what does not resemble them."[1] The Anarchists desire that there
shall be no differences of instruction or education; they demand that the obligation of manual
labour shall be incumbent upon everybody, and
that everybody shall receive a like bringing-up
and education.

During the Terror people made a show of
coarse manners, so as to escape the reproach of
being aristocrats. The Jacobins discovered aristocrats at every turn and corner, and the *sansculottes* put down shop-keepers and lawyers'
clerks as aristocrats. A delicate skin was more
than once considered as a sign of aristocracy
sufficient to call for the penalty of death. The
appellation "Mr. Delicate Skin"[2] was equivalent to a sentence of death.

When the murdered Duchesse de Lamballe was
exhibited naked in the Rue Saint-Antoine, the
whiteness of her skin aroused the fury of her
slaughterers. "Look," cried one of them, infuriated, "look how white she was. Do you see her
beautiful skin?"

[1] Tacitus, "Historiæ," Bk. I., § 45. "Annales," Bk. IV., § 33.

[2] Michelet. "Histoire de la Révolution Française," Vol. V.,
p. 97.

The history of revolutions throws a terrible light upon the ugly side of human nature. Envy and the desire to abuse are the ruling passions of the revolutionary. In England, as in France, there have been "Levellers." To-day these Levellers go by the name of Anarchists; the majority of them are at bottom mere envious individuals who are jealous of those who occupy a higher social station. They mask their greed under the cloak of a theory when they demand the expropriation of the capitalists, the suppression of the "capitalist privileges," and the triumph of the fourth estate.

Socialists and demagogues have been inflaming for a century past that hatred of the well-to-do class which to-day incites the Anarchists to perpetrate so many outrages. In the "Catéchisme Politique des Industriels" which he published in 1824, Saint-Simon addressed the very same reproaches to the capitalists that the Anarchists are now repeating. He alleged that the middle classes carried through the revolution solely in their own interest, and with a view to exploit the masses (page 8). On the morrow of the revolution of 1830 the demagogues denounced the middle class as an oppressive aristocracy that it was the duty of the masses to abolish.[1] During the reign of Louis Philippe imprudent

---

[1] De Salvandy, "Seize Mois, ou la Révolution et les Révolutionnaires," p. 322. In 1793 the middle class had already been pointed to as a proper object of the hatred of the masses. Durand de Maillane relates that at the time of the election of the Deputies to the Convention, an elector at Avignon proposed "to bring the guilty middle class to reason." ("Memoires," p. 32.)

writers inspired the poor with hatred of the rich by exaggerating the delights that accrue to wealth, and by drawing a sombre picture of the situation of the poor. Numerous are the books in which employers of labour are represented as vampires battening upon the people, and in which the workers are depicted as the victims of oppression and reduced to a state that is worse than slavery.

Among the writers who have stirred up feelings of hatred and vengeance in the hearts of the people, there is one who specially deserves to be cited on account of his great talent that bordered on genius, and of the considerable influence he exerted. The writer in question is Lamennais, who, after preaching with rare eloquence peace, concord, and union, launched out into furious anathemas against society, exciting the masses against kings and priests, the poor against the rich,[1] the workers against their masters, and even the soldiers against their chiefs. All the sophisms of Anarchism are to be found in the "Paroles d'un Croyant," which might be styled with more justice the "Paroles d'un Révolté;" the wish for absolute equality, the hatred of authority, the hatred of the rich, incitement to violence, provocation to military indiscipline. In his eighth chapter Lamennais describes what he terms the exploitation of the workers by the employers of labour, who, he says,

---

[1] It was Lamennais who said: "The paradise of the rich is made of the hell of the poor."

are continually increasing the hours of labour and diminishing the wage; they cause the death of the workers by depriving them of absolute necessaries; they are disciples of Satan, more cruel than the masters who owned slaves; there is no name for them but in hell. In chapter vi. he compares man to a bee, who is only entitled to the portion of honey necessary to his subsistence, and he asserts that whoever gathers more than he needs is an unjust man. This theory is that of socialism and of anarchism: "To each according to his needs." In chapter vii. the believer affirms that God created neither great nor humble, neither masters nor slaves, neither poor nor rich, neither kings nor subjects: "He made all men equal." Here again it is impossible not to be struck by the resemblance between these ideas of Lamennais and those of Babeuf, who wrote in his scheme of declaration: "Article 7.—In a properly constituted society there should be neither rich nor poor. Article 8.—The rich who will not abandon their superfluous possessions in favour of the indigent are the enemies of the people. Article 10.—The aim of the revolution is to do away with inequality and to re-establish universal happiness."[1] In

[1] Boireau, the accomplice of Fieschi, also declared that God had made neither kings nor subjects, nor masters nor slaves. "If God," he added, "had wished men to be slaves, He would have caused them to be born with a saddle or a pack-saddle upon their backs." The prison chaplain to whom Boireau expounded his ideas replied to him with these words of Voltaire: "Raise an outcry against law and authority, and you

chapter xix. and chapter xxxvii., the believer reverts to the idea of absolute liberty, and maintains that liberty only exists when there is nobody to dominate. "You have," he says, "but one Father, who is God, and but one Master, who is Christ. All are born equal. None comes into the world bearing with him the right to command" (ch. xix.). Elisée Reclus gives expression to the same thought, and takes his stand, like Lamennais, on the same passage of the New Testament, when he says: "It is not in the choice of new masters that salvation lies. Is it needful that we Anarchists, the enemies of Christianity, should remind an entire society that claims to be Christian of these words of a man of whom it has made a God: 'Call no man master! master!' Let everyone remain his own master."[1] The Anarchists would have neither masters, kings, nor elected representatives of the people. Up till now, they say, the sole object of the middle classes in overthrowing a Government has been to possess themselves of the vacant places. To-day we aim at suppressing all government, and all authority, in order to give mankind

have every idle fellow on your side. And when you have these fellows at your beck and call there will not be wanting shrewd persons who will fit them with saddle and bridle, and who, mounting them, will proceed to overthrow thrones and empires." Boireau reflected a moment and then said: "After all it is very possible you are right." (M. Bérenger's "Report on Penal Repression.")

[1] Kropotkine, "Paroles d'un Révolté." Preface by Elisée Reclus, p. x.

liberty. The watchwords of the new revolution should be: No more laws! no more criminal codes! no more barracks! no more prisons! no more judges! no more police!

For some time past the number of books attacking the army have been on the increase. The Anarchists advise the soldiers to refuse obedience, and adjure the conscripts to decline to perform their military service. A few years ago, at the Bouches-du-Rhône assizes, I was called upon to try Sebastien Faure on the charge of inciting to military indiscipline. I remarked that his system of defence was identical with the ideas developed by Lamennais in the 35th chapter of the "Paroles d'un Croyant," where he excites the soldiers against their chiefs and represents military service to be a diabolical invention. "The oppressors of nations," says Lamennais, "invented military service solely with a view to keep men in a state of servitude. Satan suggested to them an infernal ruse, in giving them the idea to assert that obedience is glorious, and that honour and fidelity are virtues. 'I will persuade them,' said Satan, 'that it is a glorious action. . . . . *I will make them two idols, which they shall call Honour and Fidelity, and a law which shall be called passive obedience. And they shall worship these idols!*' If Honour, Fidelity, and Obedience be idols, the conclusion is obvious: for the good of humanity these idols must be broken."

The pages written by Lamennais in condemnation

of violence and crime have never been surpassed. "The holiest cause," he wrote, "becomes an impious and execrable cause when crime is employed in its support." And yet a few pages further on, by one of those astonishing contradictions that were common with him, he advises the oppressed to resort, if necessary, to violence, to shatter the tyranny of their oppressors. "If at first," he tells them, "victory seems to elude your grasp, it is only a trial, and your day will come, for your blood will be as the blood of Abel, whom Cain slew, and your death as that of the martyrs" (ch. xii.). Thus it is that Lamennais excites the poor against the rich, and urges them to do themselves justice and to conquer their share of happiness by violence. He would have property restricted to what is necessary, and material satisfactions equalised. He inculcates to citizens the contempt for authority and to soldiers the hatred of their chiefs, telling them that honour and fidelity are idols. Does this not amount to expounding the theories of Anarchism?

Such is the violence of language to which a writer of genius allows himself to be drawn on, when he is unable to restrain the warmth of his feelings and the vivacity of his imagination. His reason wanders, and his judgment is troubled to such a degree that he no longer sees things as they are. Whichever way he looked, Lamennais thought he saw the weak suffering oppression, the just begging their bread, rogues covered with honours and abounding in riches, and the innocent condemned by iniquitous judges. On one occasion he entered court and heard the trial of a vagrancy case. To convict a person of this offence the law demands that three conditions shall be fulfilled. A vagrant is a person who has no fixed domicile, no means of existence, *and who habitually exercises no trade or profession.* The not possessing a domicile and the lack of means of existence are not punishable, unless they be accompanied by the failure to exercise a trade or profession. The law demands that every man who is without resources shall work, a wandering life without means and without work being a danger to society. Blinded by his prejudices against society, Lamennais imagined that the man whom he saw on his trial was punished because he was poor, and he left the court cursing the judges and society.[1] He had not even heard accurately the words of the presiding judge, or understood the drift of the measures for the prevention of vagrancy. If on returning to his study he had but consulted the criminal code, he would have seen that the judge had punished, not poverty, but habitual laziness.

Almost all the writers who have violently attacked society in pamphlets, novels, or plays, and have furnished Anarchism with weapons, are men who have been led astray by morbid

---

[1] Lamennais, "Amschaspands et Dasvands," third edition, p. 232. Moreover in " Paroles d'un Croyant " Lamennais says: "There are scarcely any other than bad laws in the world. Sons of Adam, these mill-stones are the laws of those who govern you, and it is you whom they crush." (Ch. xxviii.)

sensibility and a disordered imagination. They suffer at the spectacle of human misery to such a degree that they rail against God or society: their sensibility makes of them Socialists or Atheists, or even madmen. The sufferings of Ireland filled Swift with a consuming anger. "Do not the corruption and wickedness of men devour your being?" he said to one of his friends. "Do they not make your blood boil?" His friend having answered him in the negative, Swift angrily observed to him: "How is it you can contain yourself?"[1] An Anarchist, whom I tried, told me that he could not support the spectacle of the suffering and iniquity he saw in the world: to escape the sight he wished to commit suicide.

It is acute sensibility, joined to a disordered imagination, that has driven so many writers to make violent attacks on society. Their pity for the workers makes them unjust, cruel, and pitiless for the employers of labour, and suggests to them words of anger that incite the masses to civil war. Louis Blanc, for example, by calling upon the people to avenge the "tyranny of the middle class," was responsible in no small measure for the events of June, 1848. He incurred responsibility, too, by inditing such phrases as the following: "When a man demands to live by serving society, or is fatally reduced to attacking it under penalty of succumbing, it comes about that his apparent aggression is resorted to

[1] "Recollections of Jonathan Swift," by Walter Scott, Vol. II., p. 50.

in self-defence, and the society that condemns him is not his judge, but his murderer."[1] The same combination of morbid sensibility and cruelty is found in the writings of Kropotkine. His heart overflows with tenderness for working men and peasants, even when they are thieves and murderers, and he is thrilled with joy at the thought of the destructions, expropriations, and exterminations that he calls down upon the heads and belongings of the capitalists. "Let us treat as a brother," he writes, "the man who in a fit of passion has injured his fellow; . . . the greatest criminals are merely the ignoble products of the idleness of the well-to-do."[2] When, however, it is a question of expropriating the capitalists to satisfy the needs of the people, he becomes implacable. "This expropriation," he says, "must be accomplished on a vast scale. On a small scale it would have the appearance of mere vulgar pillaging; resorted to wholesale, it is the beginning of the reorganisation of society."[3] It is with enthusiasm that he recalls the exploits of the Paris Commune, unhappily put a stop to by "the murders of the Versaillais."[4]

The Terrorists of 1793, Marat, Robespierre, were all "sensitive" men who dreamed of realising the happiness of humanity by the extermination of the aristocrats. "Whoever is aglow with love of

---

[1] "Organisation du Travail," p. 26.
[2] "Paroles d'un Révolté," p. 244.
[3] Ibid., p. 337.   [4] Ibid., p. 125.

his country," said Robespierre, "should hail with transport the means of striking its enemies a blow." Fouché, at the same time that he was shedding torrents of blood at Lyons, shed tears of joy over the happiness he was procuring humanity. "I have just had two hundred heads cut off," he wrote to the Convention. "I propose to have as many cut off every day. Tears of joy and virtue, the effect of a holy sensibility, well up into my eyes. Let us take nature for our example in dealing out justice. Let us strike like the lightning, and may even the ashes of our enemies disappear from the soil of liberty."

At the period just referred to, every time that a Jacobin had an act of cruelty in view, he finished up his appeal in favour of proscription with a tirade upon his love of humanity. The executioners made a great show of sensibility. The death sentences pronounced by the revolutionary tribunal were often accompanied by sentimental allocutions.

Recently, at the Seine Court of Assizes, the Anarchist Léauthier concluded his defence by saying: "Let me tell you that I would tremble at a lizard, but that men will not make me tremble; that I would weep before a child, but that I will smile at the guillotine." The man who would tremble at a lizard did not tremble when he thrust a knife into the breast of the Servian Minister.[1]

[1] This morbid sensibility, which so readily goes hand in hand with cruelty, is another legacy from the 18th century. It was brought into fashion by Rousseau and the Romantic school.

The death of a butterfly caused him to shed tears, but the death of a capitalist made him smile.

At the international congress of students held at Liège in 1865, one of those present declared that his love "for the human community" caused him to desire the destruction of the well-to-do classes. "If property withstands the Revolution," he cried, "it must be abolished by the decrees of the people, and if the capitalist class resists, the capitalist class must be killed off. . . . The capitalists are murderers and robbers. . . . Allusion has been made to the guillotine; our sole object is to clear the way of obstacles. If a hundred thousand heads constitute an obstacle, let them fall; our love is exclusively confined to the human collectivity."

Among the innumerable sophisms that spur on the Anarchist to action must also be noted the false idea that the citizen is entitled to substitute himself for the State when it is a question of avenging offences or of preventing iniquitous acts. The Anarchist constitutes himself a dispenser of justice and proclaims himself the avenger of the oppressed. To revenge himself on the magistrates who sentence his companions, he blows up their dwellings; he explodes a bomb in the restaurant where the courageous citizens who denounced one of his accomplices are to be found; he would kill the directors of a company that, in his opinion, oppresses its workmen. Finally, if an Anarchist is condemned to death, his friends plan to revenge him by fresh outrages.

Novelists and dramatic authors have proposed to complete the "Rights of Man and Woman" by proclaiming that free love and adultery are rights, and poets have claimed that the right to be supplied with food may be enforced against society. Materialist philosophers have maintained the "right to happiness and material satisfactions," the Socialists the "right to work," and the revolutionaries the "right of insurrection." All these rights, the right to free love and adultery, the right to be supplied with food, the right to happiness and material satisfactions, the right to work, and of insurrection, are claimed by the Anarchists, who complete them by upholding the "right to rob and murder." Previously the authors of crimes, of which passion was the motive, had taken justice into their own hands and enforced their rights by recourse to vitriol and the revolver. The Anarchists claim the right to employ dynamite. When they commit murder they affirm they are accomplishing an act of justice, just as when they steal they are effecting a restitution. The thieves, according to them, are the owners of property who have been robbed; the murderers of the people are the capitalists whom they murder.

Astonishment has been expressed at the audacity of the Anarchists, at their tranquillity of mind during the proceedings in court, and at their firmness at the hour of their execution. Some writers have even compared them to the early Christians. Bayle, anticipating this tendency, had alleged a resemblance between the regicides and the martyrs. He wrote: "It is to be deplored that assassins of this kind evince as much firmness as the most illustrious martyrs of the primitive Church."[1]

If the Anarchists display firmness at their execution, the explanation is to be sought in the fanaticism that animates them and in the vanity by which they are eaten up. All fanaticism, however execrable its motive may be, conduces to exaltation and, in consequence, to courage. They are also sustained by vanity. All the Anarchists are vain. They know that the public has its eyes upon them, and that the papers publish every detail that concerns them. This sort of celebrity, of which they are greedy, affords them a kind of pleasure that intoxicates them.[2]

In reality, however, they are so far from regarding death with indifference that they make every effort to escape it. Their outrage committed, they are seen to take to their heels, to accuse the innocent so as to mislead justice, to use their revolvers on the police who try to arrest them, to

---

[1] "Dictionnaire de Bayle," V. Chastel.

[2] Léauthier, in announcing to Sébastien Faure his intention to kill a capitalist, wrote to him: "I count on you to take in hand my defence against the begowned barristers, and it will be given to both of us to pass a joyous moment exposing, at the trial, the reasons that induced me to act." The Vienna magistrates, to avoid giving the Anarchists this satisfaction, judged them *in camera*. The newspapers should refrain from keeping the public informed of what the accused do and say, and from publishing their portraits and waxing pathetic over their fate.

conceal their identity, and to furnish false explanations with a view to lessen their responsibility. Vaillant affirmed that when he exploded a bomb in the Chamber of Deputies it was not his object to kill anybody. Léauthier, who thrust his cobbler's knife into the breast of the Servian Minister, made out that he only intended to wound him.

Whereas the Christian martyrs submitted to be slaughtered like lambs, and pardoned their executioners, the Anarchists, heaping crime on crime, are like wild beasts that revel in blood and destruction. What is there in common between tigers that kill and steal and lambs that submit to being killed and despoiled?

Among the causes that have perverted the public conscience and have contributed to create the state of mind of the theorists of Anarchism, I must further point out the glorification by a great number of historians of the crimes of the Revolution, and the negation of moral ideas by contemporary materialist doctrines.

The most popular histories of the Revolution have been a school of political crime and revolutionary fanaticism for the people. They have taught the masses the paramount importance of the end in view, the lawfulness of rebellion, and even of slaughter in the interest of society; they have made them believe that a social upheaval is a factor of civilisation, that terrorism is an instrument of Government, and that progress is only to be achieved by violence. Buchez and Roux attempted the justification of revolutionary crimes. They wrote that terror may be a system of government, that it is sometimes obligatory, that it is a method that is to be judged by the end in view.[1] The September massacres seem to them nothing more than "a measure of public safety," accomplishing "a useful function."[2] H. Marest and Dupont de Bussac have termed these massacres a great act of popular justice. M. Thiers, who has insisted so forcibly in his admirable "Histoire du Consulat et de l'Empire" on the dangers and follies of a military dictatorship, is full of indulgence in his "Histoire de la Révolution" for the illegality and even for the cruelties that marked the popular dictatorship. He terms the 18th Fructidor a sad but unavoidable necessity. "Legality," he writes, "was an illusion on the morrow of such a revolution as ours."[3] The same historian appears, too, to excuse the creation of the revolutionary tribunal when he says that it was necessary to establish this formidable machine so as to withstand enemies of every kind. "Why," he writes, "had terrible circumstances obliged the creation of a government

[1] This is precisely the doctrine of Machiavelli, who remarked in connection with the murder of Remus by his brother: "The wise will not condemn a man of a superior order because, in the important matter of establishing a monarchy or founding a republic, he has resorted to an unusual expedient. The act may accuse him, but the end in view should be his excuse. The excellence of the result always justifies the act." ("Discourse upon Livy.")

[2] Buchez and Roux, "Histoire Parlementaire de la Révolution Française," Vol. XX. Preface, p. vii

[3] Fourth Edition, Vol. IX., p. 320.

of death, which would neither reign nor vanquish them by the aid of death?[1] Louis Blanc praises Robespierre and Saint Just for having "exhausted terror" and for having risen "superior to remorse."

Lamartine, as well, in his "Histoire des Girondins," has committed the error of flattering the Terrorists and of attributing fortunate consequences to the crimes of the Revolution. Afterwards, however, in his "Entretiens sur la Littérature" he nobly confessed his mistake, saying: "The historian, who furnishes crime with an excuse, and cruelty with a fallacious pretext, paves the way, unawares, for future indulgence towards the imitators of these crimes. . . This is an unpardonable error of which I have myself been guilty. Shame upon myself for this complaisance! I wished to amnesty the apologists for the Revolution, and it was on myself that I passed condemnation."[2] By glorifying the Terrorists, he gave them successors. J. Vallès, in an essay on the victims of books, has admitted that his head was turned by the "Histoire des Girondins."

Kropotkine is perfectly justified when he scoffs at the theorists of the Revolution for being astonished that their books should breed a spirit of revolt in those who read them. To excuse violence is to invite a return to its employment. The historians who have admired the Revolution without reservation, have largely contributed to the

[1] Thiers, "Histoire de la Révolution Française," Vol. VI., pp. 371, 372.
[2] Lamartine, "Entretiens," Bk. XXIII., p. 63.

progress of the revolutionary spirit and of Anarchism by this indulgent attitude towards crime and their glorification of the Terror. Every incident of the French Revolution does not merit admiration: it was a time of great virtues and great crimes, of patriots and of fanatics, of heroes and of scoundrels. The duty of the historian is to judge each party, each man, according to their works, to honour the victims and to brand their butchers, to admire the heroes and to stigmatise the false patriots. It is possible to extol the principles of 1789, and at the same time to inspire hatred for the crimes that have been committed in their name. This duty has not been fulfilled by the historians who, from party spirit or love of popularity, have extolled the works of the Revolution, without reservation, forgetting that wholesale admiration of a work in which good is mingled with evil, is a justification of the evil and, in consequence, a lesson in immorality for the reader.[1] They have lent credit to the false proposition that "force is the only means of proceeding with the economic renovation of society,"[2] that progress can only result from a cataclysm,

---

[1] These injudicious admirers of every act of the Revolution go further in their worship of the Revolution than the members of the Committee of Public Safety. Here, for instance, is what Carnot, one of the members of the Committee, said of the Revolution: "The French Revolution was a combination of heroism, of cruelty, of sublime incidents, and of monstrous disorders.... There are people who are terrified at the mere name of liberty, because they judge it by the standard of the Revolution, overlooking that *this Revolution*, on the contrary, *was one continual despotism*." (Ibid., pp. 28, 35.)

[2] G. Deville,' "Aperçu sur le Socialisme Scientifique," p. 56.

and that the situation of the working class can only be improved by a fresh revolution. "If the middle classes," Vaillant declared in his defence, "had not massacred or caused massacres during the Revolution, it is probable that they would still be under the yoke of the nobility."

In the course of the last hundred years France has undergone so many Revolutions that the discontented are always hoping for the breaking out of yet another. To provoke it they stop short at no expedient, now that they have seen the murderers and incendiaries of the Commune amnestied by the Legislature, and in some instances provided with public functions by the Government. The public conscience has been corrupted by this indulgence shown to incendiarism, robbery, and murder, resorted to to serve political ends.

The trials of Ravachol and Vaillant proved that their intellectual depravation was on a par with the perversity of their sentiments, and that it was due, in a great measure, to the sophisms of the materialist philosophers. All Atheists and all Materialists are not Anarchists, but all Anarchists are Atheists and Materialists. "We are Materialists and Atheists," declared Bakounine, "and we glory in the fact."[1]

The Communists also were Materialists and Atheists. Vaillant told the jurymen that they were mere "atoms lost amid matter," and that the history of humanity "is in truth but the perpetual

[1] Bakounine, "La Théologie Politique de Mazzini et l'Internationale," p. 7.

play of the cosmic forces for ever renewing themselves and passing through infinite transformations." He stated that he had taken his ideas from Dr. Büchner, and from supporters of the theory of fatalist evolution. Emile Henry also made a materialist profession of faith. The progress of Anarchism is one of the consequences of a materialist education. Without religious or philosophic faith humanity becomes uncharitable, malevolent, and ferocious. It is true that a few Anarchists, notably Sébastien Faure, have been brought up on religious principles, but, having lost their faith, they cease to be able to understand sorrow and suffering, which are inexplicable without hope in another life, and, rebelling against destiny, they rail against society, it being impossible for them to wreak their wrath upon nature.

The cross-examination of Ravachol showed with what rapidity the theories of the naturalist philosophers have spread among working men, who would apply to human societies the zoological laws of selection and the struggle for life, since man for them is merely an animal. The president of the Loire assizes reminded Ravachol that he had said to the examining judge: "I wish to reach my goal and to triumph over all obstacles. The hermit was an obstacle; I did away with him." Ravachol answered: "Yes, sir; that is quite right." *Query:* "A few days after the 26th June you saw this coachman again, and once more you hired his carriage. What did you propose doing?" *Answer:* "I wished to see whether he had made any communication to the police. If he had spoken, I had a dagger, I had a revolver. *My intention was to make away with him.*" Query: "Then you make away in this ready fashion with the persons who stand in your way?" Answer: "Yes, for us it is a necessity, *it is a necessity of life,* and it is the same for everybody." How often have the terrible words, "Persons who are in our way must be got rid of," been uttered by politicians! Ravachol also tried to excuse his crime by saying: "If I have committed murder, it was to satisfy my personal needs." His personal needs were numerous; they included excellent food, little work, and the luxury of several mistresses. This Anarchist put in practice the famous Socialist theory which may be thus summed up: "To each according to his needs." The Socialist writers, who make out that people have a right to what they want, are themselves the successors of the sensualist philosophers of the 18th century. It is well known that Helvétius makes the *desire* of being happy the basis of law, Destutt de Tracy the *need*, Volney the *instinct of preservation*, and d'Holbach *utility*. Contemporary Materialists serve up afresh as something novel these definitions of law, which amount to its negation, and their sophisms speedily stifle the conscience of the working class and prepare it for crime. False philosophical systems reach the masses, nowadays, with terrible rapidity by such channels as pamphlets, public meetings, and cheap newspapers. A swarm of journalists and politicians, who flatter the people so as to live at its expense, poison it by propagating the most unwholesome doctrines.

It is the fashion, at present, to make society responsible for all evils, all vices, all suffering, and even all crimes. A great number of contemporary writers repeat the unjust accusations of J. J. Rousseau,[1] d'Holbach, and Diderot. They pretend that "all vices are the fault and the crime of society."[2]

"The poor man," writes Dr. Büchner, one of the favourite authors of Vaillant, "knows no other way of escape from his plight but crime. He is the victim of his situation."[3] All these sophisms are to be met with in the examinations of Anarchists on their trial. The President of Assizes having remarked to Ravachol, "You commit murder to satisfy your passions; what can society expect of a man who manifests such sentiments?" "It is I," replied the accused, "who have something to expect of society. It is its duty to support me, and it is not surprising that one employs every means to be happy, since society neglects its members. . . . All that has happened, I tell you, *is the fault of society!* It is a phenomenon that comes to pass, and is the result of the situation of the workers,

---

[1] "Man is born good," said Rousseau. "Society depraves him." "Society," wrote d'Holbach, "is a harsh step-mother for the people, who avenge themselves by robbery and murder." ("Système de la Nature," Part I., ch. xii.)

[2] Cabet, "Voyage en Icarie," fifth edition, p. 391.

[3] Dr. Büchner," Force et Matière," p. 498.

who die of hunger amid the wealth they have produced."[1]

The "phenomenon" to which the accused referred was the murder of a poor old man, a crime he related in the following terms: "I put my hand on his mouth. Death did not follow quickly enough. I forced my handkerchief between his teeth. . . . Then, as he still struggled, I pressed my knee on his chest. He was soon dead." The "phenomenon" of murder had come to pass, because Ravachol needed to kill to effect a robbery. It was not he who was guilty, it was the fault of society that had not made him rich and happy. When this Anarchist was condemned to death his companions protested indignantly against his sentence, and maintained that it was the jury who were guilty, and that the execution of the murderer would be a crime of the capitalist class. Nor did Vaillant omit to make out that the responsibility for the crimes he had committed lay with society. "You have been sentenced several times," the President said to him. "Yes, sir," he answered, "thanks to society." *Query:* "You allege that there is no such thing as crime or criminals, that everything is merely the consequence of the influence of the environment, and again, that it is the fault of the organisation of society. You left for America after the proceedings against the Russian Anarchists, and so as to rid yourself of your wife." *Answer:* "Yes, sir."

[1] "Gazette des Tribunaux," 11th January, 1894.

The Anarchists allege that they are victims of society, and they make society responsible for everything. If an Anarchist working-man dissatisfies his employer by his laziness or is dismissed because of his insolence, he lays the blame on the organization of society, and considers his employer a task-master, who ought to be suppressed. Another working-man, being unable to satisfy his wants, blames society for making an unequal division of wealth. "Society," declared Léauthier, "is bound to assure my existence. As it does not do so, it treats me badly, and I decided to revenge myself upon the first capitalist I met." The man with a university degree, who fails to obtain in society the brilliant situation and the material satisfaction on which he had counted, proceeds to curse society.

Persons who occupy a social rank for which they were not intended, those who have failed in life, the incapable, and those whose ambitions have been disappointed detest society, because it does not offer them a situation in keeping with their demands. The fury of Marat, during the Revolution, is to be ascribed, in great measure, to the deceptions he experienced prior to 1789. The day that the Academy of Sciences declined to examine his pretended discoveries, touching the nature of light, Marat vented his rage in violent terms. An attempt having been made to console him, by the assurance that with his talents he would, sooner or later, effect his purpose, he answered, grinding his teeth: "My purpose! I would like all humanity to be contained in a bomb, to which I would set fire so as to explode it."[1]

To revenge himself for the disdain of the Academy, he afterwards denounced it as a hot-bed of aristocrats. Other Anarchists make society responsible for the inequalities of rank of fortune that exist amongst men, shutting their eyes to the fact that social inequalities are determined by physical, moral, and intellectual inequalities, and that it is nature, and not society, that makes men unequal in respect to health, intelligence, and strength of will, and, in consequence, of unequal wealth.

The violent hatred against society that animates the Anarchists must not be attributed to poverty, but rather to the belief that happiness is the final object in life, that it consists in enjoyment, and that society is bound to procure them happiness. Previous to 1789 statesmen, in general, only allowed that the masses had duties, spoke to them solely of their obligations, and consoled them for their sufferings by holding out the hope of happiness in another world, the privileged classes in the meanwhile being careful not to neglect the pleasures offered by this world. The democrats have gone to the other extreme: they omit to remind the masses of their duties, and call their attention exclusively to their rights. Assuredly they are right in wishing to improve the material situation of the masses, and in not

[1] "Mémoires de Brissot," Vol. I., p. 349.

putting off until another world their hope of a measure of happiness. Christianity does not content itself with promising happiness in another life, for it says: "Seek first the Kingdom of God and His justice, and the rest, that is to say happiness, will be given you in addition." The rich, who neglect neither their interests nor their pleasures, would show bad grace in accusing of egoism the working-men and peasants who desire a measure of well-being; they cannot demand a renunciation which they do not practise themselves.

Still, though it be absurd to invite the masses to think only of heaven, and to despise the good things of this world, it is dangerous to shut them off from heaven, and to keep their eyes fixed on the earth, by telling them that happiness is the one object in life and that it is given by riches. No doubt, the quest of happiness and wealth is most legitimate when the intention is only to obtain them by dint of work and thrift. Still it is criminal to speak to the working class of nothing but pleasures to be had and wealth to be shared; ardent covetousness and the hatred of the rich are kindled by these words. To tell them that poverty is abject[1] is to inspire them with the desire to acquire wealth at once and at all cost, so as to deliver themselves from the suffering and shame attendant on poverty. Christianity, on the contrary, taught the poor calmness and

---

[1] It was Darwin who said that poverty is abject. ("Descent of Man.")

patience, speaking to them of their dignity,[1] and honouring them as the favoured friends of God.

Moreover it is this exclusive concern for well-being that destroys patriotism. Why is it that the love of their country has become a feeling unknown to the Anarchists? It is because they say: "One's country is where one is well off, where one enjoys well-being." The man who has ceased to believe that merit attaches to suffering, who does not look to Divine justice to repay him in another life for what he has endured, and who concentrates all his thoughts on his quest for a happiness that eludes him (for there is no paradise on this earth even for the rich), experiences before long acute deceptions and great irritation against society. He desires happiness at all cost, and he therefore demands the liquidation of society by petroleum or by dynamite. Everywhere, in Italy, in France, in Spain, the aim of the Anarchists, Internationalists, and Collectivists is the same: the division of wealth, and happiness and enjoyment claimed as a right. In the manifesto of the Anarchists of La Pouille, issued in August, 1878, may be read: "The end to be reached is to assure mankind the most complete happiness possible. . . . Love ought to be free and delivered from codes and rituals." As far back as 1873 the Spanish Internationalists also declared that their aim was to assure to everybody his share of happiness. "If we lack

---

[1] One of the most beautiful of Bossuet's sermons runs upon this thought: "The exceeding dignity of the poor."

the power," they added, "to achieve our end, which is to sit down in our turn at the banquet of life, then will appear on the scene petroleum, the avenger whom the privileged classes dread, not only to accomplish the work of destruction, but to execute an act of sound and sovereign justice. A levelling down, if need be by fire and sword, is what is demanded by the dignity, so long trodden under foot, of the proletarian."

This furious desire to taste the pleasures of life is further stimulated by the materialist theories that always accompany revolutionary socialism and anarchism, and that teach the glorification of the passions and the rehabilitation of the flesh. "We desire," said the Saint-Simonians, "that humanity shall cease to be crucified, and mortified in the flesh."[1]

The passions are of Divine origin; why desire to correct the work of God? The passions should be emancipated and nature left to develop itself to the full. Morality is a false and pedantic science that for three thousand years has made a pretence of leading men to virtue and good morals, with its absurd dogmas of moderation and the repression of the passions.[2]

If, said Fourier, there still be moralists who teach that the passions are not inevitable and legitimate, "it is because the majority of them are of an age when one ceases to enjoy the favour of women."[3]

---

[1] The works of Saint-Simon and Enfantin. "Prédications," Part III., p. 363.
[2] Victor Considérant, "Destinée Sociale," Vol. I., p. 52.
[3] Fourier, "Théorie des Quatres Mouvements," p. 175.

Naturalist and sceptical philosophers are to be found at the present day, who raise the negation of morality to the dignity of a system, who extol egoism, and who proclaim the right of enjoyment. According to the German philosophers Max Stirner and Frederick Nietzche, who boldly take the title of "immoralist philosophers," one must be a simpleton to believe in moral obligation: "There is nothing sillier than the idea of morality. . . . . . A moral nation is almost always a nation without intelligence; it creates nothing, it does not progress. The desires, the aspiration to enjoy, and the intense sentiment of enjoyment without heed of moral scruples, are the soil in which the most delicate flowers of the mind grow up and bloom." Duty being suppressed, and the quest of pleasure becoming man's sole motive, it is understandable that the contemporary sensualist philosophers, like their predecessors of the 18th century, teach "the art of enjoyment," and that the Anarchists desire to put it in practice.

The fact that Christianity sees something divine in suffering and disciplines the passions is the reason why it is to-day the object of a savage hatred on the part of the theorists who deify enjoyment. Fourier violently attacks it because, he says, "its dogmas are hostile to pleasure."[1] Saint-Simon reproaches the Christian morality with teaching exclusive love and indissoluble

---

[1] Fourier, "Théorie des Quatre Mouvements," p. 207.

unions.[1] The Anarchists maintain that Christianity, by inculcating asceticism, deceives the oppressed so as to assure the security of the oppressors.

This hatred of religion and contempt for morality are also fostered by the conviction that "science alone can improve the unhappy plight of humanity."[2]

M. Renan and the writers who, following his lead, would rid humanity of what they call superstition, admit that moral abasement will be the result of the loss of religious beliefs, but they console themselves with the thought that immorality is to be preferred to fanaticism. "It is better," says M. Renan, "that a people should be immoral than that it should be fanatical; for immoral multitudes are not troublesome, whereas fanatical multitudes make the world more stupid, and a world condemned to stupidity ceases to offer any reason why I should interest myself in it: I would as lief see it perish."[3]

This contempt for morality has produced in the upper strata of society a class of "intellectual men, who care for nothing but success, cleverness, and pleasure, and in a lower rank of life another class of men, impatient to possess their share of happiness and very decided to conquer it by all means.

The most implacable Anarchists belong to the

[1] Works of Saint-Simon and Enfantin, "Prédications," Part III., p. 365.
[2] Renan, "L'Avenir de la Science." Preface, p. ix.
[3] Ibid., p. x.

new generation that has been brought up in the negation of spiritual beliefs. In this case, the beast that lurks in every man, being freed from all scruples and all beliefs that can keep it under restraint, rushes into every excess to satisfy its appetites. The new theories of "the struggle for life" and the inevitableness of evolution have introduced a further leaven of egoism and hatred into the hearts of the young Anarchists. They have taught them to consider themselves mere animals and to imitate the animals who struggle for existence heedless of right and justice. Is it astonishing, in consequence, that men should come to resemble wild beasts, and should dream of nothing but destruction and extermination?[1] No longer believing in anything, neither in God, nor the soul, nor moral obligations, nor a future life, impatient to satisfy their appetites, and no longer hoping for compensation in another world, the Anarchists demand to slake their thirst for pleasure at once, and if society does not render them happy, they do not hesitate to accord themselves the right to destroy it. "Man," said Vaillant, "comes to an end where the tomb begins; . . . in consequence, he should satisfy his desires to the fullest possible extent, and there is no reason for the existence of society unless it finally completes his well-being" (*Journal des Debats*, 6th January, 1894).

Instruction, unaccompanied by a moral educa-

[1] According to the Anarchist Vaillant the animal appetites were to be the sole law of the new society of his dreams. ("Gazette des Tribunaux," 11th January, 1894.)

tion, cannot inculcate wisdom and the spirit of justice: it merely develops pride and the desire to enjoy. The Anarchist Henry retorted to a Paris Municipal Councillor, who had said at a public meeting that working-men demanded work, that he and those who thought with him demanded pleasures. The instruction we have received, he said, "has opened the minds of a certain number, and they have asked themselves whether they have not as good a right as anybody else to the satisfactions that civilisation offers to those who have the means to pay for them. In consequence of the organisation of society young men find that they earn very little or nothing at all by utilising the instruction they have received; . . . there is no chance for these young men, as, indeed, for all those who suffer, but in a complete upheaval, which will permit them (they think so at least) to establish a society that will provide for everyone according to his needs. And these needs are not confined to the needs of the belly. . . . This is why it is that for some time past young men starting in life without a clearly defined social station, and not resigned to their lot, force themselves into notice wherever they can, and this disposition will, perforce, go on increasing until the final smash up."[1]

The philosophers who believed that an immoral multitude is not troublesome because it is not fanatical should be beginning to see that immorality does not exclude fanaticism, and that

[1] "Journal des Débats," 27th March, 1894.

the men who explode bombs in churches are more "troublesome" than those who resort to them to pray.

On the day that the pupil of the man of science who prides himself on being the enemy of Christianity threw his bomb in the Chamber of Deputies, the politicians who are in the habit of exclaiming "It is Christianity that is the enemy" must have thought that society has, perhaps, a more redoubtable enemy than religion, which teaches the respect of human life, and of property, saying to man: "Thou shalt not kill, thou shalt not steal."

Finally, it is impossible for men of science, intoxicated by their chemical discoveries, not to recognise to-day the insufficiency of science to assure the happiness of humanity when they see the most redoubtable criminals demand of science the means of destroying society. The Vendôme Criminal Court recently condemned to three years' imprisonment an ex-schoolmaster who furnished Anarchists with directions for the manufacture of explosive engines, and who wrote to his clients: "Violent means are alone efficacious. Hurrah for dynamite, milenite, panclastite, the dagger, and the revolver." This same schoolmaster declared that Ravachol (a thief and a murderer) was his Christ. Men of science, such as Paul and Elisée Reclus, approve the outrages of the Anarchists, and literary men encourage them. Emile Henry was a bachelor of science and was admissible to the École Polytechnique; Sébastien Faure has been through the entire classical course, etc., etc. G. Deville, in his "Aperçu sur la Socialisme Scientifique," invites the revolutionaries to "utilise all the resources that science puts within the reach of those who have something to destroy." Already, in his "Lettres Persanes," Montesquieu had given utterance to the fears inspired in him by "the progress of chemistry." " I have not been in Europe long," Rhedi remarks to Usbeck, "but I have heard sensible people talk of the ravages of chemistry. . . . I tremble, lest in the end people arrive at discovering some secret which will furnish a quicker way of causing men to perish and of destroying entire peoples and nations."[1]

In the study I have just made of the causes of Anarchism I have striven to make clear the share of responsibility that rests with writers. This responsibility is enormous. In general, writers do not care to have their responsibility talked about; they are fond of pretending that doctrines are without influence upon actions. I believe, on the contrary, that disordered ideas produce moral disorder, that a false thesis may call forth an infinite number of bad actions, that a sophism is often more dangerous to society than a crime. J. J. Rousseau, who has done so much harm with his political sophisms, says himself that bad maxims are often more odious than bad actions.[2]

[1] "Lettres Persanes," Letter cv.
[2] "La Nouvelle Héloïse," Part I., Letter xxx.

It is the sophisms spread abroad by writers on property, religion, government, and capital that have produced the theory of Anarchism, and put weapons into the hands of the Anarchists. The writer who puts unwholesome theories into circulation in society explodes bombs in its midst. The propaganda by ideas always precedes the propaganda by deeds. Men, and especially young men, pass rapidly from the idea to action. Intellectual disorder produces moral disorder. The world is guided by ideas. If they be sound, they conduce to wisdom and tranquillity, but if they be unhealthy they engender disorder and crime.

Recently, at the Aix assizes, we tried and sentenced, for the manufacture of an explosive powder, an Anarchist, aged thirty-three, who, since the age of seventeen, had been noted among all his employers for his assiduity at his work, the regularity of his conduct, and the kindness of his character. The only reproach his foreman had ever made him was that of working on his own account during his leisure hours at the discovery of a mechanical invention. Upon a salary of a trifle over three shillings a day, this excellent, hard-working, sober, and devoted workman kept his wife, two children, and his aged father, whom he had taken into his household. Since his sentence he cannot think without tears of his wife and children, and he implores to be given work that he may send them assistance. What made an Anarchist of this unhappy man? It was neither laziness, nor intemperance, nor cupidity: it was the sophism. His room was found to be full of Anarchist newspapers and pamphlets; they had turned his head.

There are poisons for the mind just as there are poisons for the body. Certain doctrines are veritable poisons for the soul; false maxims induce death as surely as venomous substances. The number of intellectual poisons is as great as that of physical poisons. There are doctrines which, like haschich, lull remorse and stupefy the conscience. There are others that may be compared to explosive substances; they fill the hearts of the people with virulent passions, whose aliment is destruction, expropriation, and extermination. Again, are there not newspapers that, like corrosive acids, destroy all they touch, and speeches that, like alcohol, inflame the blood, agitate the nerves, sear the brain, and dry up the heart? These intellectual poisons are to-day on offer everywhere, in the booksellers' shops, at the newspaper stalls, in places of refreshment, and in the public streets. At the shops where drink is sold, and the number of them increases every day, poisons are also on sale—the literary matter to be found there is as adulterated as the drinks. The hapless people are poisoned in every manner, in mind as well as in body. It is because society is literally poisoned by the sophists that it is diseased.

When I note the evident influence of sophisms upon the crimes of the Anarchists there is no limit to my surprise when I hear it said that no guilt attaches to opinions, that words do not constitute a danger, that pure thought is harmless (Renan). A writer with the best intentions may do a great deal of harm. To avert the danger with which society is threatened by the Anarchist passions, the public institutions must not be solely relied upon. Above everything else, it is necessary to reform the intelligences that sophism have led astray, to re-establish in the public conscience the beliefs that bring peace, to remind the working-man that he is not a mere animal, subject to no other law than the satisfaction of his instincts; it is necessary, in a word, to teach the people that they have their personal duties and responsibilities. The mischievous doctrines that lend the Anarchists their strength are more efficaciously combatted by salutary doctrine than by the scaffold, the necessity for which, however, I do not contest.

Political anarchy is the consequence of moral anarchy, which, in turn, results from intellectual anarchy. "The great political and moral crisis which societies are traversing," says Auguste Comte, "is the outcome, when traced to its final source, of intellectual anarchy."[1]

He hoped that the triumph of Positivism would put an end to this anarchy; he was of opinion that the old spiritual beliefs were unsuited to modern democracy and were only good enough for the men of the Middle Ages. The truth is a

[1] A. Comte, "Cours de Philosophie Positive," Vol. I., p. 40.

democracy stands in greater need than any other
society of spiritual beliefs, and that free thought
inculcated to working-men and students makes
Anarchists of them and partisans of revolt. Society is diseased, and to restore it to health it must
be re-endowed with moral beliefs. When the
Anarchist R——— mounted the scaffold, he re-
pulsed the priest, declaring that he did not believe
in God, and adding that had he believed in Him
he would not have committed the crimes for
which he had been sentenced. The real remedy
for the crisis we are traversing is a return to
Christianity. Since the false philosophical, political, and economic systems are making a joint
attack upon the foundations of society, the duty
of every good citizen is to contribute to their
defence to the extent that he is able. Those who
do not defend society betray it. To the proselytism of evil must be opposed the proselytism of
good. It is the strict duty of all those who have
the good fortune to hold salutary beliefs, derived
from their education, their family, or their studies,
to propagate them, and not to allow sophisms to
pass without challenge. It is cowardice to remain
indifferent in face of the monstrous sophisms
that turn out thieves and murderers. When the
house is on fire, the citizen who does not aid in
extinguishing the flames incurs responsibility
for the disaster. Attacked by such numbers of
the idle and dissolute, of the ambitious and fanatical, the object of the onslaughts of so many
sophists and revolutionaries, how can society

escape the storm that is brewing if it be only lukewarmly defended by honest men?

Moreover, men of authority and fortune can do much to re-establish order in public life and in men's minds if they decide to set a good example. The parliamentary scandals which have cropped up in recent years in France and Italy have done more for the progress of revolutionary Socialism and Anarchism than twenty years of propaganda. Fortunes ill acquired and ill employed scandalise and irritate the poor. The politicians who are guilty of venality and the rich who do not deserve respect are largely responsible for the progress of Anarchism.

CHAPTER IV.

POLITICAL HATREDS.

> The range of human hatred—War has been the normal condition of the human race—Causes of war—In international relations might is right—Man hates whatever differs from himself—Race hatreds—Statesmen inflame international animosities—Republicanism and war—Class animosities—Party hatreds—Political persecutions—Conflicts of classes in history—Contemporary class hatreds—The fate of moderate men—Political calumny—Temporary reconciliation of political parties—Political executions—The mob in politics—Political riots—Political excesses of the mob—Political vengeance—Political reaction—Political apathy—Political ferocity.

"When God made the heart of man," says Bossuet, "the innermost feelings of man, He placed there first of all kindness, after the pattern of His own character, and to be, as it were, the sign-manual of the beneficent hand that fashioned us." Is it indeed kindliness that lies at the bottom of the heart of man? One is inclined to have doubts on the point when one observes the numerous hatreds that subsist between men: religious hatreds, theological hatreds, national hatreds, social hatreds, the mutual hatreds of the patricians against the plebeians, of the plebeians against the patricians, of the rich against the poor, of the poor against the rich; and racial hatreds caused by differences of ideas, of sentiments, and of colour.

Wolves do not devour each other, but as much cannot be said for men! They kill each other in the name of religion, in the name of liberty, in the name of fraternity, in the name of equality. The noblest religious and philosophical ideas, falsely interpreted, have given rise to hatreds. In the name of a religion that enjoins love priests have burned men at the stake. In the name of doctrines whose watchword is liberty, philosophers have been persecuted. In the name of fraternity, philanthropists have been guillotined. Heretics have been burned on religious principles; women and children have been slaughtered out of patriotism; noblemen, priests, and working-men have been guillotined by their fellow-citizens. Every animal has an enemy in the shape of another animal of a different species, but man's worst enemy is man.

The history of humanity is a mere succession of wars: foreign wars, civil wars, racial wars, class wars. Wars are on record that have lasted seven years, thirty years, and even a hundred years. The wars of the Revolution and of the First Empire lasted nearly twenty-five years. Commercial peoples, such as the Carthaginians, Venetians, and the English, engaged in commercial wars, with a view to enforce treaties and tributes, and to acquire pecuniary advantages. Ambitious peoples engage in wars of conquest to extend their rule. The nation that sees another nation growing up beside it takes umbrage at its strength, and endeavours to shatter it. When Carthage became a rival to Rome, the Romans declared it must be destroyed: *Delenda Carthago.* Holland, in the 17th century, having become a rival power to England, England at once endeavoured to weaken it. Sovereigns kindle wars between their neighbours to weaken them, and to play the part of arbiters. Others seek in war a diversion from interior difficulties.[1] Political parties urge on war to supplant their adversaries or to propagate their principles.

In international relations it is might that prevails. At the present day nations resort to specious pretexts to cloak their hatred and cupidity. Among the ancients the superiority of might over right was openly proclaimed. For example, when the inhabitants of Milos refused to yield obedience to the Athenians, these latter urged that being the stronger they had the right to lord it over them. "We demand," they said, "that each shall regulate his pretensions upon his strength. . . . We are well aware, you and we, that amongst men, there is no question of the claims of justice except when the power to act is equal between the two parties, and that those that have the advantage in strength exact everything they can,

---

[1] Charles V. said to François I.: "We rule, you and I, peoples so hot-blooded, so proud and tumultuous, that if to amuse them and to take the edge off their bellicose impetuosity we do not wage war from time to time, our own subjects would make war on us, which would be much worse." (Bayle, "Dictionnaire." Charles-Quint.)

and that the weak accord them whatever is exacted of them. . . . Men have ever been determined, as if by a natural necessity, to rule wherever they have the power.[1]

The various peoples of Greece were perpetually at war. Athenians, Lacedemonians, Thebans, Ionians, Dorians, Acheans, Messinians, Etolians, and Corinthians were for ever in conflict, signing provisional treaties, breaking these treaties on the first favourable occasion, recommencing the war, devastating the country, pillaging the towns. The smaller peoples, too weak to resist, put themselves under the protection of a stronger State, that took care to fleece them. The Athenians and the Spartans put a heavy price on their protection.

Man hates whoever differs from himself; his favour is reserved for those who resemble him. The white detests the black, the black detests the white; the North American persecutes the Indian and despises the nigger. Reason, and above all Christianity, have revealed the sentiment of fraternity to some minds, but this sentiment is not general. Separated by race, climate, beliefs, institutions, and colour, men have a difficulty in considering themselves members of the same family. The hatred and contempt that the Greeks entertained for foreigners is well known. Foreigners in their eyes were barbarians. Aristotle advised Alexander to treat them as he would plants or animals; advice that is astonishing in

[1] Thucydides, "Bellum Peloponnesiacum," Bk. V., § 89, 105.

the mouth of a philosopher, and that Alexander had the wisdom not to follow. International law did not exist among the ancient peoples. Foreigners were without rights. In the East they considered them to be unclean beings. (Herodotus, Bk. II., sec. 41; Manon, XII., 43.)

At the present day the different races still mutually detest and despise each other. The war of 1870 showed that the Germans are animated by a savage hatred against the French; they were seen to be greedy of vengeance, and glad to be able to ravage with fire and sword. A Prussian magistrate, who died in 1887 in Berlin, where he was Under-Secretary of State in the Ministry of Justice, and whose letters have been published recently, wrote during the war that such was his racial hatred against us that he revelled in all the destruction and all the slaughter the German armies were committing in France. We are still far removed from international fraternity and racial solidarity. By this mistaken policy statesmen have created deep-lying hatreds between France and Germany.

Instead of calming the hatreds that arise between nations, statesmen, carried away by their own passions, foster international jealousies and rivalries, and cause the breaking out of wars that might have been averted. How many nations, under the guidance of ambitious sovereigns and ministers, have slaughtered each other without serious motives! Of how many wars might be said what Frederick II. himself said of the war between Prussia, Austria, and Saxony: ". . . In some ways this war caused a useless effusion of blood. . . . What advantage did Prussia, Austria, and Saxony derive from this war, carried on with so much determination and animosity? None but the mutual ruin of vast provinces, the slaughter of thousands of men, who, differently employed, might have been useful to their country. Moreover, the events that were fatal to so many private individuals were useless to those who initiated the conflict. . . . Europe," added Frederick II., "is a veritable cockpit." Sanguinary struggles are everywhere in progress; it might be thought that the kings had resolved to depopulate the earth. . . . Should the acquisition of two or three frontier strongholds, of a small strip of territory, a boundary of more or less extension be regarded as advantages when the excessive cost of the war is taken into account, and it is remembered how heavily the taxes that have produced these immense sums have weighed upon the people, and, above all, at the cost of the blood of how many thousands of men these conquests have been purchased?[1]

Wars do not last nowadays as long as they

---

[1] Frederick II., "Histoire de Mon Temps." The princes that have caused the most blood to be shed, Louis XIV. and Napoleon I., have regretted, like Frederick II., the wars they have carried on. "I have been too fond of war," said Louis XIV. on his death-bed. Napoleon I., after the disastrous Russian campaign, repeated the words of Louis XIV.: "I am not afraid to confess it," he exclaimed, " I have been too fond of war. I have conceived great enterprises, that were out of proportion to the strength of the nation." ("Vie et Travaux Diplomatiques du

used to do. They are finished in a few months, but the number of victims they make in a few days is greater than it used to be in several years, because entire peoples join in the struggle.

Republics are somewhat less warlike than monarchies. Still, wars between peoples take the place of wars between kings. The ancient republics and the Italian republics were fond of war. The South American republics attack each other as savagely as did the empires of former days. Nations, like individuals, are subject to the passions that make for war. Occasionally even, like women with a turn for romance, who are wearied by a quiet life, they tire of peace. Such under Louis Philippe was the condition of France. It regretted the Napoleonic wars, and it had recourse to a fresh revolution, which procured it civil war and prepared the way for the wars of the Second Empire.

Human nature is so fertile in sentiments of hatred that on occasion a nation must needs apprehend the hostility of a neighbour it has aided for the very reason that it has rendered a service. To render service to a people is often a means of making an enemy of it. The remem-

Comte d'Hauterive," p. 319.) Carnot relates that when he was alone with Napoleon I. he had often heard him deplore that "mania for conquests that had led him to commit such fatal mistakes." ("Exposé de la Conduite Politique de M. Carnot," p. 23.) Louis Philippe, on the contrary, increased the strength of France by maintaining peace. At the end of his reign the Russian Chancellor, Count Nesselrode, wrote to the Russian Ambassador in London : "France has gained more by peace than it would have obtained by war."

brance of Magenta and Solferino has something to do with the hostility of Italy towards France.[1]

Hatred of the foreigner, even when it leads to war, is less odious than class and party struggles. In the ancient societies, when slavery was in force, the class that held the power often treated the inferior classes with the most horrible cruelty. Thucydides narrates that the Spartans were in the habit of decimating the Helots when they became too numerous. On one occasion, so as to be sure that the bravest should be among the victims, they employed the following subterfuge: they promised liberty to those who should be pointed out by their comrades as the bravest. Two thousand were pointed out in this way, "but shortly afterwards they disappeared, without there being even an inkling of the manner in which they had been put to death.[2]

Down to the French Revolution class struggles form the substance of the interior history of the different peoples. The history of the Roman republic resolves itself into the history of the struggle between patricians and plebeians. The patricians treat the plebeians as a conquered race, and arrogate to themselves all privileges and dignities; they refuse the plebeians, as far as possible, any share in the government, so as to

[1] Machiavelli, noting this hatred of the person who has received a favour for his benefactor, has remarked: "A prince who desires to preserve himself from conspiracies should stand in much greater fear of those whom he has loaded with benefits than of those on whom he has heaped injuries." ("Discourse upon Livy," Bk. III., ch. iv.)

[2] Thucydides, Bk. IV., § 80.

keep for themselves the benefits of the exercise of authority. In ancient France there were three mutually hostile orders. The kings, instead of endeavouring to bring the classes together, sought to breed division between them. The history of France is the history of the struggle between those with privileges and those without privileges. The Throne supported and raised the status of the people. The abolition of privileges and the conquest of equality were the principal objects of the French Revolution. It was the obstinacy with which the nobility and the clergy clung to their privileges that made the revolution necessary.

It would seem that class hatreds should no longer exist since the Revolution, which suppressed privileges, and in consequence the classes that divided the nation against itself. Nevertheless the nobility and the middle class continued to detest each other under the Restoration and the July Monarchy, and to-day, although all French citizens have the same civil and political rights, Socialism is there to revive class hatreds on the pretext that "the working class" is oppressed by "the governing classes." The Socialist congress that was held at Brussels in August, 1891, "taking as its standpoint the struggle between the classes, and convinced that there can be no question of the emancipation of the working class so long as there shall be governing classes, . . . advises the wage-earners of the entire world to league themselves against the domination of the capitalists." The capitalists are pointed to by the Socialist leaders as being the enemies of the workmen. The workmen of the various countries are called upon to stand elbow to elbow in a struggle against them.

These social hatreds are fatal to patriotism. Formerly in civil wars the contending parties called the foreigner to their assistance. The Duke of Guise allied himself with Philip II., while the Protestant chiefs were in alliance with the German princes. At the time of Richelieu, the Protestants implored the aid of Germany. The Huguenot emigrants returned to La Rochelle on board English vessels, to defend the town against Richelieu. During the Fronde, Condé put himself in the hands of Spain, sought the support of Cromwell, and invited the troops of the Duke of Lorraine to enter French territory. Turenne invaded Champagne at the head of a Spanish army. During the French Revolution the Emigrants contracted foreign alliances. Toulon was delivered up to the English. After Waterloo the Royalists, wild with joy, received the allies with enthusiasm.[1] Since this date, up till 1871, the political parties did not dare to ally themselves with the foreigners. Since the Commune, however, anti-

---

[1] De Viel-Castel, "Histoire de la Restauration," Vol. III., p. 444. In 1814 the Royalists were even desirous of taking down the Statue of Napoleon I. from the Vendôme column. A number of young men presented the Emperor of Russia with an address in which they termed Napoleon I. a monster. There were Frenchmen who formed the project of assassinating him at the moment he was engaged in fighting the allies. ("Memoirs of Chancellor Pasquier," Vol. II., pp. 264, 276, 286.)

social passions have acquired such violence that they have stifled patriotism. On the morrow of Sedan the demagogues and their followers overthrew the Vendôme column and fraternised with the Prussians. During the siege of Paris, the same persons took advantage of our disasters to stir up riots and to aggravate the situation. The revolutionary Socialists and the Anarchists nourish a savage hatred against the army because it is the defender of order and of the fatherland. Colonel Billet, who had commanded a regiment of cuirassiers at Reischoffen, and who had crowned himself with glory by charging the Prussians at the head of his regiment, his two sons at his side, was killed in broad daylight, in time of peace, in the street at Limoges by a Frenchman animated by this hatred of the army. The revolutionary Socialists and the Anarchists do not admit a fatherland, and calumniate the army that defends it. They dare to represent it as a school of egoism, immorality, and brutality; whereas it is a school of abnegation and sacrifice. They protested against the Franco-Russian fêtes: an Anarchist working-man even fired a revolver at the crowd that was acclaiming the Russian sailors.

In times of revolution the struggle between classes has reached such a pitch as to be accompanied by the destruction of the houses of the rich, of public monuments, and even of towns. At Lyons, in 1793, the Jacobins caused 20,000 private houses to be destroyed. The convention issued a decree that ran as follows: "The town of Lyons shall be destroyed, all the habitations of the rich shall be demolished." Some of the most beautiful monuments of Paris were burned by the Commune in 1871.

By the side of these class hatreds, which hold terrible disturbances in store for contemporary society, must be ranged party hatreds. Reason and religion say to man: "Every fellow-citizen is your brother; you must love him;" but politics cry to him: "This fellow-citizen is your adversary, you must hate him and persecute him." As the result, these savage cries are heard, according to the régime: "The aristocracy is the enemy, the Liberal is the enemy, the ecclesiastic is the enemy!" And "the enemy" is combatted by street riots and by unjust laws, by decrees and with the rifle. Man is so constituted that he detests whoever does not resemble him, or whoever refuses to share his political passions. The violent hate the moderate; in their eyes moderation is treason.[1] The efforts of L'Hôpital to reconcile the Catholics and the Protestants were worthy of all admiration, and what can be sadder than the spectacle of his powerlessness to still the hatreds between the two parties. A Catholic himself, he was regarded with suspicion by the Catholics, who

---

[1] Theramenes, one of the thirty tyrants, having proposed to inflict a moderate punishment on a Spartan whom his colleagues wished to put to death, was himself condemned to drink the hemlock. Mdme. de Staël, having displayed pity for the victims of the *coup d'état* of the 18th Fructidor, was accused of treason, and was obliged to make a hasty escape from Paris.

were inclined to look upon him as a heretic, and who were wont to say that it was well to beware of the Chancellor's mass. The Protestants for their part were unable to admit that it is possible to be tolerant out of love of moderation and justice. At the time of the Bordeaux insurrection against the King and Mazarin, the moderate members of the Fronde were looked upon with suspicion by the violent party that denounced them as traitors and partisans of Mazarin. During the French Revolution, the moderates were the object of the suspicion of all parties. The Constitutionists who were banished from France met with a very bad reception at the hands of the out-and-out Royalists, and were looked at askance by the European Governments. "Scaffolds were erected for them on the frontier of their country, and persecutions of every kind awaited them on foreign soil."[1]

The Jacobins detested the moderate Republicans even more than they did the Royalists. The Girondins were proscribed as moderates, the Dantonists on the ground that they were too disposed to indulgence, and even the indifferent were outlawed. Carnot, although he was a Republican to the core, was proscribed on the 18th Fructidor as a Royalist and protector of Emigrants because he desired that the laws should be interpreted as much as possible in their favour where it was proved that they had not borne arms

[1] Mdme. de Staël, "Considérations sur la Révolution Française."

against their country. This moderation caused him to be proscribed. Lanjuinais, who showed such great courage at the Convention and at the Congress of the Five Hundred, was denounced by the ultras of the Restoration who had remained in hiding during the storm, and who now reappeared and asked to be rewarded for a devotion that had cost them nothing.

This hatred of the violent for the moderate has been observed at all periods of history. "The most moderate men," wrote Thucydides, "perish the victims of factions."[1] The English patriots, Sidney, Harrison, and Hutchinson, after being the butt of Cromwell, were banished by Charles II.

It is more particularly the struggles of the Revolution that give the measure of the intensity of political hatreds. The parties slaughtered each other like gladiators in a circus. The orators' speeches were full of vindictiveness, fury, and rage. The members of the Committee of Public Safety mutually detested each other. Carnot relates that his expulsion was proposed in his presence by Saint Just, just as some time before that of Hérault de Séchelles had been proposed, a measure that had promptly brought him to the scaffold. "I replied coldly to Saint Just," adds Carnot, "that he would leave the Committee before me, and the whole triumvirate with him, and the Committee, stupefied, remained silent."[2]

Before proscribing each other the parties resorted

---

[1] Thucydides, Bk. III., § 82.
[2] "Exposé de la Conduite Politique de M. Carnot," p. 33.

to mutual calumny, and accused each other in turn of plots and intrigue. Robespierre never ceased accusing his adversaries of being traitors and conspirators; his speeches are a mere tissue of calumnies. Calumny was the favourite weapon of the Jacobins against the Girondins; it served their purpose. "There is not a department," said Buzot, "not a town, not a trumpery club that does not dub us Royalists and Federalists."[1] C. Desmoulins' book, entitled "Histoire des Brissotins," contributed by its false allegations to the proscribing of the Girondins. When he heard their condemnation he could not prevent himself exclaiming: "The unhappy men! It is my book that has killed them."

From the outset of the Revolution the adversaries of the Throne attacked it by spreading abroad a host of calumnies against the King and Queen. Kropotkine highly approves of these tactics, and advises the Anarchists to employ them against the capitalists. "Calumniate, calumniate," the Jacobins[2] used to say, as the Anarchists say to-day, "it will always have some effect." They were aware that the most absurd imputation, if repeated at large, is, in the end, accepted as true. To excite the people against Louis XVI. this easy-going king was accused of contemplating the massacre of the Parisians. At a later period, in order to prepare public opinion for the

---

[1] "Mémoires," Buzot, p. 47.

[2] Danton declared from the tribune that it was lawful to calumniate the enemies of liberty.

massacre of the nobility and clergy, the latter were accused by the demagogues of plotting a massacre of patriots. A few days before the September massacres the rumour was spread that a plot had been hatched in the prison.[1]

It was by false accusations against the Constituent Assembly that the demagogues excited the fury of the populace in June, 1848. On the third day of the insurrection, representatives of the working-men came to the legislative body to obtain an assurance that the Constituent Assembly did not intend reducing the people to starvation, with a view to making it abhor the Republic. The Deputies who received them showing astonishment at their questions, the working-men responded: "You see when people are undergoing every sort of hardship they are ill-disposed. Besides, we do not see what is going on, we only know by the newspapers. It is the newspapers that have excited us."[2]

When political parties seem to become reconciled and to drop their sentiment of hatred, all that has happened in reality is that they have coalesced against another party that they detest still more. A common hatred has reconciled them for a moment, but once the victory has been

[1] After the massacre of Saint Bartholomew the victims were calumniated. Royal letters were sent to the provinces announcing that " the execution at Paris" had been carried out merely to nip in the bud a plot contrived by the Protestants. The King ordered the Parliament to take proceedings against Coligny and his friends, and two notable Protestants, who had escaped massacre, were condemned.

[2] Corbon, " Le Secret du Peuple," p. 19 .

obtained over the enemy they will start attacking each other afresh. The Girondins combined with the Jacobins against the Throne, but after they had overthrown it they fell upon one another. The hatred of the Jacobins against the Girondins was heightened by jealousy. The Jacobins, jealous of the talent of the Girondins, proscribed them to avenge themselves for this superiority. Danton joined with Robespierre against the Girondins, and then fell in his turn beneath the onslaught of his accomplices.

Political hatreds are so intense that the proscription of an adversary becomes a pleasure. The man who hates experiences a sense of enjoyment when he sees his victim suffer.[1] In 1793 the Jacobins found a pleasure in the spectacle of the death of the nobles and priests; they occasionally invited the executioner to be their guest. History records that there have been several emperors who took pleasure in regarding the heads of those whom they put to death. When Sylla was killed by order of Nero, "his head was carried to Nero, who remarked jokingly that it was disfigured at too early an age by white hairs."[2] The head of Plantus was also brought to Nero, who took pleasure in the sight. Otho was overjoyed to gaze upon the head of Piso; "it is said that he never cast more eager looks upon any head."[3]

---

[1] Ennius has quite truthfully remarked: "One would like to see the man whom one hates dead." (Cicero, "De Officiis," Bk. II., § 7.)

[2] Tacitus, "Annales," Bk. I., § 57.   [3] Ibid., § 44.

It was a king who remarked in the presence of the lifeless body of an adversary whom he had had put to death : "The corpse of an enemy always has a pleasant odour."

Political hatreds are not quenched by persecution. Men pardon more easily the injuries that are done them than those they inflict. The party that has had recourse to persecution, wishes to continue to persecute. Victims occasionally pardon their executioners, but the executioners never pardon their victims, whose firmness and resignation irritate them; they are even irritated against their victims when death does not supervene quickly enough. The butchers who in 1793 slaughtered children at Nantes were furious when the poor children were too long in dying.

The political party that has begun to persecute its adversaries continues to oppress them from the fear that they should retaliate; it supposes that the oppressed will desire to revenge themselves in turn ; and from fear of the reaction to bring its persecutions to a close.

Political hatreds respect nothing, not even tombs. In 1793 the ashes of the kings were scattered to the winds, and outrages were committed upon dead bodies. In England, in 1661, the bodies of Admiral Blake and of the mother and daughter of Cromwell were removed from Westminster.

It is by enlisting the support of the dregs of the population that the violent, in times of revolution, are always successful in vanquishing the moderate. "I am well aware," said Danton on the eve of the 31st May, "that we are in a minority in the Assembly; all we have to rely upon is a crowd of rascals, who are only patriots when they are drunk. We are a pack of ignoramuses. Marat is a mere yelper; Legendre is only fit to cut up meat; and the others only know how to vote by keeping their seats or rising to their feet. We are far inferior in talent to the Girondins, but if we are beaten they will reproach us with the September massacres, with the death of Capet, and with the 10th August, in which events they sided with us. In consequence, we must attack them. They are fine speakers, who deliberate and feel their way. We have more audacity than they have, *and the dregs of the populace (canaille) are at our orders.*"

The Jacobins subsidised the rough element so as to have it at their beck and call. The men under the command of Henriot, who surrounded the Convention on the 2nd June, were individuals whose services had been bought several days before. An assignat of the value of five livres was even distributed to each of them on the scene of action. "On the 2nd June," says Lanjuinais, "I saw assignats distributed publicly to the chief of the hundred and one thousand men.[1] Buzot, wishing to explain the ruin of his party, remarks: "We could only employ honourable means, and they were of no avail. Gold, gold, that was what was bound to assure success, and what did assure it. Were not emissaries seen

[1] Lanjuinais, "Fragment Historique sur le 31 Mai." The Mayor, Paché," adds Lanjuinais, " had furnished for this occasion 150,000 francs, destined to the Saint Domingo Colonists."

everywhere with money, sometimes openly, as in the case of the two millions accorded the people of Bordeaux, and more often in secret? Money was necessary and we had none."[1] The Commune of Paris allowed every working-man under arms forty sous a day until the re-establishment of public tranquillity. Danton caused the voting of the decree that raised an army of paid *sans-culottes* in every large town, and of the decree that awarded two francs a sitting to the patriots who were present at the sectional assemblies.

The Jacobins were not the only party[2] that enrolled the rough element. The Girondins also had rioters in their pay. From the opening days of the Revolution the riots were systematically organized. "The poor creatures who figure in them," says Chancellor Pasquier, "knew neither what they wanted not what they were doing, and it was clear that their fury had been paid for."[3]

Philippe Egalité, the Duke of Orleans, expended considerable sums for riots. To supplant Louis XVI. he promoted the insurrection of the 5th October. According to two Deputies of the Right, Durand de Maillane and Lanjuinais, the adversaries of the Revolution also provoked disturbances with a view to bring it into discredit.[4]

---

[1] Buzot, "Memoires," p. 140.
[2] Etienne Marcel had sent as far as Avignon to recruit ruffians.
[3] Chancellor Pasquier, "Memoires," Vol. I., p. 49.
[4] "Histoire de la Convention Nationale," by Durand de Maillane, p. 47. "Fragment Historique sur le 31 Mai," by Lanjuinais, p. 296.

A great number of popular movements, that appear spontaneous, are, in reality, mere organized affairs, got up, or at least turned to account, by political parties. Riots are seldom due to sudden explosions of popular anger; they are often ordered by ambitious agitators. The events of the 20th June were arranged for by the Girondins, who wished to force the King to take them as ministers; those of the 31st May and the 2nd June were the work of Robespierre and Danton.

When the people are let loose, an outlet is given to a torrent that cannot be stemmed. When the masses have once been allowed a taste of rioting, blood, and pillage, it becomes very difficult to keep them under restraint. "When the people have laid criminal hands on a just king, and have tasted the blood of the best citizens, when the Republic is a mere litter beneath the feet of the trampling throng, then, assuredly, there is no storm or conflagration that may not be more easily allayed than the transports of a maddened multitude."[1] The Girondins underwent this experience; after hounding on the crowd against the Throne, they saw the same crowd turn against themselves. A riot once begun, there is no knowing where it will stop. A spark often gives rise to a vast conflagration that it is difficult to extinguish. During the struggle between the Armagnacs and the Burgundians, the master butchers, at the instigation of the University, sent into the fray their assistants and slaughterers; they hoped to be

[1] Cicero, "De Republica," Bk. I., § 42.

able to keep them in hand, but this proved beyond their power. When, under Henry III., the Duke of Guise let loose the Parisian populace, he was begged by the King to appease the sedition, but he was obliged to confess that he had no hold over "these escaped bulls." During the Fronde, after the combat in the Faubourg Saint Antoine, on the 4th July, 1652, Monsieur and Condé had recourse to M. de Beaufort, merely with the intention of frightening the municipal authorities, but the unbridled crowd went further than was desired, and slew several magistrates. Popular hatreds are so blind that the people often massacre their best friends during riots. On the occasion of the revolutionary scenes that took place at the Hôtel de Ville, on the 4th July, 1652, magistrates hostile to Mazarin were massacred on the ground that they were his partisans. During the troubles of the Fronde, it was fatal to be called a partisan of Mazarin, just as later, in 1793, to be termed an aristocrat was to risk being hanged on a lamp-post. The best friends of liberty have often been slain as its enemies. In times of violent political crises, the people, led astray by the demagogues, see traitors everywhere. Generals have been denounced as traitors and slain.

Whether revolutionary or anti-revolutionary, the mob that has been freed from restraint perpetrates the most abominable excesses. The September massacrers were insatiable of slaughter. After massacring priests and nobles they hewed down old men, women, children, and sick persons at the Salpêtrière and at Bicêtre. They killed and violated young girls in their dormitories, and slew the boys shut up in the prison for juveniles. During periods of reaction, after the 9th Thermidor and in 1815, the anti-revolutionary mobs in the South of France, carried away by the passion of vengeance, imitated the fury of the revolutionaries, without equalling it, however.[1]

Men who have been persecuted are desirous of having their revenge and of causing those who oppressed them to suffer in their turn. A party that has been decimated is eager to retaliate, and even moderate men become violent when animated by the spirit of vengeance. Thucydides has described this craving for vengeance, which constrains those who have suffered to every excess. "Corcyres," he says, "was, then, the first to offer the spectacle of every excess. It was seen to what extremes the unfortunates can go in pursuit of vengeance who have long been governed with tyrannical insolence instead of being treated with moderation; what infractions of the law can be committed by hapless creatures who desire to deliver themselves from indigence, and who, led astray by their passion, are solely concerned with laying hands on the wealth of others without regard for justice; in short, what atrocities and

---

[1] After the fall of Robespierre, "the reaction of those who were termed aristocrats against the patriots was without bounds throughout the South of France. The patriots were killed there like thrushes in the fields wherever they were met with." (Durand de Maillane, *op. cit.*, 277.)

acts of fury can be perpetrated by men who, propelled less by greed than by the desire to uphold political equality, go from excess to excess, taking counsel only of their ignorance and of the insensate fury that inspires them." (Bk. III., § 84.) The peasants of the Jacquerie in the Middle Ages, and in the 18th century the negroes of Saint Domingo, returned outrage for outrage. Atrocities were committed on the side of the nobles and on the side of the peasants, on the side of the slave-owners, and on the side of the slaves. The peasants burned down castles, the nobles set fire to villages. The carnage on both sides was horrible. The Irish, so odiously oppressed by the English, also committed shocking excesses on the various occasions on which they revolted.

The reactions against epochs of violence are always violent. After overthrowing the Terror, the 9th Thermidor continued the system of the Terror, and later on the White Terror[1] succeeded to the Red Terror. The reactionaries in their thirst for vengeance begin over again the crimes of which they were the sufferers.

It is the apathy of law-abiding citizens that constitutes the strength of the violent in times of revolution. This apathy has been observed at every epoch of history. Tacitus, saddened by

[1] It is right to recognize that the White Terror caused far fewer victims than the Red Terror. " Paris, during a single day of the September massacres, was the scene of more slaughter than the entire South of France during the summer and autumn of 1815." (Viel Castel, " Histoire de la Restauration.")

the cruelty of the tyrants and by the cowardice of the victims, drops his pen in disgust, as he says: "This servile resignation and so much blood spilled in time of peace weary and afflict the soul."[1]

The "Ormée," that spread terror in Bordeaux during the Fronde, counted only 500 members. During the Revolution, the inhabitants of Bordeaux allowed themselves to be oppressed by Tallien and the 1,800 fanatics that constituted his following. At Marseilles the Jacobins were masters of only five sections out of thirty-two. Ronsin, the commander of the revolutionary army at Lyons, declared that there were not 1,500 Jacobins in the town. Paris submitted to be terrorised by a handful of assassins.

It looks at first sight as if the savage hatreds that have caused the shedding of so much blood belong to history, and as if contemporary societies would not witness again the excesses of 1793. The words fraternity, humanity, and pity are on all lips, but they have not penetrated as yet into all hearts. There are barbarians amongst us who are without ideas, who know of nothing but hatred, and who wish to destroy society. These barbarians who lurk in the purlieus of great cities are more ferocious than the barbarians who dwell in forests. It would be a mistake to lull ourselves into a false security on the score that the enemies of society are in a minority, and that the immense mass of the people is not animated

---

[1] Tacitus, "Annales," Bk. XVI., § 16.

by revolutionary sentiments. All revolutions have been accomplished by an audacious minority. The number of the violent is small, but that of the cowardly is great! In 1871 we witnessed a revival of the Terror. The excesses of 1793 were surpassed by those of the Commune, and were a fresh revolution to break out to-morrow, the acts of vandalism and cruelty of 1871 would be surpassed by the acts of barbarity of the revolutionary Socialists and Anarchists, who nourish a savage hatred against the employers of labour, the middle class, the clergy, and the army, and who desire to compass the destruction of society by every means, by the dagger, by petroleum, by dynamite, and by incendiarism.

I have been called upon to try a certain number of Anarchists, and I have noted in their words and writings an intensity of hatred that is frightful. One of them gave servants the advice to avenge themselves on their masters by depraving their children. After the outrage in the Barcelona theatre, when an engineer belonging to Aix was among the killed, an Anarchist paper wrote: "Would not each one of you feel a thrill of feverish intensity in his heart if he heard the sputtering of capitalist fat and the howls of this mass of meat struggling in the midst of the immense fabric of fire?"

Unhappily the energy of respectable people diminishes in proportion as the audacity and hate of the enemies of society augment. "We somewhat resemble persons who, when the house has been set on fire, occupy themselves in admiring the torch and the enjoying aspect of the incendiary."[1] As the result of a foolish hyper-sentimentality we have readmitted amongst us the incendiaries of the Commune, and they refuse us the pardon we have accorded them. The Anarchists, who commit the most abominable outrages, are sometimes accorded extenuating circumstances: the juries who accord them seem to be asking for them for themselves.

[1] Joubert, "Pensées," Vol. II., p. 222.

CHAPTER V.

POLITICAL HYPOCRISY.

Devices of the political hypocrite—Religion used as a cloak for political hypocrisy—Political ambition—Personal greed of politicians—The dissimulation of politicians—Politicians conceal their ambition under the cloak of hypocrisy—Cromwell's hypocrisy—Mendacities of politicians—Political persecutors—Demagogues always speak in the name of the people—Timidity of moderate politicians—The influence of fear in politics—Cowardice of the Convention—Politicians follow the crowd—Politicians as flatterers of the people—Gullibility of the people—Washington on the "Friends of the People"—The politician and the courtier—Abuse of the word Liberty—The Satanic principle—The desire for true liberty is rare—The misleading character of party names—The falsehood of official statements—Charlatanism of political parties—Criminals in revolutionary times—Goethe on the apostles of liberty.

Politics, like religion, has its hypocrites, who mask their ambition beneath big words. Molière has pilloried religious hypocrisy in an immortal masterpiece, but political hypocrisy still awaits the artist who shall unmask it.

Ambitious politicians always invoke the public good and the interest of the State. They are incessantly talking of their devotion to the Commonwealth, while, in reality, their object is power. It often happens that the minister who is for ever insisting on his concern for the safety of the

State is solely pre-occupied in his heart of hearts with the safety of his official position, and that he who is incessantly invoking the interest of the State has above all in view his own personal interests. The Government of which the ambitious politician does not form part is always a bad Government that must be overthrown—in the public interest. A policy that does not offer tangible profits is a bad policy. The good policy is the policy that procures power and pecuniary advantages. Rigid members of the Convention, who had voted the abolition of titles, finished up Barons and Counts of the Empire, zealous champions of liberty voted the establishment of the Empire, and regicides cried "Long live the King" in 1815. Implacable adversaries of Louis Philippe, who complained of the lack of liberty under his reign, became high functionaries under Napoleon III. Just as some of the regicides of 1793 became prefects and State councillors during the First Empire, so some of the Socialists of 1848 were appointed prefects and State councillors by the Second Empire. Amid a few statesmen who are sincerely anxious for the public good, how many there are who conceal their egoistic preoccupations beneath high-sounding words!

When the Duke of Berri and the Comte de Charolais rebelled against Louis XI., they declared that they took the field for the good of the community. Louis XI., however, despatched letters patent throughout the kingdom, in which he revealed the true causes of the rebellion, and explained that if he had consented to increase the pensions of the great, these latter would never have bethought themselves of the public good. The chapter of the "Memoirs of Commines" which is devoted to the narration of the revolt of the Comte de Charolais, is preceded by the following summary: "How the Comte de Charolais, with several great Lords of France, put on foot an army against King Louis XI. *under colour of the public good.*"

A great number of ambitious politicians have used religion as a cloak for their designs. "The pretext of religion," said the Duke de Nevers,[1] is no new thing and many princes have availed themselves of it, thinking to attain their end." The Duke of Guise made use of religion as a means to procure him the throne. The public interest was the pretext alleged for the Amboise conspiracy, whereas its principal cause was the Prince of Condé's hatred of the Guise family. During the wars of religion, the principal Protestant leaders were more concerned with their personal ambitions than with the interests of Protestantism. Religion was merely the pretext for the insurrection at La Rochelle in 1627, which was the outcome, in reality, of the ambition of the Rohan family, who did not shrink from seeking the support of England against the King. Charles V. concealed his ambition under the cloak of religion. "Charles," remarked Francis I.,

[1] In his discourse upon affairs of State, printed in 1590, and dedicated to Pope Sixtus V.

"wishes to encroach upon the States under colour of religion." Philip II. also used the pretext of religion for political purposes.

It was from political ambition and not in the interest of the State that, during the Fronde, the great lords posed as popular champions. Chateauneuf, one of the leaders of the Fronde, stipulated that he should be Prime Minister in all the treaties that were projected between Mazarin and his party. Another of the leaders, the Marquis de Vieuville, demanded that he should be Superintendent of the Finances, another, de Retz, the cardinal's hat, and still others places at Court and hereditary governments. When the Duke de la Rochefoucauld (the moralist) made his peace with Mazarin, he had himself allotted the respectable pension of 8,000 francs. When Condé negotiated with the Court, he demanded for his friends commissions as marshals of France, provincial governments, honours and pensions, and even a large pension for Madame de Chatillon. The tribunes of the people were just as little oblivious of their own interests. At Bordeaux, Villars, one of the chiefs of the "Ormée," demanded 30,000 crowns for himself. It is clear that the aristocracy, who incited the people to rebel against Mazarin, were pursuing their own selfish ends. This has always been the case.

The greater part of the disturbances and civil wars that ravaged France previous to 1789 were provoked by the ambition and greed of the great nobles, who were repeatedly seen to enter into close relations with the lower classes and to flatter and excite them with a view to induce them to fly to arms. What can be more contemptible, for instance, than the conduct of Condé during the troubles of the Fronde? When, at Bordeaux, the Fronde separated into two factions, one, the lesser Fronde, composed of moderate and enlightened men, the other, called the Ormée, composed of violent and passionate men of low rank, when the schism occurred, and was followed by sanguinary struggles between the two factions, Condé, the great Condé, wrote to Lenet: "If it be impossible by negotiations or craft, or otherwise, to force the Ormée to moderate its action, it will be best to range ourselves on its side. . . . I still persist in the idea that all of us shall join ourselves with those of the Ormée, since this party is much stronger than the other."[1] When the Ormée expelled several members of the Parliament who had been friends of Condé, the latter approved these acts of violence, because he thought them necessary. He even went further: he did not shrink from deceitfully throwing the responsibility upon the Prince de Conti and the Duchesse de Longueville. "I should be glad," he wrote to Lenet, "if the acts of violence of which the Parliament is to be the object could be attributed to the Prince de Conti or to Madame de Longueville."[2]

When the hero of Rocroy, led away by political

[1] Cousin, "Madame de Longueville pendant la Fronde," p. 270.
[2] Ibid., p. 318.

passion, is seen to descend to cunning, cowardice, and hypocrisy, can one be astonished at meeting with so little straightforwardness and sincerity in the political world? Princes, Kings, Emperors, Ministers, Deputies, and popular tribunes are almost all in the habit of employing words to disguise their thoughts: they make of lying a custom, a principle of government. "He who does not know how to dissimulate does not know how to reign," remarked Louis XI. Even to-day there are historians who invite the young student to admire the crafty devices of Louis XI. It has been said of several sovereigns that they lied even when they were not speaking. Hypocrisy, next to cruelty, is the dominant characteristic of almost all the Roman Emperors. Augustus concealed absolute power beneath the semblance of a republic. It is notorious what a hypocrite Tiberius was: he was always repeating that the law must be obeyed, *exercendas leges esse*. Nero was wont to dissemble his hatred beneath treacherous caresses;[1] he sought to exonerate all his crimes on the plea that they were committed in the interest of the State. To justify the murder of Agrippina he caused false accusations to be made against her; when he put to death two excellent citizens, Plautus and Sylla, he accused them falsely of being seditious spirits, and wrote to the Senate that he was watching carefully over the safety of the Republic.[2]

---

[1] Tacitus, "Annales," XIV., § 56.
[2] Ibid., § 59.

All the ambitious men who have aspired to rule have been hypocrites, alleging that they were devoid of ambition. Plutarch relates that Pisistratus gave himself out to be a man "of no encroaching disposition, content with his own, without aspiring further, hating those who might attempt to change the present state of the commonwealth, or might be plotting some new thing."[1] It was in vain that Solon, who saw through the deceit of Pisistratus, warned the people and implored them not to allow liberty to perish; in vain that he reproached the Athenians with "their foolishness and cowardice of heart;" he was unable to convince anybody, so entirely had the Athenians been lulled into a false security by the hypocrisy of Pisistratus.

Was there ever a greater hypocrite than Cromwell? He, too, hid his ambition beneath an affected humility, filling his speeches with quotations from the Bible, and with mystical effusions, often accompanied by tears, declaring that he would have been happier had he lived in the shade of his little wood and tended his flock of sheep instead of taking over the burden of government;[2] but he added that it was his duty to accept this burden in order to save the nation and in obedience to the will of God. He never spoke haughtily, like a man who makes a show of his authority, but as "an obedient colleague in the service of the people;"

---

[1] Plutarch, "Life of Solon."
[2] Villemain, "Histoire de Cromwell," Vol. VI., p. 263.

he declared himself the servant of the people. He disguised his rule under the title of Protector, just as Napoleon adopted the title of First Consul to the same end. I cannot attempt to cite all the cruel and crafty acts of Cromwell, so shall confine myself to recalling how he took the town of Drogheda. He promised those who should capitulate their lives; the besieged, deceived by this promise, surrendered, and Cromwell caused them all to be massacred. Gustave de Beaumont relates in his book on Ireland, that visiting the country two centuries after these events, he found the districts which Cromwell had traversed still full of the terror of his name. Cromwell, like so many other ambitious politicians,[1] was in the habit of slandering those who resisted him, before imprisoning them or putting them to death; he caused pamphleteers in his pay to denounce them as abominably factious characters and as men capable of every crime.

The ambitious who wish to acquire or to keep power always have their pamphleteers, their "reptiles," who slander their adversaries and dissimulate their projects. The man who proposes to confiscate liberty, vaunts liberty and declares himself ready to combat despotism. While Monk was paving the way for the return of the Stuarts, he said to Ludlow, "One ought to

---

[1] Cæsar was perpetually slandering Cato of Utica, accusing him of avarice and of being a man of bad morals. Yet Plutarch says that "Hercules might as well be accused of cowardice as Cato of avarice and of greed of gain." (Life of Cato of Utica.)

live and die for the Republic," and he swore to oppose the restoration of the Stuarts. The words of the Bible, *Omnis homo mendax*, are more especially applicable to the politician. The conqueror who oppresses a conquered country is fond of styling himself its liberator. The prince who governs in defiance of the wishes of a nation does not fail to declare that he is the people's mandatory, and the executor of the national will. The King or the Minister who is making preparations for war announces peace. Should he declare war, he endeavours by false declarations to sow division in the country he is attacking, to create a breach between the Government and the nation. Leopold declared in the manifesto he addressed to all the Powers in 1791, that he merely wished "to suppress those petty legislators of the National Assembly who, after attacking the throne and the altar, would infallibly disturb the peace of Europe." He added: "I declare to the French nation that it is not against it that I shall lead my troops." The King of Prussia resorted to the same manœuvre in 1870, declaring that he was making war upon Napoleon III., and not upon the French nation, and yet, when Napoleon III. had been made prisoner, Prussia continued to make war against the nation.

The violent affirm that order reigns when they have silenced their victims; they declare they have established peace where they have made a solitude, *ubi solitudinem faciunt, pacem appellant*. When one nation oppresses another, it does not fail to inform it that it is the bearer of the benefits of civilisation, and that it is acting in the interest of the oppressed. When the Athenians summoned the Melians to submit, they said to them hypocritically: "We speak to you at the same time in the interest of your republic. We wish to spare you a resistance that will be fatal, and to preserve you in your interest and . . . in our own."[1]

Cicero, attempting to justify the enormous tributes that the Romans exacted from conquered peoples, maintained that the Roman rule was established in their interest. The truth is that the peoples in question were robbed and pillaged with boundless greed and cruelty. The Spaniards pillaged the New World under the pretence of civilising it.

Persecutors always prate of humanity and fraternity when they are sending their victims to the scaffold. If they wish to suppress religion, it is in the name of the liberty of worship and of the liberty of conscience that they put impediments in the way of religious observances and of the recruiting of the clergy. After the 9th Thermidor the Convention proclaimed the liberty of creeds, and at the same time forbade the priests to celebrate religious services. Irreligious fanaticism is, in general, hypocritical and cruel. During the Terror it caused the murder of priests, the closing of churches, and the destruction of altars in the name of philosophy. The murderers of the

[1] Thucydides.

priests styled themselves patriots and philosophers, and gave the name of fanatics to their victims: later on the persecution was conducted in the name of legality. When persecution cannot attain its end by violence, it hypocritically assumes legal forms. When England saw that it was powerless to suppress Catholicism in Ireland by force, it authorised the exercise of that creed, but at the same time it banished the bishops so as to hinder the recruiting of the clergy. In France, the most cruel Terrorists had recourse to violence and ruse in turn to root out Christianity. Carrier, who was instrumental in drowning so many priests, and who, at his trial, declared that these drownings had seemed to him very natural,[1] also advocated the employment of ruse as an indirect means of destroying Christianity, though all the while he was proclaiming the liberty of public worship.

Confiscation, during the Revolution, was denominated at the outside sequestration or administration by the Government. The name of the Consolidated Third was given to the public debt after it had been arbitrarily reduced to a third of its value. The Convention, after the 9th Thermidor, declared that property was inviolable, and yet declared the families of the Emigrants incapable of holding property, and maintained the confiscation of their estates.

The majority of the speeches of the revolutionary period abounded in falsehoods. While the

[1] Wallon, "Les Représentants en Mission," Vol. I., p. 68.

Convention was deliberating, on the 2nd June, under menace of the guns and cannon of the Commune, Couthon spoke of the independence it enjoyed. "Now that you are reassured as to your liberty," he said, "I ask that justice be done the people, that the Deputies who have conspired be arrested." What a hypocrite Robespierre was, how all his speeches are impregnated with craft and treachery ! He is the type of the political Tartuffe. His language is always artificial and shifty; he boasts of his frankness, he affects abnegation and the absence of ambition, he pronounces devoutly the words humanity and liberty when he is proposing acts of proscription. Jealous of his adversaries who have more talent than himself, he slanders and proscribes them in the interest of the Republic, and sacrifices them in reality to his private grudges. To make himself popular he lodges with a joiner and takes his meals with the family.

Another Machiavelian expedient employed by the Governments that wish to destroy a religion consists in discrediting the clergy by choosing them badly. The Russian Government, with a view to suppress Catholicism in Poland, appointed drunken and debauched Catholic bishops.

The demagogues who wish to oppress the majority, in the name of an infinitesimal minority, always speak in the name of the people, although they represent but the least enlightened and least respectable portion of the people. It was in the name of the "people" that they demanded the execution of the King, the proscription of the Girondins, and the creation of the revolutionary tribunal. The very judges who formed part of this tribunal were given to invoking the people. . . . "The people, who knows the conspirators, desires their punishment," they said. "Inform the people that the Convention wishes to join with it in saving the Republic."[1] Factious minorities always invoke the will of the people. During the Revolution the pretended delegates of the 48 sections of Paris alleged that they alone represented the sovereign people. It has been affirmed that the 48 sections were instituted to overthrow the monarchy. The fact is that in the night of the 9th to 10th August, many of the commissaries were only elected by an infinitesimal minority. In the section of the Arsenal, which comprehended 1,400 active citizens, the election of these delegates was carried out by the members. How often, since, has the same fiction accompanied the formation of political committees and the nomination of delegates, who give themselves out to be the representatives of the majority, and who turn to account a mandate they have not received? It is thanks to manœuvres of this kind that France at times allows itself to be governed by a minority which is not the *élite* of the country. The true figures are falsified or juggled with. The minority, giving itself the appearance of being the majority, acts

[1] "Histoire de la Convention Nationale," by Durand de Maillane, p. 66.

upon public opinion and, speaking in the name of the people, directs it.

The authors of despotic or popular *coups d'état* never fail to invoke the sovereignty of the people as their excuse for outraging this sovereignty. The only sovereignty that interests them is their own sovereignty. While declaring the people to be sovereign, they impose their will upon it and treat it as their slave; they make a pretence of consulting the country, and dictate to it, in reality, the answers they demand.

At revolutionary epochs France abounds in persons who attribute to themselves the right of representing the country. If they invade the representative Assembly their object is to acquaint it with the will of the people. At the sitting of the 1st Prairial, An III., the Convention having been invaded by a seditious mob, "an individual in the costume of a gunner mounts the tribune, where, surrounded by fusiliers, he reads, in a most insolent tone, a printed manifesto, *which contains*, he says, *the will of the sovereign people in whose name he speaks.*"[1]

While the violent hide their projects under a swarm of pretexts, such as the public good, the safety of the republic and the will of the people, the moderate in turn conceal their weakness and fear beneath sophisms and falsehoods. They only yield, they declare, in order to avoid still greater evils, and to terminate a dangerous crisis.

---

[1] Durand de Maillane, "Histoire de la Convention Nationale," p. 361.

They excuse themselves for accepting the violent measures they are asked to countenance by pleading that they only vote them in the interest of those against whom they are directed. When the Jacobins, on the 2nd June, demanded the proscription of the Girondins, the Deputies of the Plain conceded the point, declaring "that after all the Deputies kept under arrest in their own houses were not much to be pitied, and that it was necessary to put an end to a terrible crisis."[1] Barrère, entrusted with drawing up a report in the name of the Committee of Public Safety, made a hypocritical appeal to the patriotism and generosity of the accused members, and asked them to consent voluntarily to the suspension of their privileges on the pretext that this was the only way of putting an end to the divisions that afflicted the Republic. The same hypocrisy was to the fore when the list of the proscribed was put to the vote: the members of the Centre, to hide their weakness, refused to vote, saying that they were not free. Their abstention allowed the Mountain to decree that the Girondins should be brought to trial.

At the present day it is fear that drives so many men of moderate opinions to howl with the extremists and Socialists; it was fear that, during the Revolution, added incessantly to the number of the Jacobins, who were at first in a minority in the Convention, and it was the same motive that

---

[1] Thiers, "Histoire de la Révolution Française," Vol. IV., p. 287.

led the Duke of Orleans to take his place with the Men of the Mountain, and to adopt the sobriquet of "Egalité."

Fear, which makes hypocrites of men, also makes them cruel. To save themselves, they cause the ruin of others; cowardice, says Montaigne, is the mother of cruelty. Numerous were the Deputies who voted the death of Louis XVI., and of the Girondins, out of fear. How many acted as did Saint-Fargeau, the former President of the Parliament of Paris! After exhibiting great hostility to the revolution he voted the condemnation of Louis XVI., and canvassed for votes in its favour. The Girondins did not desire the death of Louis XVI., but they voted for it from fear of being accused of royalism.[1] Vergniaud, who, to begin with, pronounced himself openly against the death of Louis XVI., finished by voting for it, on the pretence that it was indispensable to sacrifice one man's life to avert civil war. Many of the Deputies allowed themselves to be intimidated by the clamours of those in the public tribunes, who were murmuring against those who did not vote the death sentence. The Men of the Mountain only obtained the condemnation by the aid of audacity and terror. It was fear that, in turn, caused the Girondins to be delivered over to Danton and Robespierre, and afterwards, Danton to Robespierre. The majority in the Convention was not animated by cruel sentiments. "The

---

[1] This cowardliness did not save them. The Men of the Mountain accused them later of having purposed saving the tyrant.

majority was always sound," M. de Sevre remarked at a later date; "but it was always cowardly. It was in no sort the courage of the majority that brought the dictatorship of Robespierre to an end: it was the fear of becoming his victims that decided Tallien, Bourdon de l'Oise, Legendre, and Lecointre to attack Robespierre—they pulled him down to save themselves. Barrère, questioned afterwards upon the acts of the Committee of Public Safety, replied: "We had but one sentiment, that of self-preservation, but one desire, that of preserving our existence, which each of us thought to be threatened. One had one's neighbour guillotined to prevent oneself being guillotined by one's neighbour." To save their own heads, the Deputies sent their colleagues to the scaffold.

When Siéyès was asked, after the Terror, what he did during the tempest, he replied: "I lived." Many moderate members of the Convention did as he did: their sole thought was to save their lives by keeping silent and lying low in the "marsh." A Deputy of the Right, Durand de Maillane, has explained his attitude in the Convention in the following terms: "Robespierre's party saw no hope for the safety of the Republic and for its own security except in recourse to atrocious measures, and it resolved to rid itself of its adversaries by the sword and by assassination. Under a republic, patriotic zeal is sometimes made to serve as an excellent cloak for these horrors. For my part, deeply impressed by these shameful scenes and still more by the misfortunes they seemed to foretell, *I at once made up my mind to keep aloof and to trust for safety to my silence and insignificance;* . . . by my silence I did not provoke the anger of any member of the Left. I kept carefully present to my memory the opinion that Bodin emits in his 'Republic:' 'When one has good reasons not to declare openly in favour of the people, when it is in a state of ebullition, it is prudent, even necessary, for one's safety, not to run counter to it. . . . . It is wiser,' he adds, ' to yelp with the wolves.' "[1]

To yelp with the wolves is, in fact, the motto of a great number of moderate men, who, though they abhor extreme ideas, refrain from combating them and even pretend sometimes to hold them. If they are Senators or Deputies they vote laws that are repugnant to them, painful though it be to them to act in such fashion. The majority of politicians follow the crowd instead of guiding it; the number of those who have the courage to state their opinions and to resist the current is very small. From fear of involving themselves in trouble, people range themselves on the side that seems in the ascendant; they make a hypocritical show of extreme opinions and follow the current so as to retain popularity.[2]

[1] "Histoire de la Convention Nationale," pp. 39, 57, 33.

[2] A district councillor told me recently that he had gone to the chief town of the department to take part in a senatorial election, intending to vote for the moderate Republican candidate; "but," he added, "I saw on my arrival that the current

A great many politicians stop short at no falsehood to acquire or keep popularity. They follow with docility all the passions of the crowd. They change their ideas and programmes as public opinion veers; they defend what they used to combat, and combat what they used to defend. They are of the current opinion. If Moderation and Liberalism are in fashion they are Moderates and Liberals, but if the spirit of justice and liberty should expose them to losing their popularity, they are quick to become violent, unjust, and tyrannical, in order not to allow themselves to be surpassed in violence by their rivals. If the crowd clamour for religious persecution, they will persecute religion; if it demand iniquitous taxes, they will vote them; if it insist upon a policy of plunder, they will hasten to satisfy every form of greed and envy; even if the crowd would have blood, they will let blood flow, and will slander the victims. And yet the moment soon arrives when they lose this popularity so dearly bought,

---

did not set in his direction, and I voted for his adversary." "You are a profound politician," I answered him, expressing my irony in the form of a compliment; "you always follow the current." The councillor hesitated a moment, in doubt whether my compliment was ironical or sincere. He looked at me anxiously to see whether I was not smiling, but I managed to keep serious. Thereupon, reassured as to my intentions, and flattered at my appreciation of him, he made me this memorable answer: "Yes, sir, I always follow the current." The majority of politicians follow the current, like this district councillor, and like Alcibiades, who said: "Athens being ruled by a popular government, it is necessary to follow the impulsion of circumstances." (Thucydides, Bk. VI., § 89.)

for the people is not long in breaking its idols.¹ It was to retain their popularity that the Girondins voted the death of Louis XVI. against their conscience.

What Mdme. de Maintenon and the mother of the Regent said of the Court world may be applied to the political world: "These surroundings are terrible, and there is no head they do not turn," said Mdme. de Maintenon. "Be on your guard against all that you most esteem. I am at the fountain head, and the result is that I witness one act of treachery after the other. The very best are transformed by the Court."² Politics, also, transform the best characters. Again, the mother of the Regent said: "Since I have been here, I have been accustomed to see such abominable things, that if ever I were to find myself in a place where dissimulation was not the reigning quality, or where lying was not favoured and approved of, I should believe I had come upon a paradise."

The courtiers did not seek to enlighten the king; they merely wished to please him and to

---

[1] D'Eprem´nil, who was so popular in 1789, was in 1791 roughly handled by the populace, who wished to put him to death. Delivered from his murderers, he said to Petion, who had come to visit him, these words, which should be weighed by ambitious politicians : "I, too, have been carried in triumph by the people." In spite of the inconstancy of the people, popularity-hunting is the ruling passion of politicians. When Benjamin Constant was on his deathbed he was heard in his wanderings to murmur these words : "After twelve years of popularity justly won, justly deserved." He was bewailing the loss of his popularity.

[2] Letter of Mdme. de Maintenon, dated 15th November, 1695.

secure his good graces by flattery. The king, in their eyes, was an idol. For politicians the people has become another idol, which they flatter and worship in order to push their fortunes, humouring all its passions and applauding all its prejudices. "How great art thou, O people!" they declaim, "how noble, how gentle! All thou desirest is just!" The flatterers of the people, like the flatterers of kings, to justify its passions, give its vices the names of the contrasting virtues; they call its intolerance love of liberty, its violence love of tranquillity. They tell it that it promotes public order when it treats the representatives of authority with violence, that by interfering with the liberty of labour it upholds liberty, that by striking down the capitalist it establishes the reign of fraternity. They persuade it that by ruining the employers of labour, and by bringing about its own ruin, it enriches the country, and that by undoing itself and the manufacturers it conduces to the prosperity of the nation.

Sovereigns are sometimes sickened by the flatteries of which they are the object. Tiberius himself, every time that he came away from the Senate, could not refrain from exclaiming in Greek: "O men created for servitude!" He kept within bounds the senators who descended to excessive flattery.[1] It is rare that the people is thus disgusted by the hypocritical and gross flattery that is

[1] Tacitus, "Annales," Bk. II., § 87; Bk. IV., § 6. The Emperor Claudius declined the title of Father of the Senate, because he considered this flattery excessive. (Tacitus "Annales," Bk. XI., § 25.)

lavished upon it. It almost always yields to the seduction,[1] and especially so if the demagogues indulge as well in abuse of the rich, saying: "They are overflowing in riches, . . we are lacking in even the necessities of life; they own two or several palaces, while we have nowhere a resting place."[2] Poor people! It likes to be flattered, and does not even perceive that its flatterers live at its expense.

To excite the working-man against his employer, the soldier against his chiefs, to stir up the jealousy of the poor against the rich, to make him promises that are unrealisable, to demand the confiscation of the property of the rich, such are the habitual tactics of demagogues.[3] How is it possible for the good sense of the people to resist such culpable excitations, especially when their authors (as has happened more than once in France) are those in authority? "Workers in towns and factories," said the Minister of the Interior on the 28th March, 1848, "it is essential that you should be conscious of your sufferings, your rights, and your just pretensions. Publish them abroad. . . Working-men, declare what you have suffered, . . . declare that your life has been a martyrdom, . . . reveal these horrors to an appalled world; relate that your daughters of tender age had no choice between suicide and prostitution; relate that aged men

---

[1] "The people is gullible." Aristophanes made this remark.
[2] Salluste, "Catilina," § 20.
[3] "To-day," said Aristotle, "to please the people the demagogues make the tribunals order vast confiscations." ("Politica," Bk. VII., ch. iii., § 2.)

were abandoned to their fate when death struck you down before them, and that women have been seen stretched on the stones of the mortuary, their own corpse clutched by the corpse of their child. . . . Martyrs of labour, rise and speak. Tell how the food and remedies ordered you in the hospitals by the doctors were made the occasion of pilfering speculation! . . . Tell how fraud was everywhere, what poisons were mingled by speculation with the bitter bread you ate. . . . Society owes it to you henceforth to probe your wounds and to provide the remedies. It owes it to you to see to the preservation of your life, your health, your intelligence, your dignity. *It owes you work, food,* instruction, honour, air, light! . . You are about to have a hand in the fashioning of society. Working-men, this is an edifice that you are about to construct for society; do not permit that it be raised for the advantage of only a few, while humanity remains outside, naked, a-hungered, debased and desperate."

How redolent of hypocrisy is this rhetoric, now bland, now incendiary, of the flatterers of the people! What an infinity of promises made in bad faith!

[1] Recently, at a public meeting, a Radical Deputy from the South of France declared that all peasants and working-men ought to receive at the age of fifty a pension from the State of 400 francs. At the close of the meeting, the mayor, who had been present, talking privately with the Deputy, observed to him that what he had promised was impossible. "I am quite aware of it," answered the Deputy, "but these promises always give them pleasure." The leaders of the Babeuf conspiracy wrote to their partisans: "Do not be sparing of promises; it will always be possible to elude fulfilling them, according to circumstances." (De Barante, "Histoire du Directoire," Vol. I., p. 257.)

When will the people understand that every flatterer lives at the expense of whoever listens to him, and that "the name of friend of the people, of good Republican, is within the reach of everybody? Anybody can acquire it, but the keenest to make use of it are those who deserve it the least."[1] How many are there among those noisy friends of the people whose affection for the people is real, whose desire to improve its situation is sincere, and who prove their devotion otherwise than by words? Unfortunately in certain electoral districts it is sufficient for a person of dubious social status to cry "Hurrah for the Commune!" to wear a blouse, to slander the priests who bring up the people's children, and the Sisters of Mercy who devote their lives to tending the sick—this is sufficient to induce the belief that he is a friend of the people, the champion of the working-man, the protector of the widow and orphan and the promoter of social reforms. These pretended friends of the people are its greatest enemies. Washington stood in greater dread of these than of the English. "I shed tears of blood," he said, "over the future of my country, if the wisdom of the American people does not keep it out of the hands of such men. They are compromising all that we have accomplished. They are establishing a government of perpetual agitation, and of demagogic societies in opposition to the National Congress. *Imperium in imperio!* And what

[1] Æschines, "Discourse upon the Crown."

manner of government? The government of the most audacious, the most impudent, and the most perverted."

Fénelon, discussing the profession of Courtier, said that "the narrowest and most corrupted minds are those that acquire this unworthy profession the best."[1] This observation is applicable to those who court the people. In Paris, as in Athens, "it is the most ignorant and the most perverted who are the most skilful in charming the multitude."[2]

Like courtiers, the flatterers of the people worship the rising and turn their back on the setting sun.[3] Just as the courtiers of a king readily become the sycophants of the people in time of revolution, so on the morrow of a *coup d'état* or of a monarchical restoration the flatterers of the people are sure to become the courtiers of kings;[4] Jacobins under the Terror, they are Senators under the Empire, Legitimists under the Restoration, whereas moderate men, who have flattered neither the mob nor kings, are looked at askance by all parties.

"Ambition coupled with idleness, meanness coupled with pride, the desire to grow rich without working, dislike of truth, flattery, treachery, perfidy, the breaking of all pledges, contempt for

---

[1] Fénelon, "Direction pour la Conscience d'un Roi."
[2] Aristotle, "Rhetorica," Bk. II., ch. xxii.
[3] Tacitus, "Annales," Bk. VI.
[4] When Etienne Marcel was assassinated, says a contemporary chronicler, his friends concealed their red hoods and, crying louder than the others, rushed to meet the Dauphin.

the duties of the citizen . . . form, I think," says Montesquieu, "the character of the majority of courtiers."[1] This portrait is as applicable to the flatterers of the people as it is to the flatterers of kings. Courtiers whisper to young princes: "Free yourselves from all tutelage, from the state of dependency in which you are kept, listen to nobody, that is to nobody except us." The flatterers of the people address the people in identical language. They excite its suspicions against those who might enlighten it; they calumniate the true friends of the people.

Courtiers, the better to obtain a hold over young princes, endeavour to deprave them. The flatterers of the people follow the same course; they distribute among the working classes printed matter to which they apply the epithet literary, but which is, in reality, pornographic. The reason is that they are aware that by corrupting the workmen they will the more easily inoculate them with revolutionary passions. There is a close connection between actions and ideas, a mutual action of the one upon the other. A working-man who leads a steady life is, in general, refractory to anti-social passions. A dissolute working-man, on the contrary, is an easy prey for the demagogues. Whoever creates himself numerous needs and who works but little is very inclined to say, "To each according to his needs." The sober and laborious man

---

[1] Montesquieu, "Esprit des Lois," Bk. III., ch. v.

understands that the true doctrine is, "To each according to his works."

It is with a view, too, to perverting the people that its flatterers make of irreligion a means of government. As religion enjoins obedience and respect for authority, those whose aim is revolt and the upheaval of society endeavour hypocritically to wean the people from religion so as to be able to incite it to rebellion the more easily.[1]

The flatterers of the people, who scoff inwardly at liberty and the public good, always agitate these great words as they might a banner.[2] The love of liberty and its comprehension presuppose respect and love for others. However, those who talk the most of liberty desire liberty for themselves, but do not admit it for others. Their view is that liberty is a high-sounding word that it is well to pronounce incessantly as a means to popularity, though they nourish the while in their hearts the hatred of religion, the hatred of social superiorities, the hatred of authority, and the hatred of property. The love of liberty is not composed of this plenitude of hatreds. How many men are there who truly love liberty? For the

---

[1] Robespierre was less intolerant, for he said: "Every institution, every doctrine that consoles and that elevates men's minds, should be welcomed. . . . In the eyes of the legislator whatever is of use to the world, and in practice excellent, is the truth. The idea of a Supreme Being and of the immortality of the soul is a constant reminder of justice ; it is therefore social and republican. . . ."

[2] Commines relates that on arriving in Florence he found the town in insurrection. The factions were shouting, "Liberty, liberty!" and "The people, the people!" words they thought likely to induce the people to embrace their party.

one, liberty is hatred of the nobility, for another, hatred of religion and of priests; in 1793, for certain Jacobins, it was love for the estates confiscated by the nation and hatred of aristocrats and priests; in 1830, for some of the July conquerors, it was the love of place, for others the hatred of social superiorities. The spirit of envy masquerades as the love of liberty. One man loves liberty because of the oratorical bouts and the emotions it serves to procure him;[1] another because he sees in it a means of arriving at power and fortune; another, fascinated by the romance of the history of the Revolution, dreams of being a Robespierre, and yet another, of being a Danton. Young people believe they love liberty because they love noise, change, and revolt. Subordination wearies them, tranquillity bores them, stability irritates them. What more tedious than order, what more insipid than absolute calm? Commotion is life; a little disorder breaks the monotony of existence. One feels oneself live when one breaks a few street lamps and a few shop windows; there is some emotion to be had breaking the heads of policemen. Many working-men, for their part, confound liberty with the vociferations of public meetings. Restless spirits imagine they love liberty because all authority is repugnant to them, and they often hate the Government because they have been summoned for some trifling breach of

---

[1] The passion for gambling that is often found in politicians comes from the thirst for emotions they have contracted from their experience of party conflicts.

the police regulations. The spirit of opposition to the Government is general: it is found even in those who solicit favours of the Government. The citizen who misconducts his business or who has a bad harvest vents his spite upon the Government.

The man who has not been rendered wiser by experience and family duties has an inborn antipathy to discipline and lack of respect for authority. It is because Anarchism glorifies revolt that it takes the favour of so many young men.[1]

"What we, for our part, call liberty," says Bakounine, "is something very different; it is the *Satanic* principle and the natural fact that is termed revolt, that sacred and noble thing, revolt.[1] . . . ." There is a sort of intoxication in the way in which Anarchism exalts revolt and brings out its Satanic character. Satan is not, as a foolish people imagines, the personification of evil and egoism. "Satan," says the Anarchist theorist, "is in no way an egoist; he did not rebel in his own interest, but in that of all humanity, and he sacrificed himself in the most real manner, since rather than renounce the principle of revolt, which is to emancipate the human world, he let himself

[1] I have seen students, who had come out of mere curiosity to the Bouches-du-Rhône assizes to hear Sébastien Faure speak in his own defence, leave the court troubled and unsettled by the revolutionary language of the Anarchist and half won over to Anarchism.

[2] Bakounine, "La Théologie Politique de Mazzini et l'Internationale," p. 50.

be condemned to eternal torture, if the Holy Scriptures are to be believed."[1]

In a general way politicians and political parties understand by liberty the right of doing what they wish and of imposing their will upon others. Under aristocratic Governments the preservation of privileges is styled liberty: under demagogues this name is given to license and to the oppression of the majority by the minority. It would seem that local tyrannies should not exist in a democratic society, but in point of fact the government that is styled free has nothing free about it but the name; all that has happened is that the oppression is exercised from a different quarter. Nobody wishes to be oppressed, but everybody wants to be the oppressor; or, at any rate, the number of those who desire liberty for all is inconsiderable—people desire liberty for themselves and their friends. All parties endeavour to seize on power to oppress their adversaries. Those who cry the loudest against oppression when they are in opposition forget their principles as soon as they are in power: after having been the anvil they wish to be the hammer in their turn. An assembly can be as tyrannical as a

---

[1] The first number of the "Revue Anarchiste" contains some verses by Clovis Hugues on Satan, in which the following lines occur :

"We love thee, we offer thee the incense of our prayers,
We worship the flame that flashes in thy eyes,
O! magnificent Demon, O! heavenly Titan,
We cast at thy feet laurels and roses,
And we respect thee in thy metamorphoses
Whether thou be Vasouki! Prometheus! or Satan!"

military dictatorship. The transfer of all power from a sovereign to an assembly means not the establishment of liberty, but the displacement of a despotism.

Whenever political parties wish to persecute their adversaries, they invoke the public safety, satisfying their private grudges under pretext of the security of the people. By what they term the "public good" they mean their own personal good, and by a law providing for the public safety they understand a law that assures the safety of their domination. They are given to confounding their own interests with those of society, which are quite different, and they detect a national peril where it is merely their ambition that is in danger.

Politics almost always wear a mask. Each party wishes to destroy its adversary, and hides its ambition and greed under high-sounding pretexts. Thucydides has described this party hypocrisy. "Those who in each town," he wrote, "held the first rank, decorating with honourable names the authority they had usurped and proclaiming themselves the defenders, these of political equality—the boon of popular government—the others of a well-balanced aristocracy, were all agreed in pretending that the state of things they were in favour of was the reward of their deplorable struggles. Leaving no stone unturned to supplant each other, their audacity stopped short at no excess. . . . Their quarrels were the outcome of their desire to rule, a desire inspired by ambition and cupidity, principles that are the source of the ardour of all men, whom rivalry pits against each other."[1]

If it be wise not to judge men by their appearance, it is no less prudent not to judge political parties by the label they give themselves. Men whose aim is to make society return to the barbarity of the primitive ages style themselves "Progressists." Others, who are ignorant that society can only be preserved by successive ameliorations, give themselves the name of Conservatives, although incapable of being the guardians of anything whatever. In the language of the revolutionaries, the working-men who do not work are called the "workers." The assassins of the Commune spoke of the soldiers who were fighting on the side of order as assassins, and represented themselves as the victims of middle class tyranny. The September massacrers and the revolutionaries who passed their time in orgies arrogated to themselves the epithet "virtuous." Henriot, and his accomplices, who lived by pillage, declared that they only aspired to be rich in good morals, virtues, and love of their country. The extremists, who are always crying out against functionarism, are the first to demand the creation of public functions they are incapable of filling, and to denounce capable and honest officials in the hope of taking their places. The Directory, a corrupt and violent Government, was

[1] Thucydides, Bk. III., § 82.

always prating of virtue, humanity, and legality, even on the morrow of the 18th Fructidor. When the transportation law was voted, its seconder pretended that it was in accordance with justice and humanity; he called attention to the fact that not a drop of blood was to be shed, and that the enemies of liberty were being got rid of in a humane manner. In the eyes of the authors of proscriptions, the friends of liberty are always the enemies of liberty. Men who have no love for anybody style themselves the friends of the people; others, who do not love their country, pretend to an ardent affection for humanity. The Anarchists allege that they renounce their country the better to serve humanity.[1]

In politics, to secure the voting of "laws of exception," they are declared to be temporary, but when they are once voted, the attempt is made to convert these temporary laws into permanent laws. Political parties too often get laws of exception passed by agitating the spectre of a conspiracy or some other imaginary danger. They count upon fear to get them voted. The real reason for the passing of a law should not always be looked for in the reasons given officially when the measure was introduced: the apparent reasons are not always the true reasons. Saint Evremond, in a witty comedy, entitled "Sir Politick," in which he satirises the deceit practised

---

[1] Diderot had already raised the question whether it was not better to serve the human race, "which will last for ever," than a country "which is destined to come to an end." ("Vie de Sénèque.")

in politics, makes one of his personages remark: "Never say what you think in your speeches, and believe what is said to you just as little." What a number of speeches, proclamations, and official discourses are a mere tissue of falsehoods. "The Moniteur" itself has been falsified on several occasions, and has published accounts intentionally untrue.[1] Statesmen are given to saying that the people likes to be deceived; "it is necessary that princes or their ministers should study to direct it and persuade it by fine words, to seduce and deceive it by appearances, . . by means of clever pens, that turn out clandestine books, manifestoes, apologies, and artistically concocted declarations, so as to lead it by the nose, and to make it approve or condemn without its knowing what it approves or condemns."[2]

Fourier wrote a pamphlet to denounce "the traps and the charlatanism of the sects of Saint Simon and Owen;" they are the blind leading the blind, he said, false brethren whose only aim is "to have a finger in the government, the finances, and the estates of private persons." I should require a large volume to point out the charlatanism of all the political parties. I shall confine myself to presenting a few more short reflections upon this inexhaustible subject, paying more particular attention to the present time.

What is to be thought of the sincerity of politicians who vote Radical laws while declaring

---

[1] *Vide* Mortimer-Ternaux, Vol. III., p. 215.
[2] Gabriel Naudé, "Les Coups d'Etat," ch. iv.

themselves to be Moderates? If there be anything moderate about them it is above all their courage and sincerity.

What is to be thought of the good faith of those who, called upon to judge the Communists, do not dare to approve them for fear of incurring public contempt nor to disapprove them for fear of losing a profitable *clientèle*?

Are the Socialists very sincere when they declare they have nothing in common with the Anarchists, whom they, nevertheless, make their allies, protesting, too, against the measures of repression of which they are the object? Is it in absolute good faith that Radical journalists and Deputies attribute bomb explosions to the police, the middle class and the clergy? Do they not act in this way so as to misdirect public indignation? Again may it not be argued that the clamouring of the Socialist party against clericalism is merely a skilful manœuvre? The stratagem serves to divert attention from the Socialist peril which is alone to be feared. In the same way is it not with a view to discredit the moderate Republicans that the Radicals and Socialists brand them Reactionaries and Clericalists the moment they find them combating revolutionary intrigues?

Is it solely to their tenderness of heart that is to be attributed the sombre picture they draw of the misery of the people, contrasted, in order to heighten the effect, with the exaggerated happiness of the rich? Is not this antithesis a manœuvre to stir up popular anger? Catiline had already resorted to it when he said: "While they are raising the level of the sea and reducing the height of mountains, we are at a loss for a shelter. . . ." The politicians who exaggerate the good fortune of the rich augment the envy of the poor and give greater acuteness to their suffering.

Can it be held that the different language in which the Socialist addresses the peasants and the working-men respectively is a model of good faith? They promise the former that they will protect and respect small properties, while they offer the latter free trade and the destruction of property. Are they entirely sincere when they promise the suppression of social inequalities, of suffering and poverty, riches and happiness for everybody, the transformation of the earth, that "vale of tears," into a paradise, where men will all be angels, and laws, courts of justice, and prisons will have become useless? Would it not be proper to apply to these lying promises this passage of Tacitus: "There are words that are seductive and specious: they carry with them a shadow of liberty and they pave the way for a fall into the worst slavery"?[1]

Is it in reality solely with the interests of the people that these makers of fine promises who are so greedy of personal advertisement are preoccupied? The most elated among them frequently cause to be written or write themselves the most laudatory articles in their own favour, thus putting

---

[1] Tacitus, "Annales," Bk. I., § 81.

in practice the recommendations of Bacon, who advised those who desire to make their way to resort to advertisement. "In the absence of merit," he said, "make a show of its appearances. In consequence, vaunt your virtues, your talents, even your fortune. It is with ostentation as with calumny; it always leaves some impression on the mind, and the esteem of the multitude atones for the contempt of the wise, a detestable maxim where morality is concerned, but useful in politics."

Do they really hope to prepare the reign of fraternity by inciting the different classes against each other, and to lead the country to peace and union by getting ready all the elements of a new civil war? Are the demagogues whose sole occupation is the fomenting of disturbances and strikes really animated by a sincere love of the people? The agitators keep clear of the danger when a riot breaks out; they do not throw bombs, they get them thrown by others. They imitate those revolutionaries who lie low during the insurrections they have provoked, and await in safety the termination of the conflict.

To spur the crowd to action, the agitators always avail themselves of a pretext, of sensational cries. During the revolution, a number of riots took place amid cries of "Bread and the Constitution!" Those who clamoured for bread did not always need it. For instance, when the Convention was invaded on the Prairial, An III., by men and women demanding bread, the pockets of the first rioter arrested were found to be full of bread.[1] Fear of hunger, which has been the cause of many insurrections, has also been often but a mere pretext. Insurrections are always organized in the same way: women, children, and idle sight-seers are sent to the front, followed by an immense gathering that surrounds the assembly it is desired to invade, or the soldiers it is wished to hem in. To quicken the excitement the ring-leaders take care to have a few shots fired, and if the soldiers kill an insurgent in self-defence, the ringleaders have the corpse carried through the streets, and declare that the Government is assassinating the people. They also press into their service the criminals that abound in great cities, and especially in Paris, or who hasten there in the hope of pillage when a riot is brewing.

Criminals take advantage of disturbed times to rob and kill under pretext of the public interest. During the massacre of Saint Bartholomew, "a number of Catholics," says Naudé, "were victims of the tempest." There were individuals who took advantage of the disorder to kill their enemies under colour of religion. During the Revolution, acts of vengeance, due to private enmities, were committed in the name of liberty. Under the Directory, men who had taken part in the rioting and the popular insurrections left the towns to commit new crimes in the name of the reaction on the high roads. In the South of France especially, giving a political tinge to their acts of

[1] Thiers, Vol. VII., p. 405.

brigandage, "they murdered on the pretence of hunting down the Jacobins with a view to robbery those who had acquired the estates confiscated by the nation, . . . they attempted to possess themselves of the deposits of public funds, and betook them to the very tax-gatherers to seize upon the State moneys, under pretext of combating the Government."[1] Again, in times of trouble, debtors have been seen to denounce their creditors out of patriotism, or to search their dwellings with a view to removing the proofs of their indebtedness. In 1793 there were debtors who wiped off their debts by getting their creditors arrested as aristocrats.

To provoke insurrections the ringleaders sometimes hold out the bait of pillage. The leaders of the Babeuf conspiracy adopted this course. "To set the soldiers to work," they wrote to their partisans, "magnificent and long speeches are unnecessary; wine and the hope of pillage suffice. . . . "[2] One would say that they had read the passage of Tacitus: "Nothing tends to incite the multitude to civil war more than rioting and pillage."[3] C. Desmoulins, to rouse the people to revolt, promised them that "40,000 private houses, palaces, and country seats, two-thirds of the property in France, would be the reward of their valour" (France Libre, August, 1789).

[1] Thiers, "Histoire du Consulat et de l'Empire," Vol. VIII.
[2] De Barante, "Histoire du Directoire," Vol. I., p. 257.
[3] Tacitus," Historiæ," Bk. I., § 83. *Vide* also Bk. III., § 83. Plato also had remarked that "to keep their hold on the people . . . the demagogues are wont to promise them the spoils of the rich." "Res Publica," Bk. VII.)

The hypocrisy of the Communists has not attracted sufficient attention. In their proclamations to the people they never ceased to accuse the "Versaillais" of having started the conflict, and to spread false news. Delescluze was always lying.[1] During the siege of Paris the men who were afterwards the authors of the Commune professed the most violent hatred for the Prussians, but in point of fact they abstained from fighting. They only proclaimed war *à outrance* so as to possess themselves of the artillery. The reason General Clément Thomas was assassinated by them was that he had dared to denounce their hypocrisy.[2] The spectacle was then afforded of those who had been the loudest in their outcry against the despotism of the Empire, practising themselves the most abominable tyranny.

Our time is fertile in men who, in opposition, talk of liberty in order to overthrow the Government, and who, having acquired power by these tactics, refuse liberty to others.[3] Those who have been foremost in clamouring against tyranny themselves become veritable tyrants, and those who have been the loudest in denouncing the abuses of authority, themselves perpetrate these abuses, and others still worse. Goethe remarked of these hypocritical apostles of liberty: "I have always had an antipathy for the apostles of

---

[1] Dauban, "Le Fond de la Société sous la Commune," p. 355.

[2] Trochu, "Une Page d'Histoire Contemporaine," p. 148.

[3] "To overthrow the Government they talk of liberty. The Government overthrown, they attack liberty themselves." (Tacitus, "Annales," Bk. XVI., § 22.)

liberty : the final object they always have in view is the right for themselves to act arbitrarily." It is only when the man, arrived at power, puts in practice the liberal principles he professed when in opposition, that it is possible to believe in the sincerity of his liberalism.

CHAPTER VI.

POLITICAL SPOLIATION.

Wars made for purposes of robbery—Enslavement of the vanquished—Labour degrading, but pillage honourable—The Romans converted war into an instrument of pillage—Militarism a means of getting rich—The feudal system was the exploitation of the conquered—Pillaging expeditions—The English in Ireland—Armies and plunder—The right of shipwreck—The old régime a form of spoliation—Confiscation and Civil wars—Material interests and revolutions—The Roman Republic fell from economic causes—The Reformation partly a movement to despoil the Church—Confiscations of Louis XIV.—Rapacity of courtiers—Spoliation during the French Revolution—A revolution means a transference of property—Civil wars and pillage—Politicians in alliance with financiers—Politics and finance in ancient Rome—The difficulty of convicting politicians of peculation—Politicians and financiers corrupt the press—Deputies sell their votes to financiers—Progress in spite of corruption—Socialist charges against the middle class—Social equality.

While conscience and religion said to man, "Thou shalt not take what belongs to another, thou shalt earn thy bread in the sweat of thy brow," cupidity, the frenzied desire for pleasures, and laziness cried to him, "It is pleasant to pillage the possessions of others; it is agreeable to live by the labour of others."

For the ancient peoples war was a means of growing rich at the expense of the vanquished. Is not this still often the case with modern nations? "It is a maxim that has held good everywhere and of all time," said Cyrus to his soldiers, "that in a town taken from the enemy during hostilities, everything, whether persons or property, belongs to the conqueror!"[1] In the "Iliad" Achilles recounts that he has ravaged twelve cities, and that in all of them he seized upon a great quantity of booty. When he quarrels with Agamemnon, he threatens to depart, and to carry away with him all the plunder that had fallen to his share, "the gold, the ruddy bronze, the gleaming iron, the beautiful girdled women."[2] Achilles is always complaining of the greediness of Agamemnon; he calls him "the most insatiable of men, a man abounding in impudence and eager of gain." He is incessantly reproaching him with gorging himself with riches, and with allotting himself the lion's share of the booty. "At the division of the spoils," he says to him, "your share is far superior to mine, and as for me, I have to content myself with carrying in my vessels an inconsiderable portion, after wearying myself on the battlefield. . . This great king," he exclaims with bitterness, "distributed a small part of the plunder to the soldiers, kept the best part for himself, and gave the remainder to the kings and the chiefs of the army."[3]

Conquerors do not merely divide among themselves the wealth of the vanquished: they also take their women. Agamemnon took Chryseis, whom he preferred to Clytemnestra, and Achilles

---

[1] Xenophon, "Cyropædia," Bk. VII., ch. v.
[2] Homer, "Iliad," ch. ix.   [3] Ibid., ch. ix., v. 330, etc.

Briseis of the beautiful cheeks. When a town was taken the victors burned it, slew the men, and carried away the women and children. Frequently, again, instead of killing the men, they made them slaves.[1] When Alexander took Thebes he destroyed the town and sold the inhabitants to the number of 30,000. In the East, the vanquished were relegated to inferior castes.

All the reasons that have been urged in justification of slavery have been mere pretexts to hide the monstrous wish to transform men into beasts of burden with a view to take from them the product of their labour. The victors forced the conquered, whom they had reduced to slavery, to support them. The philosophers and statesmen of antiquity declared it to be needful that citizens should have leisure to occupy themselves with public affairs, and that it was requisite that they should relegate to slaves the material pre-occupations of existence. Even in Sparta, where there was no luxury, every citizen had several helots in his service.[2] It is notorious how considerable was the number of slaves in Rome.[3]

[1] The ancient peoples regarded the slavery of the vanquished as so legitimate that the Romans considered as slaves their fellow-citizens who had been made prisoners, and refused to ransom them. (Livy, XXII., 59-61.) If the prisoners came back they found their social status lowered on their return to Rome.

[2] When the Ephorians sent 5,000 Spartans to assist the Athenians against Mardonious, each Spartan was accompanied by seven helots. (Plutarch, " Life of Aristides.")

[3] After the war conducted by Lucullus in the Pontus the number of slaves became so considerable that the price of a slave fell to 4 drachmas, or about 2s. 9d. (Wallon, " Histoire de 'Esclavage," Vol. II, p. 36.)

The ancients esteemed manual labour to be servile. "It is fitting that men should be victorious in war," says a personage of Menander; "to cultivate the soil is the work of a slave." The most illustrious Grecian philosophers, Plato, Aristotle, and Xenophon, professed the utmost contempt for manual labour. "Nature," says Plato, "has created neither shoemakers nor blacksmiths; such occupations degrade the persons who exercise them."[1] The poet Hesiod, and Solon, the sage, are alone in praising labour. In Rome only agriculture was honoured: all the other industrial professions were despised. "All the workers, of whatever trade they may be," says Cicero, "form a base class and are unworthy of being citizens."[2]

The ancients who saw something shameful in manual labour, saw nothing of the kind in pillage. They considered it quite natural that the stronger people should seize upon the possessions of a weaker nation. Their statesmen founded colonies by expelling the vanquished from their territory, and repeopling it with their fellow-citizens, among whom they divided the houses and the land. After a victorious expedition against the Persians, a Grecian general is found saying to those of his compatriots who had not accompanied him "that if they live in poverty it is their own fault," and informing them "that they

---

[1] Plato, "Republic," Bk. V. See also Aristotle, "Politica," and Xenophon, "Œconomicus."
[2] Cicero, "De Officiis."   [3] Diodorus, Bk. XII.

could send their fellow-citizens who were without fortune, and they would speedily see them in the utmost opulence, for all these possessions are the prizes that await the conqueror."[1] The philosophers expressed no indignation at these acts of pillage. Plato only blamed them when they had been committed by one Grecian city at the expense of another.[2]

War, too, was an industry for a great number of barbarous peoples. "You will never succeed," says Tacitus, "in convincing men that it is better to till the soil and to await the harvest than to raise up enemies and to seek for wounds; they go so far as to believe that to acquire by labour what can be obtained by bloodshed is to give evidence of sluggishness and cowardice." Tacitus expresses his astonishment at the customs of these peoples, and yet the Romans had converted war into an instrument of pillage since they took possession of the territories of the conquered peoples. They confiscated the countries they overcame in virtue of the right of conquest, and created the *ager publicus*. This land was either sold for the profit of the State or conceded on a lease or for purposes of colonisation. Under pretext of providing neighbouring peoples with laws, the Romans sought for wealth by pillage, and they overwhelmed with taxes the provinces they conquered. "Our provinces groan," says Cicero, "free peoples are loud in their complaints;

---

[1] Xenophon, "Anabasis."
[2] Plato, "Republic," Bk. V.

kings cry out against our greed and injustice. As far as the distant shores of the ocean there is no spot so obscure, so hidden though it be, to which the exorbitant pretensions and the iniquitous doings of our fellow-citizens have not penetrated." When Appius left Cilicia, Cicero found the province ravaged to such a degree that "it might have been thought that a wild beast and not a man had traversed it." Appointed governor of the province ruined in this way, Cicero was still able to drain from it in one year two million two hundred thousand sesterces, *salvis legibus*.

In ancient times, booty taken from the enemy was sent to Rome or sold by the Generals, who paid in the proceeds to the public treasury.[1] When a soldier joined the army he was made to swear not to steal more than one "object a day of greater value than a silver piece."[2] Soon, however, the Roman Generals took to distributing a portion of the booty amongst the soldiers. When Macedonia was conquered Paulus Æmilius handed over a portion of the spoils to the soldiery, but without satisfying their greed; the army, considering the share that had fallen to it too small, endeavoured to have Æmilius refused a triumph. With Lucullus these habits of pillage became general. When Mithridates was pursued by the army of Lucullus, he made good his escape by leaving behind him on the passage of

---

[1] Plutarch, "Life of Fabius Maximus."
[2] "Aulus Gallius," Bk. XVI., ch. iv.

his pursuers the mule that carried his gold; the Roman soldiers abandoned the pursuit to seize upon the money.[1] On the occasion of his triumph Lucullus caused a register to be borne in the procession, setting forth that he had made a gift of 950 drachmas to every soldier. Military service had become a means of acquiring wealth by pillage. The soldiers complained when the Generals treated with towns instead of taking them by storm. The soldiers of Lucullus, Plutarch recites, "complained of their captain, because he negotiated capitulations with all the towns, and took none of them by force, and gave them no opportunity of enriching themselves by pillage." They bitterly compared their lot with that of the soldiers of Pompey, who, they said, "were already reposing in their homes with their wives and children, possessed of good estates, and living in fine towns like important and rich citizens."

During the last years of the Republic the Generals encouraged the greed of the soldiery in order to render themselves popular, endeavouring by their munificence to attach the soldiers to their person. Sylla allowed them to plunder both private individuals and the State.[2] Pompey distributed money amongst them. Cæsar enriched them; "he subdued the Gauls by the arms of the Romans, and won over the Romans with the money of the Gauls." He was particularly liberal

---

[1] Plutarch, "Life of Lucullus." Cicero, "Pro Lege Manilia," § x.
[2] Sallust, "Catilina" § xi.

in his gifts to the Spanish and German soldiers that formed his escort. It was by conciliating the soldiers by means of liberal gifts and the multitude by distributions of wheat that Augustus was successful in concentrating the entire authority in his own hands.[1] The successors of Augustus became dependent upon the Pretorians, who ended by putting the empire up to auction. For example, in 193 A.D., they disposed of it to Didius Julianus at the price of 6,250 drachmas per soldier.

The Romans have not been alone in pillaging the world under pretext of civilising it. How numerous are the peoples that other peoples have treated as their prey! How many thousands of men have been expelled their country, slain, or reduced to slavery by other men! The needy peoples of the North made their way to the South in search of a richer country. War has been a means of expropriation and of appropriation. When the Normans, for instance, invaded England, they took possession of the soil and of the conquered men, whom they called "subjects," that is those who had been subjugated. The vanquished were obliged to labour for the benefit of their conquerors, and political writers affirmed that the conquerors had the right to own the conquered.

[1] Tacitus, "Annales," Bk. I., § 2. When Napoleon invaded Lombardy in 1796 he followed the example of Cæsar and Augustus when he issued the following proclamation to his soldiers: "Soldiers, you are badly fed and almost naked. . . . . . I am going to lead you into the most fertile plains of the world. You will find there great cities and rich provinces; you will find there honour, glory, and riches"

The feudal system, at bottom, was merely the organisation of a victory, the exploitation of a conquest. The serfs were the vanquished, who were obliged to cultivate the soil for the benefit of their conquerors.[1]

Just as the Old World was pillaged by the Romans, so the New has been ravaged by the Spaniards and Portuguese; India by the Moguls, the Afghans, and the English; Italy by the Germans, Austrians, French, and Spaniards; Ireland by the English, etc., etc. How often have European nations made war upon the peoples of Asia, Africa, and America with a view to forcing upon them their wares, their clothing stuffs, and their alcohols! It is this spirit of greed evinced by the European peoples in their dealings with the peoples of other parts of the world, that has checked and often entirely put a stop to the civilising work of missionaries.

The struggles between England and Ireland have always ended in confiscations. Elizabeth distributed 200,000 acres to colonists of English birth. James I. confiscated another 500,000 acres, and allowed the Scotch concurrently with the English a share in the confiscated land. Under Charles I. Lord Strafford stripped of their estates the inhabitants of Connaught and Galway. Ireland having revolted in 1641, one of the Lord Justices, Sir William Parsons, fomented the revolt and connected as many people with the movement as possible, " in order that, the

---

[1] The serfs were even obliged to pay tribute.

number of the guilty increasing, the harvest of confiscations that would follow the war might be the more fertile." (G. de Beaumont, "L'Irlande," Vol. I., p. 67.) When England paled off the Irish Catholics in one of the four Irish provinces, their estates were divided between Cromwell's soldiers and the speculators who had advanced funds to the English Government. The owners of these confiscated estates were alarmed when the Restoration took place, but they were confirmed in the possession of their domains by Charles II. The Irish did not obtain justice, and the King himself appropriated a part of the spoil.

Armies have almost always claimed a share in the plunder of conquered peoples. Neither the English during the Hundred Years' War, nor the Germans, French, and Spaniards during the wars in Italy[1] and Germany, nor the armies of Louis XIV., of Frederick II., and of Napoleon, nor the allied armies in 1815, nor the German armies in 1870, distinguished themselves by much respect for private or public property. The armies of the First Republic exhibited splendid heroism, but their disinterestedness was not always equally remarkable. "In 1793, in the Deux-Ponts country," says M. Arthur Chuquet, "Hoche,[2] admirably aided and seconded by the orderly commissary Achier, who bled the district to the last drop,

[1] When Rome was pillaged, in 1527, by the army of the Constable of Bourbon, the Spaniards and Germans, of which the army was composed, committed the greatest atrocities. For an account of this pillage see Guicciardini.

[2] Arthur Chuquet, " Les Guerres de la Révolution."

despatched to the interior mirrors, clocks, mattresses, furniture, bells, and other valuables. 'Were the wretched "sans-culottes" to labour for ever without profit?' he wrote to Bouchotte. 'No, they should have, besides liberty, velvet knee-breeches, satin waistcoats, and the large-sleeved coats of the aristocrats.'" In 1814 the Cossacks came to Paris to sell the objects they had stolen from the country folk.[1] In 1815 the foreign armies seized in a number of towns upon the public coffers, and committed numerous acts of pillage.

In former times armies were not content with pillaging the foreigner, but plundered their fellow-countrymen as well. "The men-at-arms," says Commines, "are not content with a modest life and with what they get from the peasants and that is paid for; on the contrary, they belabour and assault the poor folk, compelling them to procure them bread, wine, and victuals from elsewhere, and if the good man have a pretty wife or daughter, he will do well to keep close watch over her." During the Vendean war, several Republican generals pillaged the Vendeans. The Conventionalist Lequinis, despatched on a mission by the Convention, recognised that pillage was preached to the utmost possible extent, and that the generals encouraged the practice in their soldiers, so as to hide their own achievements in the same field. (Wallon, "Les Représentants en Mission," Vol. I., p. 255.)

The ancient peoples were not content with

[1] "Mémoires du Chancelier Pasquier," Vol. II., p. 274.

saying "Woe to the vanquished!" they also said "Woe to the shipwrecked!" Side by side with the right of conquest, they created a still more odious right, *the right of shipwreck*. In virtue of this pretended right, the vessels that were stranded on the coasts were confiscated, and the crews and passengers reduced to slavery. This singular mode of spoliation, transformed into a right by politicians and jurists, has existed among most maritime peoples, who took advantage of the rocks on their coast to enrich themselves at the expense of the shipwrecked; among the English, for instance, the inhabitants of Brittany, the Sicilians, the Greeks, the Danes, and the Venetians. Barbeyrac, who annotated Grotius, affirms that this barbarous custom existed even in his time in certain countries.[1]

The right of "aubaine," like the right of shipwreck, was a spoliation. The Treasury seized upon the property that a foreigner left behind him when he died. This right was still in existence at the time that Vattel was writing.[2]

The nations have disputed the possession of the sea in the same way as that of the land, endeavouring to secure themselves a monopoly to the detriment of other nations. After the discovery of America, Spain laid claim to the exclusive ownership of the ocean. Portugal claimed the sole right to the Indian trade. England, again, attempted to accord itself exclusive

---

[1] Note to Grotius by Barbeyrac, Bk. II., ch. vii.
[2] Vattel, "Le Droit des Gens," Bk. II., ch. viii.

domination over the seas between the coasts of Great Britain and the United States. France demanded the liberty of the seas and equality of rights for all nations. Several centuries have been necessary to secure the recognition of these elementary principles.

The social organisation of the old régime was nothing more nor less than a form of spoliation, since the nobility and clergy exonerated themselves from taxes, the burden of which they threw upon the "third estate." The peasants in particular were bowed down by taxes, and politicians rejoiced in their poverty, which they regarded as a guarantee of their obedience. "If the people were well off," says Richelieu, in his Political Testament, "they would with difficulty keep within bounds."[1]

To keep the plebeians in their dependence the Roman patricians maintained them in a state of poverty.

Confiscation has always been at the bottom of civil wars. Proscriptions are not solely inspired by political hatreds and rivalries; greed is a further motive for them. The authors of proscriptions yearn for the wealth of their victims as well as for their blood; they do not always kill for the sake of killing; they often kill for the sake of robbery. Plutarch, narrating the proscriptions of Sylla, says: "Men were slain to secure their property, and those who killed them might pro-

[1] Properly indignant at this hateful policy, Fénelon refuted it in his " Instructions pour la Conscience d'un Roi."

perly have said: "His fine house is the cause of this man's death, his fine garden of the death of this other." The utterance of Quintus Aurelius is well known. Never having taken part in political struggles and thinking he had nothing to fear, he went out to scan the list of the proscribed; to his profound astonishment he saw his name upon the list, whereupon he exclaimed: "My house at Alba is the cause of my death."

As a general rule political agitators are poor, and seek fortune by the overthrow of the established order of things: this boldness comes of the fact that they have nothing to lose. "*Sylla inops*," says Tacitus, "*unde præcipua audacia;*"[1] they are still more audacious if they are loaded with debts and athirst for pleasures and power. Ruined rakes have need of a revolution to pay their debts and re-establish their fortune.

I will not say with the First Napoleon that the belly governs the world—the statement is too absolute, for ideas also govern the world—but it is the truth that the appetites and material interests exert as great an influence as ideas upon revolutions. Conflicts concerning ideas are often conflicts of pride and ambition for the leaders and for the people, conflicts in which the stomach is primarily involved. While a few desire the triumph of ideas, without personal preoccupations, others far more numerous seek in revolutions a means of self-aggrandisement, domination, or of revenging and enriching themselves.

[1] Tacitus, "Annales," Bk. XIV.

The struggles that took place in Rome between the patricians and plebeians in connection with the agrarian laws bore upon a question of property. The republic had become an association of some hundreds of families, who had usurped the immense domains of the State, and reduced the people to poverty.[1] The patricians stood out against the agrarian laws, whose object was to set a limit upon their immense possessions, and to create small proprietors. The republic perished because it did not effect the reforms proposed by the Gracchi.' The Empire was accepted because it assured the triumph of the small proprietor.

The wealth of the Jews was one of the principal causes of the persecutions they underwent during the Middle Ages. The kings and nobles, who were in debt to the Jews, resorted to proscriptions to free themselves from their obligation. Again, it was to possess himself of their wealth that Philip the Handsome, a king who was a false coiner, caused the slaughter of the Templars.

The Reformation was not solely due to a religious sentiment. A great number of German princes embraced the reformed faith merely with a view to seizing upon the property of the Church. In England, the primary cause of the Reformation was the desire of Henry VIII. to repudiate his wife and marry another woman; the King only quarrelled with Rome because the Pope refused to approve his divorce. However, the rupture

---

[1] Fustel de Coulanges, " Les Origines du Système Féodal," pp. 90, 92.

between Henry VIII. and the Pope was due in part to a desire to appropriate the wealth of the monasteries. The nobility hastened to approve the move, to secure their share of the spoil.

Confiscation was never left out of sight in the edicts of the Kings of France against the Protestants. "We will and intend," said Louis XIV., when he revoked the Edict of Nantes, "that the possessions of those who within a space of four months do not return to our kingdom, or to countries and lands under our sway, that the possessions they shall have abandoned be confiscated in consequence of our declaration of the 20th August." A portion of the confiscated possessions was given to the courtiers.

The greed of the courtiers was so great that it was on the score of the danger that threatened them from this source, to which he called the attention of the Minister of Henry II., that President Séguier, in the name of the Parliament, opposed the registration of the edict ordering the establishment in France of the tribunal of the Inquisition. "As soon as your enemies," he said to them, "shall be sure of obtaining from the King the confiscation of your possessions, it will be sufficient to make sure of an Inquisition and of two witnesses, and though you be saints you will be burned as heretics."

The report which Necker, at the time Director-General of Finances, presented to Louis XVI., in 1781, contains the most melancholy details touching the greed of the courtiers and the enormous sums they cost the Treasury. The pensions amounted to twenty-eight millions a year. "I doubt," said Necker, "whether all the sovereigns of Europe together pay away more than half such a sum in pensions." Favours emanating from the Throne had become "the universal resource. The acquisition of remunerative posts, marriage, and educational projects, unexpected losses, unfulfilled hopes, all these occurrences had become an excuse for recourse to the munificence of the sovereign. It might have been thought that it was incumbent upon the Royal treasury to conciliate all interests, to smooth away all difficulties, and to make good all disappointments. Moreover, since the method of pensions, although developed to the utmost, was insufficient to satisfy these pretensions and to serve the turn, to the extent desired, of this shameful greediness, other expedients had been devised and were being invented every day: interests in farms, in Government takings, in posting stations, in many financial posts, in the supply of provisions, in contracts of every kind, and even in the supplying of the hospitals, everything was good enough, everything had become worth the attention of persons who often by their position had least to do with such matters." The courtiers even demanded the cession of forests they pretended were abandoned. When Calonne negotiated a loan of one hundred millions, three-quarters of the sum was distributed among the King's brothers, the friends of the Queen, people in favour, and noblemen deeply in debt.

During the Revolution the spoliation continued, but in the opposite direction. Instead of contenting themselves with the abolition of privileges, and the establishment of equality, the covetous caused a third of the country to be confiscated and sold as national property.[1] To gain adherents to the Revolution the leaders of the movement gave away estates or sold them far below their value. By this means they won over to the movement those who acquired these properties, these persons being interested in the maintenance of the new order of things, and having become the enemies of the despoiled proprietors. A law of the 9th February, 1792, confiscated the estates of the Emigrants. Extraordinary taxes were imposed upon the fathers and mothers of Emigrants. (Decree of the 12th September, 1792.) The persons who did not leave within twenty-four hours Lyons, Marseilles, Bordeaux, Caen, and the towns that had risen in arms against the Constitution were accounted Emigrants. The priests, too, who had refused to pledge their submission to the Constitution were considered as Emigrants, and their parents were taxed on the same footing as those of the Emigrants. To hasten the sale of the estates of the Emigrants the Convention, on the 11th September, 1793, decreed the following provisions: "The administrators who shall refuse under any pretext whatever to proceed with the sale of the estates of the

---

[1] Léonce de Lavergne, " Economie Rurale de la France depuis 1789," p. 20.

Emigrants, and of the other national domains, in the fortnight allotted for the making of tenders for the said estates, shall be punished with ten years' imprisonment in chains." Again, on the 19th March, 1793, the estates were confiscated of persons condemned for crimes against the Revolution. On the 1st August, 1793, the penalty of confiscation was pronounced against those who had been outlawed, and later against those who had allowed any indications of the old monarchical order of things to subsist upon their properties. Confiscation following upon condemnation, fathers of families were seen to kill themselves in the earlier period so as to be able to leave their possessions to their children. To avert this danger the Convention voted the law of the 29th Brumaire, An II., by which confiscation is made to date from the accusation.

By the 73rd article of the decree of March 28th, 1793, the Convention allotted a reward to informers, according the tenth part to the citizen who should reveal the possessions of Emigrants that had been overlooked or concealed. It thus returned to the hateful practices of the Roman Emperors, who allowed informers to enrich themselves and even to attain to positions of dignity. The famous passage of Tacitus is well known in which he speaks of "the informers, encouraged by rewards as odious as their misdeeds, sharing the spoil amongst themselves, some taking priestly offices and consulships, others the governments of provinces, or posts of authority at home, laying hands upon whatever came their way."[1] The two principal informers against Thrasias and Soranus received a reward of five millions of sesterces, and an accomplice one million two hundred thousand sesterces and the insignia of the questorship.[2]

"By whatever high-sounding terms of liberty, equality, or fraternity a revolution announces itself, it is essentially," says M. Taine, "a transference of property."[3] I am of opinion that there is some exaggeration in this statement, for the love of equality, the hatred of privileges, and the desire to secure liberty of conscience and political liberty were the principal motives of the Revolution. Still, the French Revolution, like all revolutions, was marked by a transference of property.

All the confiscations decreed by the State turned to the profit of private individuals, who purchased the confiscated estates for much less than their real value. In any case, the Revolutionaries considered that the object of the Revolution was the despoiling of the rich and the enriching of the poor. The revolutionary committees of Bordeaux, Lyons, and Marseilles practised extortions upon the rich, selling their possessions, ransacking their dwellings, and even their cellars,[4]

---

[1] Tacitus, "Historiæ," Bk. I., § 2.
[2] Ibid., "Annales," Bk. XVI., § 33.
[3] Taine, "La Révolution," Vol. I., p. 386.
[4] Revolutionaries never omit a visit to the cellars. In 1871 the cellars of the archbishop's palace were rifled by the Communists. In 1793, at Lyons, Albitte and Colot requisitioned 700 bottles of good wine for their own table.

on the pretext of searching for the arms of the aristocrats, and declaring that "the superfluous belongings of every private person are the patrimony of the 'sans-culottes,' and that everything he detains beyond what is strictly necessary constitutes a theft that he commits to the detriment of the nation."[1]

Danton was responsible for the decree ordering those domiciliary visits which gave the sans-culottes the opportunity of appropriating the furniture, jewels, and wine of the aristocrats. The Paris Commune seized the plate belonging to the churches and the furniture of the Emigrants. Even the belongings of the prisoners who perished in the September massacres were stolen. Each of the members of the Watch Committee chose himself a watch.[2] One of the principal slaughterers, who had committed the most impudent robberies, complained later, on the 31st May, that there had been no pillaging, saying: "On such a day as this I ought to have had as my share at least fifty houses."[3]

Similar scenes of pillage have always accompanied civil wars. At the time of the struggles between the Armagnacs and the Burgundians, when Paris was delivered over to the latter, the great nobles of Burgundy mingled with the pillagers in order to secure what they could. According to Brantôme, several of his friends, of

---

[1] Taine, "La Révolution," Vol. III., p. 50.
[2] Michelet, "Histoire de la Révolution Française," Vol. VI., p. 128. [3] Ibid., Vol. V., p. 86.

good birth, were the richer by ten thousand crowns after the night of the massacre of Saint Bartholomew.

In connection with all proscriptions, these words of the Bible may be applied to their authors: "And they covet fields and seize them, and houses and take them away; and they oppress a man and his house, even a man and his heritage."[1] Agitators have recourse to specious pretexts to stir up the people, but as a rule their only aim is the satisfaction of their appetites.

This summary study of political spoliations would be incomplete were I to omit to touch upon the spoliations committed in the past by courtiers and at the present day by politicians in league with financiers. In the preceding chapter, devoted to political hypocrisy, I have already called attention to the numerous points of resemblance between the flatterers of kings and the flatterers of the masses. It remains for me to prove that the latter are every whit as greedy as the former. When Fénelon indited his examination of conscience concerning the duties of royalty, he put the following question: "Have you not been too indulgent to the courtiers who, under pretext of sparing your purse, have proposed to you what is termed a stroke of business when asking you for rewards?" Courtiers are fond of these "strokes of business," and politicians have a weakness for them as well. To support themselves those who till the soil are obliged to sow, to weed, to

[1] Micah, ch. ii., v. 2.

harvest, to thrash the wheat, and to carry it to the mill. Politicians, like courtiers, neither sow nor weed, nor harvest, nor fill barns: politics afford them their living. Working-men, from morning till evening, or from evening till morning, hammer iron, shape wood, melt lead, dig the earth, or erect buildings at the price of their lives; they spin and weave stuffs. Politicians, like courtiers, do not fashion either iron or wood; they knead the electorate, as dough is kneaded, and instead of mixing with it good yeast, they ferment it with the leaven of civil war, with sophisms and lying promises, with calumnies and unwholesome theories; they neither spin nor weave, and yet they are better clad, better fed, and better housed than those who labour.

Like courtiers, politicians have a keen eye to all posts that become vacant, to concessions and monopolies. If the fortunes of politicians before and after their arrival at power be examined, it is found that they were poor before they entered office and that they leave it rich. Might not the question which Cicero put to Antony be addressed to them: "Through what prodigy have you, who owed four million sesterces at the Ides of March, come to owe nothing whatever at the Kalends of April?"[1]

At every period, politicians have been seen to ally themselves with shady financiers. A race of civilised brigands has been formed, who, proceeding with their spoliations on cunning

[1] Second Philippic, § 37.

lines, plunder the State and strip the public. As far back as 1868 Father Gratry quoted with indignant eloquence a passage of the "Moniteur" for March, 1866, where it was stated that "in eighteen months more than forty companies had been called upon to render an account to justice (that had shown itself, and properly so, severe) of more than eighty millions cast away in the abyss of guilty speculation."[1] This figure of eighty millions, of which the public had been lightened, has since been far surpassed in connection with the gigantic swindles that have been perpetrated in recent years. A single company has been successful, thanks to the connivance of certain politicians and by dint of false statements respecting the time required for construction, the amount of the expenses and the possible profits, in getting 1,300 millions paid into its coffers, three-quarters of which sum has been lost. According to M. Léon Say, the financial crisis of 1882 cost France several milliards, a drain equal to that imposed by the Germans. More than a milliard has been lost in connection with the Uruguay, Brazilian, Portuguese, Spanish, and Greek loans.[2] Two passages of the Bible may be applied to the financiers, who have become the world's masters, and to their accomplices the politicians: "*Mercatores tui erant principes terræ,*[3] *principes vestri socii furum.*"

[1] P. Gratry, "La Morale et la Loi de l'Histoire," Vol. I., p. 120.
[2] "Sciences et Travaux de l'Académie des Sciences Morales," December, 1893.   [3] Revelation xviii. 23.

This alliance between financiers and politicians, which exists at the present day throughout Europe as it does in America, in France as in Italy and England, existed also in Rome, in Florence, and in the France of former days. At Rome the consuls, pretors, and knights engaged in vast financial operations. The men who farmed the taxes gave them an interest in this undertaking in order to gain their support. Atticus was interested in the operations of those who exploited Cilicia. Cicero himself had business relations with the farmers of taxes. He speculated in financial affairs and won large sums of money. In the year in which he was appointed augur he was a poor man in February, while in October he had suddenly become wealthy.[1]

The governors who pillaged the provinces had a secret understanding with the tax farmers, with whom they divided the spoils of the allies. The power of these tax farmers was great. When governors like Lucullus wished to prevent their exactions, they went to Rome to complain, and silenced their adversaries by the aid of orators in their pay, "which it was the easier for them to do, inasmuch as they were careful to have a hold upon those who negotiated business operations in Rome."[2] On more than one occasion they were successful in procuring the recall of governors who were opposed to their fraudulent practices. As a rule, however, they were in league with the governors.

---

[1] Deloume, "Les Manieurs d'Argent à Rome," p. 88.
[2] Plutarch, "Life of Lucullus."

Verres, for example, did everything he could to be agreeable to the company that farmed the custom-house duties and the rights of pasturage, and decreed whatever was demanded of him by Carpinatius, the vice-director of the company. In exchange for their services the company had the letters destroyed which had been written by the employés of Verres with a view to call attention to his extortions and to the frauds he had committed at the expense of the custom-house. By referring to copies of letters Cicero lighted upon "an account relating to payments extending over many months, which had been inscribed in the name of Verres without corresponding receipts." By searching the registers of the company he was able to trace the frauds of Verres, despite the fact that numerous entries had been deleted in the registers. He discovered in the same way that Verres had had business relations with the company under the fictitious name of Caius Verratius.

It is difficult to convict politicians of peculation. The guilty party does not sign a receipt; the sum is handed him directly or by intermediaries,[1] by men of straw, by secretaries, in which case he defends himself by saying: "Personally, I have

[1] In the advice he gives his son, Louis XIV. alludes to the employment of intermediaries as one of the underhand methods resorted to by corrupt Ministers to enrich themselves. (Louis XIV, "Mémoires," Dreyss' edition, Vol. I., p. 163.) "Very few corrupt Ministers," he says, "have the audacity to rifle their master openly, and to seize without subterfuge upon the possessions with whose administration he has entrusted them, because to do so would be a crime of which it would be easy to

received nothing." This was the system of defence of Verres when he was accused of having pocketed 40 million sesterces. It was demolished by Cicero, who admitted that not a single piece of money had been paid into the hands of the Pretor, but added: "Your hands were your prefects, your scribes; . . . all that has been pocketed by each one of them has not only been remitted to you, but has been paid into your hands: it is impossible to take any other view. Judges! the truth is, if you allow this defence, 'Verres has received nothing in person,' you do away with all trials for peculation. No accused or guilty person will ever be brought before you to whom it is not open to avail himself of this mode of defence."[1]

At the present day, as in Rome, politicians are seen to put their influence at the service of shady financial companies. The companies that give politicians a seat upon their board of directors do not do so in order to profit by their business ability, but with a view to being able to rely, if necessary, upon their support and to inspire the shareholders with confidence.

In the hands of politicians and financiers the newspaper press has become an instrument of

convict them. The mode of robbery they find the easiest and esteem the most likely to escape future researches, is to appropriate in the name of another what they intend shall profit themselves. The crafty devices they make use of to this end are of so many different kinds, that I shall not attempt to explain them in detail, and shall merely say that they always augment the theft they are intended to hide."

[1] Cicero, "Secunda Oratio in Verrem," Bk. II., § 10.

spoliation. Great financial companies are not content with purchasing merely the advertisement newspapers can give them. They also pay the papers to praise their undertakings so as to deceive the public; they even make the papers fixed payments at regular intervals. According to the report of M. Machard, Inspector of Finances, the Crédit Foncier, from 1877 to 1890, spent 116,102,513 francs in expenses of emission. ("Gazette des Tribunaux," 27th January, 1893.) Charles de Lesseps has admitted having expended a hundred millions of francs in advertisement and kindred expenses. The articles in praise of the Panama Canal, published by the papers, were written by the directors of the Company.

When stock is to be issued, the board of directors places an important sum at the disposal of the directors with which to purchase the support, or at any rate the neutrality, of the Press, so that in the case of journalists it is literally true that speech is silvern and silence golden. When the proprietor of a paper is a politician it receives larger sums from the financial companies than would otherwise be the case. As soon as a financial undertaking is announced the journalists are found demanding money, and threatening the company with their hostility if it be not granted them. The men who call themselves the friends of the people are not behindhand in trafficking in newspaper articles that deceive the people, and contribute to its being fleeced.

Again, deputies, senators, and ministers are found to sell their votes to financial companies. They resort to the most crafty tactics to make sure that their influence shall be bought. In a case of recent occurrence, being called upon to examine a scheme in which a great company was interested, they did not reject it, but they adjourned it to allow the company to come to terms with them in the interval with respect to the sums demanded. The sums changed hands directly, or through the medium of middle-men, or under the guise of an interest in guarantee syndicates. These fictitious syndicates were merely a surreptitious mode of rewarding a criminal complicity, for the members of the syndicates ran no risks whatever. Seven millions of francs were allotted a single banker to purchase the parliamentary support of which the company stood in need. It is on record that a Minister of Public Works replied to a company that was asking for the authorisation to issue lottery bonds, that the scheme would not be introduced unless he was presented with a million. A first payment of 375,000 francs was made him the day the Bill was laid before the House, and he only failed to receive the remainder of the million because the measure had to be withdrawn in face of the hostile attitude of the Chamber.

Thousands of families have been ruined by the gigantic swindles of financiers and politicians. The director of the Dynamite Company, who was sentenced at the Seine Assizes, was an exprefect, an ex-deputy, an ex-senator, and an ex-Director of Departmental and Commercial Affairs at the Ministry of the Interior.

In spite of fortunes acquired with scandalous rapidity by means of Stock Exchange speculations, fraudulent artifices, and political transactions, contemporary society has realised immense progress as compared with the ancient peoples and the old régime which lived on spoliations. Slavery and serfdom have disappeared from the civilised world. The spectacle is no longer afforded of a handful of citizens oppressing a great number of slaves, or of a small number of men living on the labours of the great majority. Labour is free and held in honour.[1] Privileges have been abolished. All citizens are equal before the law. Privileged persons have ceased to impose the burden of taxation upon the people and to receive honours and dignities for themselves. The French Revolution has caused the disappearance of these social iniquities. While it is necessary to point out the errors and crimes that have been committed in the name of the Revolution, one should not tire of recalling the immense social progress it has brought about.

The Socialists deceive the people when they declare that all the Revolution has done has been to substitute the privileges of the middle class for those of the nobility, and that the people is oppressed by the middle classes in the same way

[1] An edict of Henry III. contains this abominable declaration: The right to work is a royal right and that attaches to the domain.

as it was oppressed by the nobility prior to 1789. The middle classes have no privileges; they do not constitute a closed caste; they cannot be compared to the nobility of the old régime—they despoil nobody; on the contrary, they enable a great number of working-men and employés to live by the work and wages with which they furnish them. The men whom the Socialists denounce as privileged individuals have attained to fortune by dint of labour, intelligence, and thrift. Where does the middle class end, where does the people begin? Every day men hailing from the lowest ranks of society raise themselves to the highest and become members of the "classes," while idle and spendthrift members of the classes fall back into the lowest ranks of society. Are not the small tradesmen, the foremen, and the workingmen, who establish themselves on their own account, members of the middle class? Does not the business man, the contractor, the barrister, the doctor, or the manufacturer belong to the people, and do they enjoy special privileges? It is difficult to see in consequence how the foundation of society can be changed, unless the system of privileges is to be re-established for the benefit of the working-men. Absolute social equality is an unrealisable dream,[1] because men are unequal,

[1] Marshal Bugeaud, wishing, in 1842, to found a number of villages in the vicinity of Algiers, divided the land in equal parts between the soldiers of the 48th Regiment of the line. When he visited the country in 1845 he found there were colonists in the possession of from five to six thousand francs, worth of cattle, while there were others that had not even been able to keep the live stock that had originally been allotted

and because the idle, the debauched, and the unskilful will never be able to acquire or keep the same fortune as laborious, thrifty, and intelligent men. "For each estate Jupiter dressed two tables; the dexterous, the alert, and the strong take their seats at the first, and petty folk eat what they leave at the second."[1]

Still, although absolute social equality is a dream, there is nothing Utopian in the wish to raise the social level and to lessen inequality. These desiderata are realised progressively by the action of economic laws, by the increasing dearness of labour, by the lowering of the rate of interest, by the spread of education, and the development of the spirit of solidarity. The great differences that existed in the past between the rich and the poor in respect to dress, education, and habits are steadily lessening.[2] It is becoming more and more difficult every day to live without working.

---

them. (Marshal Bugeaud, "Les Socialistes et le Travail en Commun," p. 24.) The fact that equality is destroyed by the force of circumstances is the reason why Rousseau does not hesitate to demand that the State shall intervene to re-establish it. ("Contrat Social," Bk. II., ch. xi.)

[1] La Fontaine.

[2] Especially in the South of France. In Provence the peasants obtain possession of the land by the nature of things. Only the peasants who own the land they till can make agriculture pay in the district in question. I am acquainted with a number of these cultivators, who are richer than many members of the middle class. On a recent occasion I asked one of these men why it was that the peasants declined to purchase the land which middle-class owners in straitened circumstances were anxious to sell them. I obtained the reply: "We possess more land than we can cultivate."

There still exist iniquities for which individuals are responsible, spoliations which come under the criminal law, but the iniquitous organisation of society is a thing of the past, and it would be possible, by a stern application of justice, to put an end to the swindles of shady financial companies and politicians.

Doubtless much remains to be done in the way of improving the situation of the poor, but these improvements can be accomplished without violence. The new revolution, desired by the Socialist, would be a fresh spoliation and the most disastrous of all.

CHAPTER VII

CORRUPTION AMONGST POLITICIANS.

POLITICAL CORRUPTION IN ROME.

(I.) Political corruption in Rome—Corruption may prevail under any form of Government—Bribery in Rome—Venality of demagogues—Responsibility does not necessarily moralise politicians—Peculation in Rome—Corruption of judges among the Romans—Political corruption in Athens—Alcibiades—Pericles—Aristophanes on demagogues.—(II.) Political corruption in England—Lord Bacon—Corruption among Members of Parliament—Louis XIV. as a corrupter of foreign politicians—Corruption in England after the Revolution—Walpole's methods of corruption—Corruption as practised by George III.—Purchase of seats in Parliament—(III.) Political corruption in France—Richelieu's views—Peculation under Louis XIV.—Louis XIV. on the necessity for watching Government officials—La Bruyère on the financiers of the 17th century—The nobility and the financiers—Peculation in the 18th century—Political corruption under Louis XV.—Corruption during the Revolutionary period—Political morality under the Empire—Venality of Talleyrand—Political morality during the Restoration—Political corruption under the July monarchy—Deputies as directors of public companies—Heine on corruption in France.—(IV.) The causes of political corruption—Levity of life among politicians—Instances from Ancient Rome—Influence of women in politics—Love of luxury and display among politicians—Simplicity of life the best safeguard against political corruption.

Lord Brougham has affirmed that " sobriety, integrity, love of the public good, and disinterestedness, virtues foreign to a court, spring up naturally on a democratic soil."[1] Virtues never spring up naturally; it is only vices that spring up without effort as weeds do; virtues, like useful plants, require to be cultivated if they are to spring up on democratic soil. Corruption is prevalent under all forms of government. Tribunes of the people are corruptible as well as senators. During the last years of the Roman Republic they showed themselves every whit as greedy as the patricians for the gold of Jugurtha. The King of Numidia made grants to begin with to all those whose influence

[1] Lord Brougham, "De la Démocratie et des Gouvernements Mixtes," p. 143. This passage of Lord Brougham's seems to be borrowed from Sidney's book on Government, the 19th section of which is accompanied by the following summary: "Corruption and venality, which are so common in the courts of sovereign princes, and in their States, are rarely found in Republics and mixed governments." Montesquieu, wishing to establish that virtue is not the mainspring of a monarchical Government, adduces a passage from Richelieu's political testament. "Should there be found," he says, "amongst the people some hapless honest man, Cardinal Richelieu insinuates in his political testament that the monarch will do well not to have recourse to his services; so true is it that virtue is not the mainspring of this form of government." ("Esprit des Lois," LIII., ch. v.) Robespierre expressed the same thought when he said: "You are acquainted with the ingenuous utterance of Cardinal Richelieu, contained in his political testament, and to the effect that kings should carefully abstain from making use of men of probity, since their services would be unprofitable." (Report drawn up in the name of the Committee of Public Safety, upon the relations between religious and moral ideas and republican principles.) Montesquieu and Robespierre have misinterpreted the passage from Richelieu's political testament; it runs as follows. "These officers," he says, referring to magistrates, "are chosen from amongst the best and most enlightened men of the States, and, if the republics be well ordered, the richest are usually preferred to the poor, and nobles to those of low birth, because it is supposed that they are more virtuous and more enlightened, and that, in consequence, they are less capable of certain base actions, to which necessity and absence of breed-

in the Senate was great;[1] the moment his emissaries made gold to gleam before their eyes, the senators were fascinated by the huge sums offered them. Jugurtha, however, did not overlook the tribunes of the people, for he had advised his emissaries "to try the effect of gold upon all consciences." Babius, a tribune of the people, was no more incorruptible than Calpurnius or Scaurus. All, patricians and plebeians alike, were glad to be bribed, and Jugurtha, on leaving Rome, disgusted at so much greed, could not refrain from exclaiming: "Venal city, that will speedily perish if it finds a buyer."

Aristophanes in his admirable comedies has scourged not only the impudence of demagogues, but their venality as well. A pork-butcher, addressing Cleon, says to him: "You resemble those who fish for eels; in clear water they catch nothing, but if they only stir up the mud they make a good haul; in the same way it is only in

---

ing might incline them." (Ch. viii.) Richelieu is of opinion that it is more difficult for a poor than for a rich functionary to remain honest; he advises the King to choose rich magistrates, because he considers them likely to be more virtuous and independent. This opinion had already been expressed in ancient times by statesmen, who had made it a rule of government even under constitutions that were not monarchical. The Carthaginians were persuaded "that a poor citizen is unable to leave his affairs and conduct those of the State with honesty." (Aristotle, "Politica," Bk. II., ch. viii., § 5.)

[1] Sallust, "Jugurtha," § 12. "Men invested with this magistrature have been seen," says Aristotle again, "to be accessible to corruption and to sacrifice the interests of the State to private consideration." ("Politica," Bk. II., ch. vi.) The Swiss and Dutch Deputies accepted pensions from Louis XI. and Louis XIV. as eagerly as did the great noblemen of England and Poland.

times of trouble that you line your pockets. . ."
The people: "Ah! rogue, so this is how you rob
me, I who loaded you with crowns and presents."
Cleon: "*I stole in the public interest.*" The people:
"Quickly return me that crown." Cleon: "Good-bye,
crown; . . . so another is going to possess
you; assuredly he will not be a greater thief, but
perhaps he will be luckier. . . . I admit that
I am a thief. Do you allow that you are another?"
Cleon's rival has no scruples in making the admission; he hastens to add that he has been guilty
of perjury as well, and that, being the greater
rogue of the two, he deserves to come off best.
"To steal, to commit perjury," he says, "that is
the way to reach a high position." These being
his principles, a brilliant future had been predicted
him while he was young. "There is the stuff of a
statesman in him."

It would seem that when a man is called upon
to take part in the conduct of public affairs the
sentiment of his responsibility and his concern
for the public good should raise him morally to
the level required by his situation. Unhappily,
considered closely, many great politicians from
the moral standpoint are very petty; their lives
often offer the spectacle of irregularities and vices
that create astonishment, and that contrast with
the fine sentiments with which they adorn their
speeches. Disinterestedness is not, as a rule,
a virtue of statesmen. But there have been
politicians who have become famous solely
because they were honest.

At Rome, during a long period, politicians were conspicuous for their disinterestedness. Paulus Æmilius brought back to Rome all the treasures of Macedonia without keeping back any portion. Scipio Africanus "returned home empty-handed, after having destroyed Carthage."[1] However, from the time of Sylla onwards, the public men preyed upon the Republic. "To prey upon the Republic," exclaimed Cicero, "is not merely shameful, but an abominable crime." The crime became general.

The crime of peculation became so frequent that Menenius said: "It is held of no account since we have made a practice of it, . . . so profoundly has avarice, like a contagious plague, affected men's souls."[2] Cato exclaimed in his indignation at the impunity accorded those guilty of peculation: "Those who rob private persons pass their lives in chains; robbers of the public live resplendent in gold and purple."[3] The Romans passed numerous laws to suppress corruption: the Cornelian law, the Calpurnian law, the Tullian law, the Aufodian law, the Licenian law. All these laws, however, did not suffice to suppress the evil, because the judges themselves were open to corruption.

According to Cicero, "in the space of nearly fifty years, during which the order of knights was charged with dispensing justice, not the least suspicion ever arose of a Roman knight having

---

[1] Cicero, "De Officiis," Bk. II., § 22.
[2] Sallust, "Jugurtha," §§ 31, 32.
[3] Aulus Gellius, Bk. XI., ch. xviii.

received money to render a judgment," whereas "during the ten years that justice has been in the hands of the Senate" it is impossible to conceive "all the vile and infamous acts that have marked the administration of justice." Cicero affirms that when Clodius was acquitted, thirty judges out of fifty-five had accepted money from the accused. "Do you wish to know," Cicero wrote to Atticus, "how the acquittal was procured? It was through the poverty and infamy of the judges."[1] When the Senator Septimius was convicted of the crime of peculation, the fine he had to pay was regulated by the sums he had received while a judge. Cicero says further that "a case is known of a senator who, while judge, accepted money during the same trial on the one hand from the accused to be distributed to the other judges, and on the other from the accuser to condemn the accused."

The governors who pillaged the provinces set aside a portion of their ill-gotten gain for the judges before whom they would have to appear to answer for their crimes. Verres declared that he had distributed in this fashion what three years of his Sicilian pretorship had brought him in; that he considered himself fortunate if the product of a single year remained for himself, and that he had reserved for his judges that of the third year, the best and the most fruitful.[2] According to

[1] Cicero's "Letters to Atticus," No. 23. Seneca, "Letters to Lucilius," XCII. Plutarch, "Life of Cicero."
[2] Cicero, "First Speech in *Verrem*," § 14.

Cicero it would have been to the advantage of the plundered provinces not to prosecute those who had preyed upon them; the reason being " that if there were no trial in prospect, each governor would merely strip the provinces of what seemed to him sufficient for himself and his children, while as it is, with the courts of justice constituted as they are, each governor carries away with him what he requires to satisfy himself, his protectors, his legal counsel, the pretor, and his judges. Under these conditions there is no limit to the exactions. It is possible to satisfy the cupidity of the most avaricious of men, but not to make the cost of a trial more disastrous than all possible acts of pillage." Cicero in his correspondence allows his indignation against these corrupt judges to find vent at every turn in the most vigorous language. "No gambling hell," he exclaims, "ever saw such a company gathered together; tarnished senators, knights in rags, tribunes, guardians of the treasury, as burdened with debts as they are light of money. . . . . What a sore this man is! What rogues!"[1] He alleges that Antony had introduced acrobats and musicians into the third decury of judges. "What a tribunal, ye gods! A Cretan has a seat in it, and the worst of them all. . . . Can he even speak Latin?"

Political Corruption in Athens.

Political corruption also existed in Athens and

[1] Cicero, "Letters to Atticus," No. 23.

even at the most glorious period of its history, the century of Pericles. Politicians were wont "to occupy themselves with the conduct of public affairs with the intention of making money out of their posts and of pushing their own interests."[1] The orators Stratocles and Democlides "used to invite each other to proceed to their golden harvest, referring mockingly in these terms to the rostrum whence they addressed the people." Æschines and Demosthenes mutually accused each other of venality. Demosthenes was convicted of malversation.[2] The Grecian historians record a number of piquant details touching the venality of the politicians of this period.[3] The conquest of Greece by Philip of Macedon was effected as much by his gold as by arms. Wishing, on one occasion, to capture a stronghold, Philip told off a number of his soldiers to reconnoitre the place; the men declared upon their return that it was impregnable. He then asked them if it was so inaccessible that an ass laden with gold would be unable to approach it, for he had often easily acquired possession by gold of places he was unable to reduce by force of arms.[4]

[1] Plutarch.
[2] Plutarch. Aulus Gellius (Bk. XI., ch. ix.) also relates that Demosthenes received money to keep silent, and that he appeared in the Assembly, his neck wrapped up in wool, because he was suffering, he said, from a quinsy. "Say rather from a 'silver malady,'" cried some one in the crowd.
[3] Plutarch, "Life of Phocion."
[4] It would seem that Horace had this historical incident in his mind when he wrote in Ode XVI. of his third Book:

        Aurum per medios ire satallites
        Et perumpere amat saxa, potius
        Ictu fulmineo.

Alcibiades appears to have been a most typical example of the sceptical politician who is at once a man of pleasure and a man of business; ambitious and unscrupulous, a fascinating speaker, of supple and shifty character, he played all parts and assumed all masks, varying his language according to circumstances, "for ever transforming his appearance, and with more ease than does a chameleon." To attain to power he did not rely solely upon his talent as an orator, or his numerous connections, but made himself popular by flattering the people, offering them games and even horse races. "The sums he expended in keeping horses to run in races were much talked about." Not content with owning racehorses, he indulged in amatory escapades and neglected his wife for courtesans. He was fond of scoffing at religious ceremonies and of scandalising serious people by his freedom of speech. A clever and very agreeable talker, he was versed in the art of making witty remarks. On one occasion he went to visit Pericles, who sent him word that he could not see him, as he was busy considering how he should render his accounts to the Athenians. "Would it not be better," was Alcibiades' answer, "that he should consider how he might manage to render no accounts at all?"[1] His death was worthy of his life; he died a violent death in the house of a courtesan, leaving a daughter, who became the celebrated Lais.

The politicians of the period kept up their

[1] Plutarch, "Life of Alcibiades."

popularity by gifts to the people; corrupt themselves, they were the corrupters of others. Pericles himself, as the author of the measure by which those who attended the public deliberations, the public games, and even the fêtes received payment, introduced corrupt habits into Athens, which, in the end, caused the democracy to degenerate into a demagogy.[1] The people kept honest citizens out of the public functions, reserving them for the demagogues who flattered them and made them distributions of money.

Aristophanes has drawn a portrait of these flatterers of the people that has remained so true a likeness that it is worth while to recall it. When the pork-butcher, whose political education had been obtained in kitchens and slaughter-houses, vies with Cleon for the popular favour, he begins by invoking the gods of rogues and boasters, the gods of simpletons, lick-spittles, and insolent fellows. "Give me," he begs, "boundless audacity, an inexhaustible gift of the gab, an impudent voice. . . . *Cleon:* Let my dear lies hasten to my aid. I will crush you or I will lose my reputation. . . . I will drag you before the people; they will settle your pretensions. *The pork-butcher:* I, too, will drag you before the people and I will surpass you in slanders. *Cleon:* Poor fool! The people have no faith in you, while I

---

[1] Aristotle, "Politica," Bk. II., ch. ix., §§ 3, 4. Already in Xenophon's time it used to be said: "With money much can be accomplished in Athens." ("De Republica Atheniensium," ch. iii.)

make sport of them as I please. *The pork-butcher:* So the people belong to you, are yours to do what you will with. *Cleon:* The reason is that I know the words that please them. Oh! *you will not get the better of me in abject flattery.*" This last thrust recalls the saying of a minister and courtier: "My enemies can do what they will, they will not effect my overthrow. Thank Heaven, I have not my better at the court as a valet."

Political Corruption in England.

England also has traversed periods of corruption. The most precise details are found in the Memoirs of Commines, touching the venality of the chief personages in England under the reign of Edward. Louis XI. paid "some sixteen thousand pensions to ministers, great persons, and courtiers." Lord Hastings, the Lord Chamberlain, let himself be bought like so many others by the King of France; "he raised great difficulties before he would become a pensioner of the King," because he was already in receipt of a pension of a thousand crowns from the Duke of Burgundy, but yielding to the pressure brought to bear upon him by Commines, he was induced to accept the offers of Louis XI., who had him offered double what the Duke of Burgundy was giving him. Louis XI. ordered Pierre Claret, his steward, to remit him two thousand crowns, and to demand a receipt, "so that in the time to come it should be patent and known how the Lord Chamberlain,

Chancellor, Admiral and Equerry of England, with many others, had been the pensioners of the King of France." Pierre Claret had an interview with the Lord Chamberlain in private. "After having said to him what was necessary on the part of the King, he handed him the two thousand crowns in gold, for money was never given great foreign personages in any other form." The emissary of Louis XI. asked Lord Hastings for a receipt, or at least for a brief letter, so that he might not be suspected by his master of having kept the money for himself. The Lord Chamberlain, however, replied: "This gift comes to me of the good pleasure of the King, your master, and not at my request; if you wish me to take it, you will place it here in my sleeve, and there will be no letter or witnesses, for I do not wish that by my fault it shall be said, 'The Lord Chamberlain of England has been the pensioner of the King of France,' nor that my receipts be found in his office of accounts."[1]

Chancellor Bacon was also guilty of peculation, and was a corrupt magistrate. Brought up before the House of Lords, he confessed his errors in these terms: "After examination of the accusation made against me, sounding my conscience, and recalling my conduct as far back as I am able, I confess fully and sincerely that I have been guilty of corruption. I renounce any attempt to defend myself, and abandon myself to the clemency and mercy of your Lordships." A

---

[1] Commines, "Mémoires," Bk. VI., ch. ii.

commission of the House of Lords waited upon Bacon to inquire whether he was really the author of the letter containing these confessions, which he then renewed, saying: "My Lords, I am indeed the author of this letter in which I accuse myself. The letter is my work, the work of my hand and of my heart. I implore your Lordships to be full of pity for a poor broken reed."

Several Kings of England bought the votes of Members of Parliament at the price of a pension. This expedient, says Voltaire, shortens difficulties and averts conflicts; it was extensively resorted to by Charles II. "The second Parliament, summoned in 1679, started proceedings against eighteen members of the House of Commons in the preceding Parliament . . . they were accused of having received pensions. However, as there was no law forbidding the acceptance of gratuities from the Sovereign, it was impossible to bring them to trial!"[1] The court of Charles II. was most corrupt. Louis XIV. says in his "Mémoires,"[2] that "it is a court at which much may be done with the help of money, and

---

[1] Voltaire, "Essai sur les Mœurs." England under Charles II.

[2] "Mémoires de Louis XIV.," Vol. II., p. 448. He failed, however, in his attempts to bribe Chancellor Hyde, whose support he was anxious to have for his scheme of a marriage between Charles II. and the Infanta of Portugal. Louis XIV. gives the following account of this endeavour to corrupt Hyde: "I entered in private upon the most secret negotiations with him, negotiations of which even my Ambassador in England was ignorant, and I sent him a clever man, who had with him, ostensibly in order to purchase lead for my ships, letters of credit to the value of 500,000 francs, which he offered the Minister from me, merely asking him for his friendship. He refused my offers." ("Mémoires de Louis XIV.," Vol. II., p. 448.)

the Ministers of this nation have very often been suspected of being the pensioners of Spain." In his negotiations with the court of Charles II., as in those with the other European sovereigns, Louis XIV. was in the habit of showing himself exceedingly liberal to Ministers, Kings and Queens. He expended large sums in pensions to foreign Princes and Ministers.

The Dutch Deputies and the great Polish nobles were no more incorruptible than were the Ministers. "Amongst the Dutch," says Louis XIV., "there were several Deputies to whom I caused pensions to be paid. I gave considerable pensions, too, to several Polish nobles, in order that I might dispose of their votes at the election which was in prospect. I had pensioners in Ireland, whose work was to stir up the Catholics against the English. I was further in treaty with certain refugees from England, to whom I promised important sums, that they might revive the activity of what remained of the Cromwell faction. I gave the King of Denmark one hundred thousand crowns to induce him to join the league against the King of England, and later I presented the Queen, his wife, with a necklace of pearls; I gave another necklace to the Electress of Brandenburg, and made the Queen of Sweden an important present, having no doubt but that these princesses, overlooking the general interests of their States, would feel themselves honoured in their own persons by the pains I took to secure their friendship. Being aware of the influence enjoyed in Sweden by the Chancellor, and that the Prince of Anhalt and the Count of Schwerin had the ear of the Elector of Brandenburg, it was my wish to secure their good offices by my liberality."[1] It is clear that Louis XIV. spared no expense to procure himself allies in the foreign courts. "It often happens," he says, "that moderate sums, dispensed opportunely and with judgment, keep States from incomparably greater outlays and losses. In the absence of support it was possible to acquire at small cost, it is sometimes necessary to raise great armies. A neighbour, who might have been made our friend with a slight expenditure, sometimes costs us very dearly when he becomes our enemy." When engaged in a negotiation with the House of Austria, in the interest of the Duke d'Enghien, he purchased the good offices of a high functionary attached to the person of the Emperor for 100,000 crowns.[2]

Corruption continued to be prevalent in England after the revolution of 1688. Numerous scandals cropped up in the course of 1695; the Speaker, Trevor, was convicted of having accepted a thousand guineas from the City of London to procure the passing of a Bill. "In the same year, Mr. Grey, Secretary of the Treasury, was imprisoned in the Tower of London for having accepted a bribe of two hundred guineas, while Mr. Hungerford was expelled for having received twenty

---

[1] Louis XIV., "Mémoires," Vol., II., pp. 174-176.
[2] Ibid., p. 163.

guineas in return for services rendered when he was chairman of a committee."[1]

William III., in order to gain the support of Members of Parliament, gave them posts whose emoluments were paid out of the Civil List. Parliament protested, and demanded the exclusion of functionaries in receipt of a salary or a pension from the Crown. In 1707, after a long discussion, only the functionaries appointed since 1705 were deprived of their seats, those who had entered upon their posts prior to 1705 being compelled to seek re-election. Under Queen Anne, under George I., and more especially under George II., the Crown continued to award pensions to Members of Parliament. The writings of the period abound in strong protests against the intrigues of Ministers and the habits of corruption that had been introduced thereby into Parliament and thence throughout the country.[2]

The cynical manner in which Robert Walpole purchased the consciences of Members of Parliament and boasted that he had the tariff at his fingers' ends is notorious. Macaulay, none the less, judges his conduct with surprising indulgence. "Walpole governed by corruption because in his time," he says, "it was impossible to govern otherwise. . . . . The House of Commons was in that situation in which assemblies must be managed by corruption or cannot be managed at all. The fault was in the constitution

[1] De Franqueville, "Le Gouvernement et le Parlement Britannique," Vol. III, p. 352; Vol. II., p. 2.
[2] Condillac, "De l'Etude de l'Histoire," Part III., ch. i.

of the Legislature, and to blame those Ministers who managed the Legislature in the only way in which it could be managed is gross injustice. They submitted to extortion because they could not help themselves. We might as well accuse the Lowland farmers who paid blackmail to Rob Roy of corrupting the virtue of the Highlanders as accuse Sir Robert Walpole of corrupting the virtue of Parliament. His crime was merely this, that he employed his money more dexterously, and got more support in return for it, than any of those who preceded or followed him." Lord John Russell admits political corruption to be a political necessity.

During the Ministry of Lord North, George III. formed, by dint of corruption, a party that was called the "party of the King's friends"; its members regarded politics solely as a means to satisfy their covetousness. A new mode of corruption, which has since been widely practised in France as well as in England, was added to the old by the Court; it consisted in granting Members of Parliament lucrative contracts. Fox attacked the corrupt influence of the Court and demanded the exclusion of Members of Parliament interested in contracts. The struggle between the Court and the opposition was keen. A Ministry would purchase votes in the interval between two sittings of the House. Fox[1] got

[1] Fox's integrity has not been suspected in spite of the irregularity of his private life, of his passion for gambling, and of his want of scruples. "At a period when numerous and striking examples seemed to authorise politicians to have an eye to their

wind of the fact, and denounced the traffic in a speech. "Around me," he exclaimed, "are contemptible creatures, who have betrayed their faith. Let them rise and leave the ranks of my friends and seat themselves in the ranks of my enemies." Lord North's Ministry was overthrown and replaced by Lord Rockingham's Ministry, which passed the Bill excluding from Parliament members interested in contracts.

The English Members of Parliament who sold their votes paid heavily for their seats. Lord Chesterfield wrote to his son (letter of the 19th December, 1767) that he had entered into negotiations with an agent for the sale of rotten boroughs for the purchase of a seat in Parliament, and that he had offered him £2,500, but had received the reply that it was no longer possible to find a borough at the price, the rich Indian merchants having bought up all that were in the market at much higher prices. The purchase of a borough was a speculation; seats were bought that votes might be sold.[1] The electioneering agents "even attempted to procure a quotation for seats on the Stock Exchange, and it actually came about that a tariff was established for certain boroughs."

own interests, he refrained from seeking wealth, and constantly abstained from taking those recognised precautions against poverty (what a euphemism!) to which, thanks to the abuses prevalent at the time, it was possible to have recourse without loss of reputation." ("Rémusat l'Angleterre à XVIIIe Siècle," Vol. II., p. 482.) Fox, when he was in Paris, in 1776, astonished Mdme. du Deffand by his scepticism. "He is not a bad man at bottom," she wrote to Walpole, "but he has no sort of principle, and he looks with pity upon those who have."

[1] De Franqueville, op. cit., Vol. II., p. 468.

The spectacle was witnessed of boroughs offering themselves to the candidate who bid the most. Oxford offered to elect the candidate who would pay the debts of the town, and concluded the bargain with the Duke of Marlborough.

According to Lord John Russell £5,000 was paid for a seat in Parliament during the early years of the 19th century. Wilberforce admitted that his elections had cost him £8,000. The rotten boroughs were suppressed in 1832. Electoral and political corruption have since diminished, but they have not disappeared. In 1878, two English men of business boasted in public that they possessed infallible means of influencing the members of a committee entrusted with the examination of a Bill.

Political Corruption in France.

Numerous were the Ministers who were convicted of peculation under the old régime. Numerous, too, were the courts of justice instituted with the object of forcing the financiers to disgorge the money of which they had robbed the Treasury with the connivance of the Superintendents of Finance. Enguerrand de Marigny, Minister of Philip the Handsome, was accused, during the reign of Louis X., of having ruined the finances, and was hanged on the gibbet of Montfaucon, which he had himself constructed. Girard de la Guette, who had been Superintendent of Finances under Philip the Tall, was hunted down under Philip the Handsome, and arrested for depredations; he was questioned under torture, which was inflicted so severely that he died while undergoing it; his body was dragged through the streets and exposed in Paris on a gibbet.[1] On 25th April, 1328, Pierre Rémi, principal treasurer to Charles the Handsome, was hanged, under Philip of Valois, for malversations committed in Guyenne and for "great thefts of royal moneys"; in a few years he had amassed one million two hundred thousand francs, which represents twenty millions of modern French money. He was hanged on the gibbet of Montfaucon, which he caused to be reconstructed, and the King regained possession by confiscation of what he had been robbed.[2] In 1409 Jean de Montague, who had enriched himself in the financial administration, was condemned to be beheaded. During the reign of Charles VII., Jean de Xaintoings, Receiver-General of Finances, was arrested "for having dissipated and wrongly employed the moneys of the King, extensive sums of which it was proven he had stolen." He was also declared guilty of forgery. Still he was only condemned to a few years' imprisonment and to the confiscation of all his possessions. He was soon released from prison, after paying over to the King sixty

---

[1] Jousse, "Traité de la Justice Criminelle," Vol. IV., p. 34.

[2] Peculation, says Montesquieu, being a common crime in despotic States, confiscations are useful in such States. "By their means consolation is afforded the people; the money they bring in represents a considerable tribute which the prince would raise with difficulty from semi-ruined subjects." ("Esprit des Lois," Bk. V., ch. xv.)

thousand crowns. In 1453 took place the trial of Jacques Cœur, who was the victim of the jealousy of the great nobles, who were his debtors, and of the envy of people, who did not believe it was possible to grow rich without peculation and recourse to the magical arts. The son of a furrier of Bourges, Jacques Cœur had made an immense fortune in commerce: he had established branch houses at Montpelier, Marseilles, Lyons, Tours, and factories in Africa and Asia. On several occasions he advanced considerable sums to the King for war expenditure; he entered the King's Council as treasurer, but with the authorisation to continue his commerce. The land he acquired and the castles and houses he built excited the jealousy of the great nobles and of the officers of the royal household, and they persuaded Charles VII. to have him arrested. He was at first accused unjustly of having poisoned Agnes Sorel, and, when this accusation had been shown to be baseless, of alleged extortions. His enemies, charged with judging him, declared him guilty of peculation and of exporting money out of the kingdom. By the sentence passed by the King, from his Bed of Justice, he was condemned to apologise and to pay a fine of one hundred thousand crowns. His possessions were confiscated and a portion of his estates were distributed amongst his accusers.

In the 16th century, in the reign of Francis I., occurred the trial of the Superintendent of Finances, Samblançay, who died a victim of the greed and perfidy of the Queen Mother, Louise of Savoy. Having been denounced to the King by Samblançay, for having appropriated 400,000 gold crowns intended for Lautres, Governor of the Milanese, the Queen Mother swore to revenge herself. In 1527, during the absence of Francis I., she had the superintendent brought up on a trumped-up charge of malversation before a commission of judges arbitrarily chosen by Chancellor Duprat. Although innocent, Samblançay was sentenced to death and hanged. Some time afterwards his innocence was recognised; when the Queen Mother died 1,500,000 gold crowns were found in her coffers, including the 400,000 crowns destined for Lautres.

In 1527 Jean de Porcher, who had administered the King's finances, was accused of peculation, and condemned to be hanged. The same sentence was passed in 1536, on René Gentil, President of Appeals. The same year Admiral Chabot was tried for embezzlement of the royal moneys, stripped of all his honours, sentenced to a fine, and banished. By a decree dated the 23rd April, 1545, Chancellor Poget was condemned for the crime of peculation and other malversations to a fine of one hundred thousand francs, to be degraded from his office, and to five years' banishment. Marshal de Biez was accused of having appropriated a part of the money destined for the payment of his company of gendarmes; declared unworthy to occupy his post, he was condemned by a decree of the Parliament of

Toulouse to make restitution, to be suspended from his functions of Marshal of France for five years, and to be banished from court. In 1565 François Allamant, President of the Audit Office, was pronounced guilty of peculation and condemned to pay a fine of sixty thousand francs. By decree of the Parliament of Paris, dated May 29th, 1583, Jean Poisle, counsellor of the Parliament, was sentenced "for peculation and corruption, double dealing, extortion, and violence."

It was in the 16th century that the commissions instituted to judge persons accused of peculation took the name of "Chambers of Justice." Rigorous regulations were passed in 1532, 1545, 1557, and 1559 to repress this crime, which had become frequent. Chambers of justice were also instituted in 1566, 1578, 1584, 1593, 1601, 1607, 1624, 1645, and 1652.

When L'Hopital was present at Bordeaux with Charles IX., he protested, at the Bed of Justice that was held there, against the peculation of certain magistrates and the venality of the courtiers. "Gentlemen," he said, "I fear that there is avarice in our midst, for I have been told that some there are who take money to grant an audience, and when they are blamed, they reply it is much worse at the Court, for there it is that the great rogues are; but it is not well, neither here nor there."

When Sully became Minister, "disorder and brigandage were everywhere. . . . The friends of the King took their part of the product of the farms, and of the contracts made with the purveyors. The Treasury was administered by dishonest persons; those who should have kept the accounts kept no accounts whatever."[1] François d'O, Superintendent of the Finances under Henry III., was, says Henri Martin, the great robber, the chief of all the robbers. Sully restored order to the finances, and put a stop to the exactions of the military governors.

Marshal de Marillac, sentenced to death under Richelieu for peculation, could not understand such severity. "A man of my station condemned to death for peculation!" he cried. Richelieu showed himself pitiless. He considered "the art of finance as one of the principal parts of politics; it is the more indispensable in a State," he adds, "in that money is the soul of all affairs. A commonwealth is only strong in proportion to the richness of the public treasury."[2] Mazarin was far less severe upon those guilty of peculation: it is known that he was not above reproach himself, and that he left behind him after his death a fortune of 50 millions, which would represent 200 millions to-day.

The commencement of the reign of Louis XIV.

[1] "Les Chambres de Justice," by Petit-Jean, Procureur-Général at the Audit Office.
[2] "Testament Politique de Richelieu," ch. x. "The King," he says, "receives a great deal of money from the tax upon salt, but the people pay far more than they should do over and above what enters the royal coffers." Richelieu accuses those who farmed the salt tax of drawing up false reports and of pillaging and ruining poor private persons.

was marked by the Chamber of Justice of 1661, which tried Fouquet and a great number of financiers guilty of peculation. Over five hundred persons were convicted; according to the Procureur-Général Petit-Jean the total fines and confiscations amounted to one hundred and ten millions.

M. Cousin has written that the fortune of Colbert was no better acquired than that of Fouquet, for to all appearance, he said, "he did not manage to provide the three duchesses, his daughters, with dowries, and to build his magnificent house at Sceaux out of what he saved out of his salary."[1] M. Cousin forgets, however, that under the old monarchy the Kings made liberal presents to their Ministers. "Just as those who remain for some time in the sun are warmed by its heat," says G. Naudé, "so it is necessary that he whom a prince or a sovereign places near his person shall feel the effects of his power and of the friendship he bears him in the shape of the recompense due for the services rendered."[2] The Kings said to their Ministers, "Look after my interests and I will look after yours," in order, Naudé adds, "that being no longer the prey of that horrible monster poverty, they may bring a mind entirely free and liberated from all passions to the conduct of affairs."

Still the memoirs of Louis XIV. leave the impression that Fouquet was not the only Minister who declined to be content with the royal liberality.

[1] Cousin. "Madame de Longueville pendant la Fronde," p. 216.
[2] G. Naudé, "Considérations Politiques sur les Coups d'Etat," ch. v.

Thus the King, in the advice he gives his son, insists at length upon the necessity of keeping a watch upon the Ministers; one must not, he says, "be content with examining men before appointing them to a post, because the majority easily adopt a disguise for a time, in their passion to acquire the authority that is the object of their ambition." On the contrary, he adds, it is necessary "to observe them still more carefully when they are actually entrusted with the conduct of affairs, because, being then in possession of what they had desired, they often follow the more freely their evil inclinations."[1] It would seem that when a Minister has been convicted of dishonourable conduct, the only step to take is to dismiss and punish him. Louis XIV. is less severe; he counsels his son to reclaim an unfaithful Minister by good advice, to keep him if he has qualities that make it worth while to put up with him, taking precautions the while against the harm his avarice might cause affairs, and only to dismiss him if he is incorrigible.[2]

We also learn from the journal and memoirs of Louis XIV. that "in certain provinces the people were tormented by certain persons who abused the title of governor to practise unjust exactions." "I instal men everywhere," says Louis XIV., "expressly that I may be the more surely informed of their peculations, so as then to punish them if they deserve it."

The "Great Days" that were held in Auvergne

[1] "Mémoires de Louis XIV.," Vol. I., p. 185.   [2] Ibid., p. 186.

in 1665 pronounced a large number of condemnations for peculation.[1] "The court in its ardour," writes Fléchier, "took note of the crimes and had scarcely time to consider the station of the persons judged, whence it resulted that M. de la Tour was sentenced in the first instance to be hanged; however, when it was learnt that he was of excellent birth he was accorded the honour that was his due, and was condemned to be nobly beheaded." A nephew of Turenne, the Marquis de Malause, was sentenced to a substantial fine and to make restitution of a sum of 18,000 francs. Bourdaloue declared, at a rather later period: "A man who handles public money absolutely without reproach, and who retires from certain posts with absolutely clean hands, is at present almost a prodigy."—("Sermon sur la Religion et la Probité.")

In the preamble[2] to the decree announcing the institution of the Chamber of Justice of 1661, the King declared: "In these recent times, a small number of persons have built up rapid and prodigious fortunes by illegitimate means. Their immense acquisitions, their insolent pomp, their boundless opulence, offer an example calculated to corrupt all the maxims of public honesty." The persons referred to in the preamble of this edict were the financiers, who occupied a prominent position in the society of the 17th century. La Bruyère depicts them buying titles of nobility

---

[1] Fléchier, "Les Grands Jours d'Auvergne."
[2] This preamble was written by Colbert.

and marrying their daughters to courtiers. "If a financier is unsuccessful the courtiers say of him he is a commoner, a nobody, a vulgar fellow; if he is successful they demand the hand of his daughter. . . . A very rich man may . . introduce a duke into his family and make a nobleman of his son. . . . Thanks to his money, Sylvain has acquired breeding and another name. He is lord in the parish where his ancestors paid tithes; formerly he could not have entered the house of Cléobule in the capacity of page, and he is his son-in-law. . . . After wearing livery, Sosie has made his way from a petty post in the finances to one of considerable importance; and by peculation, violence, and abusing his powers, he has at last attained to rank at the cost of the ruin of several families; become ennobled by tenure of office, it only remained for him to be able to pose as a good man; he is now a churchwarden, and the prodigy is realised."[1]

The spectacle of the nobility manœuvring to be invited to the houses of financiers is not peculiar to our own time. The greatest names of the nobility were found under the roof of Samuel Bernard, the celebrated farmer of the revenue, who occupied a most prominent position in the reign of Louis XIV.; the attractions were suppers, gambling, and fêtes. President Hénault, describing the revenue farmer's establishment, says: "It was a house where one gambled and dined

[1] La Bruyère, "Des Biens de la Fortune."

well, and that was the meeting-place of the best company. .... There were to be seen the Cardinal de Rohan, to whom nature had accorded all external talents; the Prince de Rohan, his brother; Mdme. de Montbusson, whom they disputed between them; Dessorts, since Controller-General; Mdme. Turgot, M. d'Aumont, Mdme. Martel. ... Marshal Villeroi, attracted by Mdme. de Sagonne, the daughter of Bernard, and who was the object of the most delicate attentions with a view to inducing him to shut his eyes to what had passed at Lyons, where Bernard had gone bankrupt for 32 millions."

A new and very severe decree against peculation was issued in 1701; it ordained that those convicted of this crime should suffer the death penalty. Nevertheless the depredations of the financiers continued.

At the death of Louis XIV. public opinion again demanded the repression of the abuses committed by the financiers. A new Chamber of Justice was instituted in March, 1716.[1] It gave the judges who were to compose the chamber power to pass capital and penal sentences, and to impose fines. It was authorised, too, to take proceedings against persons of every kind,

---

[1] Montesquieu refers to it in his "Lettres Persanes": "What is termed a chamber of justice," he says, "has just been established. It is so called because its object is to strip them of all they possess. It is impossible for them to dispose fraudulently of or to hide their belongings, for they are made to declare them accurately under pain of death; in this way they are made to traverse a very narrow pass—to choose, I mean, between their life and their money." (Letter XCVII., Usbeck to Isben.)

of whatever birth and station, who should have been guilty of peculation. These severe dispositions did not last, and a decree dated September 18th of the same year, 1716, permitted capital and penal sentences to be transmuted into fines. In the end the Chamber of Justice concerned itself with decreeing taxes rather than with anything else. According to the Procureur-Général Petit-Jean, out of the 812 millions of property it left the owners in possession of 412 millions, deducting therefrom 219 millions supposed to represent taxes, but which were never entirely paid. On the 22nd March, 1717, d'Aguesseau, who had just replaced the Chancellor Voisin, announced the suppression of the Chamber of Justice; it was the last. On this occasion the new Chancellor made an observation with respect to the character of the French people the justice of which has recently been instanced in connection with the Panama scandals; the people passed from the keenest indignation to the most absolute indifference, and from hatred to compassion. The people, said d'Aguesseau, always subject to inconstancy, "likes to witness a prompt and rigorous punishment, but the matter must not be allowed to drag, or, allowing its initial indignation against the guilty to cool, it accustoms itself to believe them innocent when it has seen them for long in a state of misfortune.

The history of the Chambers of Justice comes to an end here, but the history of crimes of corruption does not terminate with it. On the contrary, under the Regent with Law and the Cardinal Dubois, and under Louis XV., corruption continues on a growing scale. The King himself speculated in wheat, and was one of the shareholders in the notorious company of the "compact of famine," which brought about the artificial famines of 1768 and 1769. The corrupt practices of this period are so generally known that I consider it useless to relate them over again.

It is easier for a people to carry through a political revolution than a moral revolution, to change its régime than to change its conscience. During the Revolution the politicians continued to make money, and the financiers did not cease to league themselves with the politicians. The most passionate demagogues combined business with politics. Hébert was on terms of close intimacy with the banker Koch, who was suspected of being in the pay of the foreigner. Morris, who represented the United States in Paris in 1789, expresses himself in the following terms when speaking of Narbonne, de Choiseul, and the Abbé de Périgord: "They are three young men of good family and of parts, who lead a life of pleasure. They were, all three of them, fast friends, and all three of them while following their ambitions have been primarily concerned with restoring their dilapidated fortunes." Montmorin admitted to Alexandre de Lameth that "in a short space of time he had expended seven millions in buying Jacobins and corrupting writers and orators."[1] Theodore de Lameth went to see Danton in the hope of saving Louis XVI. Danton answered him: "I consent to attempt to save the King, but I require a million to purchase the necessary votes. . . . I warn you, that if I cannot procure him his life, I shall vote for his death. I am willing to save his head, but not to lose my own."[2] Mirabeau, anxious to limit the opprobrium attaching to the bargain he had driven with the Court, declared that he had been paid, but that he had not sold himself. It was at this period that Fouquet laid the foundation by dubious means of his large fortune. Other Deputies contrived to have rich estates adjudged them for a handful of "assignats." Some, entrusted with missions, committed embezzlements. Ronsin and his friends pillaged Vendée. The Deputy Perrin was sentenced to the hulks for robbery. Chabot, a former monk, became suddenly rich and married the daughter of a banker. At the trial of Fabre d'Eglantine for forgery in favour of the French East India Company, Chabot declared "that a hundred thousand francs had been remitted him for the purpose of corrupting Fabre, but he added that he had not dared to speak to him of the matter: he discreetly kept the money."[3]

Pillage was rife at the War Office while Pache was in authority there. Several members of the Committee of General Safety compromised them-

[1] Michelet, "Histoire de la Révolution Française," Vol. II., p. 338.
[2] Taine, Vol. III., p. 177, note 3. [3] Michelet, Vol. VIII., p. 285.

selves in financial affairs. The Paris Commune never rendered its accounts, although frequently summoned to do so by Cambon. The Convention was never able to secure the production of the accounts and the punishment of the dishonest, who had powerful protectors in the Assembly.

On September 25, 1793, Thuriot bemoaned before the Convention the fate of the Republic, which had become the prey of the most despicable of men. "Can it be," he said, "that we have struggled as we have to give the power to robbers, and to men upon whom is the stain of blood? We drag royalty from its throne and put up roguery in its place."[1] A certain number of the Jacobin Deputies were worthless and debauched men, gamblers who speculated in "assignats" and the State properties. Amongst them were men who divided their time between murder and loose living. Rossignol, for instance, and Carrier, who ordered massacres without interrupting their orgies. Henriot had himself allotted 8,000 francs "to cover his expenses incurred in watching the anti-revolutionary massacres," and afterwards another sum of 300,000 francs, that were to serve "to frustrate plots and to assure the triumph of liberty." It was Henriot, again, who invited his friends to join in the quest for spoil in a resolution worded as follows: "I am glad to inform my brothers-in-arms that all posts are in the gift of the Government. The present Government, which is revolutionary, . . . searches even the

[1] Michelet, op. cit., Vol. VIII., p. 112.

attics for virtuous men, . . . for poor and pure sans-culottes." The poor and pure sans-culottes did not always wait until search was made for them in their attics, which they hastened to leave to devote themselves to place-hunting; they joined, too, the revolutionary committees which appropriated enormous sums of money. "The three or four millions of gold and silver extorted before the close of 1783, the hundreds of millions extorted in 1793 and 1794—in a word, almost the entire product of all the extraordinary taxes, were swallowed up on the spot by the sans-culottes." (Taine, op. cit., p. 346.)

To rehabilitate these demagogues it has been stated that many of them died poor, but this poverty is no proof of their morality. They died poor because they dissipated their ill-acquired riches; their hands were empty but not clean; their pockets were emptied as soon as they were filled.[1]

Corruption under the Directory attained still further development. The type of the politicians of this period is Barras, an avaricious, unprincipled rake, who pledged himself to all parties and had a finger in every conspiracy. Bonaparte called him the most corrupt of the corrupt. After the 18th Fructidor, those condemned to transportation were conveyed in iron cages to the ports where they were to be embarked, and the command of the escort was given to General Dutertre, who two years before had been sentenced to the

[1] Taine, op. cit., Vol. III., p. 280.

galleys for acts of pillage committed in Vendée. (De Barante, "Histoire du Directoire," Vol. II., p. 415.)

Political morality improved under the Empire and the Restoration. The passion for military glory, the reawakening of the religious sentiment, and later the love of political liberty raised the moral level. Devotion to the national flag silenced the love of riches; the feelings uppermost in the minds of the soldiers of the Empire were esteem for courage and the sentiment of honour; consideration and honours were the reward of military virtues. Napoleon I., as M. Thiers remarks, had a liking for honest men.[1] Still he more than once endeavoured to corrupt men,[2] and he took for his Ministers men of dubious honesty, such as Fouché and Talleyrand. At the close of

[1] Thiers, op. cit., Bk. LXII.
[2] Here is an instance of which Mdme. de Staël was a witness. Wishing to render unpopular the Duke de Melzi, a former vice-president of the cis-alpine Republic, Napoleon, in 1805, appeared in person before the Legislative Assembly of Lombardy, and announced his intention of granting the Duke de Melzi an important estate in return for his services. "Being at Milan at the time," says Mdme. de Staël, "I saw M. de Melzi in the evening and found him absolutely in despair at the treacherous trick Napoleon had played him without a word of warning; but as Bonaparte would have shown himself vexed at a refusal, I advised M. de Melzi to at once devote the income forced upon him to some public establishment. He followed my advice, and the following day, while out walking with the Emperor, told him that such was his intention. Bonaparte seized him by the arm, and said: 'I wager that what you just said was suggested to you by Mdme. de Staël. But, believe me, you had far better have nothing to do with such 18th century romantic philanthropy. There is only one thing to be done in this world, and that is to be for ever acquiring more money and more power; all else is a dream." ("Considérations sur la Révolution Française," Part IV., ch. xviii.)

his reign he regretted his action and said: "For the future I wish to have none but honest men about me."[1]

Thanks to the writings of Governor Morris, United States Minister in Paris in 1789, and to the revelations of Count de Senfft, the Saxon Minister in Paris in 1806, it has long been known that Talleyrand had the keenest possible passion for money, and was always trying to add to his fortune by speculation and the presents he received from the Powers. The Saxon Minister relates that during the negotiations which preceded the Treaty of Posen in 1806 Talleyrand was presented with a million by the Saxon plenipotentiary, and that several German princes obtained their admission to the Rhine Confederation by dint of money remitted to Talleyrand by M. de Gagern, Minister of the Duke of Nassau. The Pasquier Memoirs, which appeared recently, offer confirmation of the venality of the former Minister for Foreign Affairs. They show that Talleyrand took advantage of the treaties he was preparing, to enrich himself. "That of Lunéville, in which it was stipulated that Austria should take up the paper it had issued in Belgium, gave him an opportunity of making enormous profits by buying the paper before anybody was aware of the stipulation." The Vienna Cabinet was particularly generous to Talleyrand in order to be sure of his good offices in connection with the treaties he was negotiating. "The secularisation of Germany

[1] "Vie du Comte d'Hauterive," p. 320.

and all the arrangements in that country connected with the portioning out of territory were a fresh source of profits that considerably surpassed the first. "I have heard them estimated," writes Chancellor Pasquier, "by well-informed people at at least ten millions. This justice must be rendered M. de Talleyrand, that he did not keep the proceeds of his venality entirely to himself. He felt the necessity of allowing a good number of those who had assisted him to share in the spoil. The method was an excellent one for creating useful and devoted instruments."[1]

Napoleon did not ignore the venality of his Minister. Questioning him one day upon the origin of his fortune, he suddenly put to him this query: "Monsieur de Talleyrand, what have you done to become so rich?" "Sire," the Minister cunningly replied, "the means are very simple. I bought Government stock on the eve of the 18th Brumaire and sold it immediately afterwards." In 1807, when Talleyrand requested that he might be granted, in return for his services, the dignity of Vice-Grand Elector, which would have brought about his retirement from the Ministry, the Emperor, much annoyed at this resolution, said to him: "I do not understand your impatience to

[1] "Mémoires du Chancelier Pasquier," Vol. I., p. 249, 339. The Vienna Cabinet, in buying the good offices of Talleyrand, continued the traditions of the old diplomacy, which always endeavoured to bribe the Ministers of foreign Governments. The Versailles Cabinet frequently paid pensions to English, Austrian, and other Ministers. "Thugut, who succeeded Kaunitz in Austria and who preceded Metternich during the Revolution, drew a pension from France since 1768." (Wallon, "Journal des Savants," December, 1893, p. 742.)

become a great dignitary, and to leave a post to which you owe your reputation, and from which, as I am aware, you have reaped great advantages." Talleyrand's successor was M. de Champagny, whose honesty Napoleon thus vaunted: "I am sure of never finding him mixed up in any money-making affair."[1] Finally, when the Emperor, informed of the reconciliation of Talleyrand and Fouché, and of their plots against him, returned from Spain to foil them, he addressed Talleyrand, in the presence of several Ministers, in the most violent terms, covered him with insults, and called him a thief.[2]

Louis XVIII. allowed a great many of the courtiers of Napoleon to keep their seats in the Senate, and accepted Fouché for Minister. Chateaubriand, seeing Talleyrand enter the King's apartment leaning on the arm of Fouché, remarked: "There goes vice supported by crime." With a few rare exceptions, however, the Ministers of the Restoration were honest, and, speaking generally, they governed by honest means.

Baron d'Haussez, Minister of Marine in the Polignac Cabinet, alleges in his recently published Memoirs that the Government of the Restoration was too honest, and only fell because it would not create itself a majority by recourse to bribery, and by purchasing a small number of votes that were certainly on sale. "And yet but

[1] "Vie du Comte d'Hauterive," p. 217.
[2] "Mémoires du Chancelier Pasquier."

a slight effort was necessary," he says, "to detach from the Opposition the small number of votes on which the majority depended. A few posts or little money would have sufficed, . . . we were in possession of the tariff of consciences; it was not high, each member being put down at barely more than he was worth. On the Opposition benches, among the men who, from sheer love of the people, were so ardently opposed to the Legitimist cause, there were not wanting speculators who offered to drive a bargain. Had they been brought face to face with each other one could doubtless have obtained a reduction in terms. The King and the Dauphin rejected the suggestion without awaiting that the Council should express its opinion." Baron d'Haussez proposed to them to have recourse to the Civil List for the money required to secure the twenty votes that were wanted. The Dauphin refused. "The Civil List was not encroached upon," adds the Minister of Marine, "but two months after this session the King was on the road to Cherbourg."[1]

On the morrow of the Revolution of 1830, the greed of the July conquerors inspired Barbier to write the celebrated verses entitled "The Quarry" and "Popularity." Some years later there was played at the Théâtre Français C. Delavigne's comedy "La Popularité," in which political corruption, which was making headway at the time to a disquieting extent, is scourged

[1] "Mémoires du Baron d'Haussez."

in fine verse. One of the personages of the comedy is made to utter the following lines:

> To what a pass has corruption come?
> All my actions are pure, and my life is known:
> Two men visited me this morning,
> One to sell himself to me, the other to buy me.
> You desire, you say, to establish republican laws.
> And on what? On morals? Where are our Roman morals?
> This man who decries an abuse, grows fat on an abuse still greater;
> Votes, turned to base uses, are to be bought at current prices;
> Infamy, with the aid of gold, transforms itself into glory;
> He who builds thereon, builds on mire.
> —(Act IV.)

Already, in 1838, M. de Tocqueville expressed the disgust he felt at the sight of public men trafficking in their influence.[1] It was then that financial companies began to induce Princes, Dukes, Marquises, Counts, and politicians to figure on their Council Boards.[2] Procureur-Général Dupin strongly blamed the participation of public men in undertakings upon which the Chambers would be called upon to vote, and declared that the shares distributed to the Deputies served as a screen to prevent their consciences being touched by considerations of right, truth, and justice. In a speech on March 17, 1846, and in a letter of July of the same year, addressed to his electors, M. Thiers points out the progress of corruption, and deplores the spectacle of the bartering of electoral

---

[1] Tocqueville, "Œuvres et Correspondance Inédites," Vol. II., p. 85.

[2] Heine, noticing the number of naval officers who were members of the council boards of financial societies, jokingly asked whether their presence was not a precaution on the part of the companies, taken in view of their coming one day into collision with justice and being sentenced to the galleys. ("Lutèce," p. 209.)

influence. When Rothschild's firm, already all-powerful, tendered for the Northern Railway concession, there were Deputies who hurried to their offices with the request that they should be allotted at par shares which were already several hundred francs above par: in granting their demands the Rothschilds simply made them a present. "But everybody is begging of him at present," wrote Heine at the time.[1] The low moral tone of the political world had become so patent that several years prior to 1848 de Tocqueville, Heine, and a few other clear-sighted men saw in the fact the premonitory symptoms of a new revolution.[2] In 1847 General Desbans-Cubières, peer of France, ex-Minister of War, was convicted of having paid over, in concert with the director of the Gouhenam mines, 100,000 francs to Teste, Minister of Public Works, with a view to obtain a concession. Malversations were proved to have been committed at the Toulon, Rochefort, and Cherbourg arsenals. These scandals, by bringing the authorities into disrepute, contributed to the fall of Louis Philippe. This discredit, that ought only to have overtaken the guilty, attached itself at last to an honest sovereign, who was

[1] Heine, op. cit., p. 330.

[2] Tocqueville, op. cit., Vol. II., p. 133. Heine, who, like all great poets, was often more perspicacious than statesmen, had announced in 1841 the new revolution that was preparing. "The day is not far off," he wrote, "when the entire middle-class comedy in France, with its heroes and lesser actors, will come to a terrible end amid hisses and hootings, and be followed by the playing of an epilogue entitled "The Reign of the Communists." ("Lutèce," p. 209.)

unfortunate enough to have faithless servants and dishonourable Ministers.

In order to leave this book the impartial character of an historical study, I shall abstain from recounting the progress made by political corruption under the Second Empire and the Third Republic, and shall conclude this chapter, already rather long, with an examination of the principal causes of corruption.

The Causes of Political Corruption.

It is particularly in the case of politicians that it must be said: Seek for the woman, and you will have the explanation of their corruption. They often prefer the *foyer* of the opera to their homes.[1] At Rome, towards the close of the Republic, the politician lived in the intimacy of women of bad reputation, whose number had become considerable. Then, as now, women let themselves be carried away by the frenzied love of luxury and pleasures. Roman ladies of illustrious birth led the lives of women of bad reputation, frequented the waters of Baia, and gave sumptuous banquets to which they invited wits, writers, and politicians. In several contemporary comedies there have figured among the personages politicians and financiers of humble birth, who, to give their pleasures the added zest that comes

---

[1] Mirabeau preferred Coulon, the dancer, to his wife; the Girondins and Jacobins were assiduous frequenters of the *foyers* of the theatres, even during the struggles of the Revolution.

from satisfied vanity, pay highly for the favours of great ladies, whom debts and their need of luxury make accessible to plebeians.[1] This craze was common in Rome. It was for this reason that Fausta, the daughter of Sylla and the wife of Milo, was much courted; "men attached themselves to her because it flattered their vanity to be on good terms with a woman of such high rank, and to have the honour of being in their turn the son-in-law of the Dictator." Sallust, who wrote history from the point of view of the austere moralist, was surprised with the noble patrician by Milo, her husband, and well beaten with leather straps.[2] This adventure left him for the future less infatuated with women of quality, and induced him to content himself with women of a lower class, with whom he did not run the same risk.

The case of Sallust is that of a great number of his contemporaries: fond of pleasures, passing whole nights at table, greedy for money, he entered public life to satisfy his wants. "I sought," he says," like others, to raise myself to State dignities. I encountered many dangers. Impudence, intrigue, and corruption had taken the place of modesty, merit, and integrity. In my heart I despised these odious practices; but youth is imprudent, and ambition cannot resign itself to renouncing the struggle." The truth is that Sallust, incited by that thirst for power and

---

[1] See "Le Député Levreau," by Jules Lemaître.
[2] Aulus Gellius, Bk. XVII., § 18.

riches which he blames in others, played every part according to his interest at the moment; now a flatterer of the people, now one of Cæsar's courtiers, he achieved dignities by intrigue and corruption, and took advantage of his position to enrich himself. He pillaged Numidia, where he was appointed Governor, returned to Rome, built himself a sumptuous palace with gardens and magnificent baths, and continued in his writings to wax indignant over the despicable actions which politicians are induced to commit through ambition and cupidity. He would not be the type of the corrupt politician unless he had added hypocrisy to his vices.

Then, as now, divorce made it extremely easy to exchange one wife for another. The politicians made extensive use of this method. After repudiating his wife Antustia, Pompey married Emilia, and then Mutia, whom he in turn repudiated to marry Julia. Lucullus repudiated Clodia, married Servilia, sister of Cato,[1] and then repudiated her. Cæsar, a veritable Don Juan, married four wives in succession, without counting the considerable number of his concubines, among whom there were women from the provinces and Queens.[2] The dissoluteness of Antony is notorious; he

[1] Cato had two sisters. One was the wife repudiated by Lucullus, the other was seduced by Cæsar. The conduct of his wife, Attilia, was so bad that he was obliged to divorce her, although he had two children by her. He then married Martia, whom he afterwards lent to his friend Hortensius. (Plutarch, "Life of Cato of Utica.") Plutarch cites as exceptional the case of Lelius, the friend of Cicero, who had only one wife.

[2] Suetonius, §§ 47-49.

travelled through Italy accompanied by his wife and the actress Cytharis, with whom Cicero and Atticus dined on one occasion. Cicero himself divorced his wife Tertullia, married at the age of sixty-three, to pay his debts, a rich young girl, and contracted a liaison with a woman of bad reputation of the name of Cerillia.[1] Cicero's wife, after her divorce, was married by Sallust.

Ambitious men frequently owe their advancement to women. When Cethegus was all-powerful in Rome the authority was, in reality, in the hands of the courtesan Procia. It was solely due to the influence of Procia, who ruled Cethegus, that Lucullus obtained the governorship of Cilicia and the command of the expedition against Mithridates. All the other means that he had tried having failed, Lucullus "set to work to win her to his cause, and to insinuate himself into her good graces by presents and every sort of

---

[1] Cicero, said Montesquieu, "had a fine genius but a vulgar soul." ("Grandeur et Décadence des Romains," ch. xii.) His finer feelings had been blunted by politics. By ambition, love of popularity, interest, and to be agreeable to his political allies, Cicero gave his support to bad causes; he admits that he did so in his twenty-second letter to Atticus. Referring to a demand for annulment made by the persons who had tendered for the Asiatic tributes, he writes: "The fact is the demand was indefensible. Still I supported it and succeeded in giving it a semblance of justification; . . . a dirty business, a humiliating step. . . ." In another letter to Atticus, the twenty-sixth, he adds: "The claim of the farmers of the tributes to annul their engagements was of unparalleled impudence," and yet he supports it. On another occasion Cicero is found supporting before the Senate a plea introduced by the knights, who felt themselves injured because proceedings had been taken against judges who had accepted bribes. In his pleadings he attached small importance to truth; he was wont to throw dust in the eyes of the judges.

flattery he could devise, apart from the fact that it was already a very great satisfaction to a proud and ambitious woman, as she was, to find herself necessary to and sought after by such a great personage as Lucullus."[1]

The Grecian courtesans also exerted a great influence over politicians. At the time of Pericles, Aspasia "had entangled in her toils the principal men who were then concerned in the conduct of public affairs." Pericles was one of her assiduous visitors, and he separated from his legitimate wife; to such an extent was he under her influence that at her request he decided upon the Samian war in favour of Miletus. The Kings of Persia, who were aware of the influence of the Greek courtesans upon the politicians, had recourse to them more than once to gain the latter to their cause.[2]

I believe I have said sufficient to prove that when politicians embark upon dishonourable

---

Munatius, whom he had caused to be acquitted, having instituted proceedings against a friend of Cicero's, the latter, much annoyed, reproached him with his ingratitude, saying to him: "You know very well, Munatius, that on a recent occasion you were not absolved because of your innocence, but because I threw dust in the eyes of the judges, and to such good purpose that they were unable to perceive the reality of your misdeeds." (Plutarch, "Life of Cicero.")

[1] Plutarch, "Life of Lucullus."

[2] Plutarch, "Life of Pericles." Epaminondas having caused a man of humble station to be thrown into prison for a slight fault he had committed, his friend Pelopidas came to beg him to give him his liberty; "this he refused to do, but shortly afterwards a woman with whom he was intimate made him the same request, and he yielded to her demand, saying that these were the kind of favours that should be granted women friends and concubines, but not to captains."

courses, it is often in order to satisfy the desire for luxury of their wives and mistresses. Political corruption has, however, other causes. It often happens that the politician who is guilty of peculation is a collector of artistic treasures, antiquities, statues, and pictures. The Prætor Licinius, when hunting for art treasures, used to be borne through the streets on a litter strewn with roses. Verres, a man of revolting licentiousness, also entertained a passion for statues. "Statues" is the title of Cicero's ninth speech against Verres (Bk. IV.); it is entirely taken up by an enumeration of the artistic treasures stolen by the dishonest pro-consul. It is possible to be fond of statues and yet to lead a regular life, although it has been said: "Statues and good morals do not go together!" It is certain that artistic tastes can go hand in hand with great corruption. It would seem that in the heat of political strife the love of pleasure should abate, and that ambition should stifle sensuality. History shows, however, that politicians are given to pursuing their pleasures simultaneously with their more serious concerns, that they do not renounce enjoying themselves even during civil war, that orgies often accompany proscriptions, and that war, whether civil or foreign, is a further zest to their pleasure.[1] When Antony was preparing to make war against Cæsar he was engaged in every description of orgy in the isle of Samos, while "the entire compass of the habit-

---

[1] Tacitus, "Historiæ," Bk. III., § 83.

able globe was in lamentation, groans, and tears."[1] Even after his defeat at Actium Antony resumed his life of debauch. The period that extends between Pharsalia and Actium was marked by fêtes that recall those that were given in Paris, on the morrow of the disastrous war of 1870 and the crimes of the Commune. At the fêtes in question persons of considerable standing appeared disguised as animals. "An important politician, the Consul Plancus," says M. Boissier, "was then seen to adapt the tail of a fish to his person, to paint himself sea-blue, and, his head crowned with reeds, to execute the dance of the sea god Glaucus at a dinner given by Cleopatra."[2] Montaigne cites a King of Naples "who made the satisfaction of his passions the chief object of his ambition." (Bk. II., ch. xxxiii.) As much may be said of a great number of politicians, who regard politics merely as a means of procuring themselves pleasures and of exciting their thirst for enjoyments.

Public calamities, such as wars and civil strife, do not recall corrupt and cynical men to serious thoughts; often, on the contrary, they merely excite their consuming thirst for pleasure. During the plague the Athenians gave themselves over to the quest of pleasure with a veritable fury: "with no prospect beyond short-lived joys, holding their lives and possessions to be ephemeral they considered it meet to devote all

[1] Plutarch, "Life of Antony."
[2] G. Boissier, "Revue des Deux-Mondes." December 1, 1872.

their thoughts to pleasure."[1] During the Terror, "with the executions going on, the theatres were as full as usual."[2] Dancing went on at the Court of Charles VI., while the Cabochiens were slaughtering the King's friends. At the Court of Henri III. duels and assassinations alternated with the balls and fêtes. Under Charles II. of England orgies followed executions. During the wars of religion habits at once cruel and licentious prevailed. Catherine of Medicis surrounded herself with ladies-in-waiting in order to gain the party leaders.

At all periods of political corruption luxury in the matter of eating becomes excessive. "The luxury of the table," says Tacitus, "was the cause of unheard-of prodigalities during the hundred years that intervened between the battle of Actium and the conflicts that gave Galba the Empire." Unbridled gluttony was ceaselessly searching to "create new dishes, to procure fresh delights to the taste." The sums paid for a good cook were very considerable. Sallust paid a hundred thousand sesterces for a cook. Antony presented a cook with the house of a citizen of Magnesia because he had prepared his supper to his liking. His house was always full of "clowns, buffoons, jugglers, and jesters, besotting themselves and making good cheer."[3] During his consulship Pompey "amused himself with revels and festivities." One day as he was having his

---

[1] Thucydides, Bk. II., § 53.
[2] Mdme. de Staël, op. cit., Part III., ch. xvi.
[3] Plutarch, "Life of Antony."

bath, and was about to sit down to table, Hypteus, a man of consular rank, approached him to request his assistance. Pompey "passed proudly by him, without making him any other answer than that he was spoiling his supper." The banquets of Lucullus have remained famous. An improvised repast which he offered Cicero and Pompey cost him 50,000 silver drachmas.[1] Sylla also was of most intemperate habits; when his wife Metella died, "he comforted himself in his mourning by indulging in his usual festivities, which included every form of enjoyment and dissoluteness." A few months after the death of his wife he met Valeria, the widow of Hortensius the orator, at the theatre, and married her, but he none the less continued to entertain in his house "women musicians and dancers, . . gay jesters, singers, and minstrels, in whose company he drank and besotted himself the day long on little low beds."[2]

"Crates the philosopher," says Plutarch, "esteeming that civil strife and tyrannies are brought about in towns as much as a luxury or as pleasure as for any other cause whatever, was wont to say, as he played according to his custom: 'Be careful not to engage us in civil strife by increasing the meat in place of the lentils, that is by spending more than your income admits of; everybody ought to exercise control over himself.'"[3] The

[1] Plutarch, "Life of Lucullus."
[2] Plutarch, "Life of Sylla." Béranger in one of his political songs makes a Deputy of the Restoration say: "What dinners, what dinners the Ministers gave us!"
[3] Plutarch.

Chancellor de L'Hopital made the same observation at the time of the wars of religion; he had remarked that the love of pleasure, extravagant expenses, and in particular excessive luxury in connection with the pleasures of the table, promoted civil wars. He promulgated sumptuary laws, which, like all such laws, were without effect. He himself set the example of extreme simplicity at his repasts. Brantôme relates that he dined at L'Hopital's table off "boiled meat only"; in the place of dishes there were "many fine speeches and fine phrases," and occasionally "witty sayings that raised a laugh."

Simple and modest tastes, a regular life and sobriety are the best preservatives against political corruption. When the emissaries of the Samnites sought out Marcus Curius to offer him a large quantity of gold, they found him eating a frugal repast, and when they urged him to accept their present he replied to them, that the man who was content with such a supper had no need for gold.[1] Epaminondas, talking of his table, which was most frugal, remarked: "Such a repast is never visited by treachery."[2] Alexander having sent Xenocrates a present of 50 talents, the latter invited the ambassadors to supper, and had them served a frugal repast; the next day, when they wished to hand over to him the 50 talents, he said to them: "What! was it not clear to you yesterday from the frugality of my table that money is

Plutarch, "Life of Cato."   [2] Ibid., "Life of Lycurgus."

useless to me?"[1] Helvetius relates that an English Minister on visiting a member of the Opposition with the intention of purchasing his vote, found him taking his meal, which consisted of a little mutton and water. "I should have thought," retorted the member of the House of Commons, "that the simplicity of my meal would have protected me against the insult of your offers." Saint Paul uttered the truth when he said: "Be sober." Sobriety, seemingly a modest virtue, has a considerable influence in reality upon men's conduct. If Mirabeau had practised it, if he had been less fond of pleasures, those of the table included, he would not have accepted from the King four bills of 250,000 francs, a pension of 6,000 francs a month, and the payment of his debts. Unfortunately, even when he was overwhelmed with debts, he could not get on without a cook, a valet, a coachman, horses, and the luxury of several mistresses.[2]

Danton paid his debts with the money (53,000 francs) given him by Marie Antoinette, because he was fond of pleasures, women, and high living.[3] It is well known what an important part the pleasures of the table played in the life of Talleyrand and other contemporary politicians.

The explanation of political corruption is to be

[1] Cicero, "Tusculanes," Bk. V., § 32.
[2] "Correspondance de Lamarck avec Mirabeau," Vol. I., p. 171. See, too, in the "Mémoires de Brissot," Vol. II., p. 392, the causes of Mirabeau's death. Mirabeau killed himself by the abuse of pleasure. He might have said, like Danton: "I have enjoyed myself to the top of my bent, it is time to sleep."
[3] Taine, "La Conquête Jacobine," p. 258.

sought most often in intemperate and luxurious habits and in the love of pleasure. Machiavelli wrote "The Prince" to please the Medici who had imprisoned him and subjected him to torture; he sought to obtain a post from them by recourse to base flatteries and by abandoning his old convictions, because he was needy and dissolute. He himself admitted that he had contracted the habit of extravagance, and that he was unable to force himself to exercise economy. It was in order to pay for his dissolute pleasures that Louis XV. speculated in wheat and became a shareholder in the association known as the "Compact of Famine Company." Despans-Cubière and Teste were men of pleasure.

CHAPTER VIII.

ELECTORAL CORRUPTION.

Corruption under universal suffrage—How votes are purchased—A wire-puller's manual—Cicero on the way to win votes—Political condottieri—Corruption of electorate by rich candidates—Electoral returns—Demagogues in political assemblies—Aristotle and Montesquieu on democracy—Democracy and merit—Political apathy of honest citizens—Evils of political indifference—Cato on public duty—La Bruyère on public life.

Machiavelli's counsel to Leo X. was: "Leave the people its elections in appearance, but tamper with the results, if they are not as you would wish, by buying votes or altering them during the poll." How many princes, ministers, and village Machiavellis have put this advice in practice in order to raise themselves to power or to maintain their hold upon it!

When Francis I. and Charles V. were disputing the title of Emperor of Germany, it was with purses full of gold that they fought each other. The issue was long uncertain, since four electors were perpetually selling and reselling themselves. And yet the Imperial Crown was in the gift of only seven electors, all of them high dignitaries of the

Empire. Charles V. gained the day because at the last moment he distributed 300,000 crowns.[1]

In Poland, where the throne was elective, the election of the King was usually a matter of money. "The throne was so often bought and sold," says Frederick II., "that it seemed as if the sale was effected in public in the market-place."[2] Condillac was so struck by the anarchy and corruption that reigned in Poland in the 18th century, that he foresaw that these vices would bring about the ruin of the kingdom.[3]

Before it was established it was believed that universal suffrage would make corruption impossible, and this passage of Aristotle was invoked: "A large quantity is always less corruptible, as is for example a large volume of water, and in the same way a majority is less easily corrupted than a minority.[4] Machiavelli remarked: "It takes but little to corrupt a few." At the time when the restricted suffrage was seen to be susceptible of intimidation and corruption, it was thought that universal suffrage would be able to maintain its independence. "It would be necessary," wrote de Tocqueville, "to buy too many persons at once to attain the end in view."[5] Unfortunately these optimistic previsions have not been realised; universal suffrage equally with restricted suffrage

[1] Bayle, "Dictionnaire," Article "Charles V."
[2] Frederick II., "Essai de Critique sur le Prince de Machiavel," Part II., ch. xx.
[3] "De l'Etude de l'Histoire," Part II., ch. ii.
[4] Aristotle, "Politica," Bk. III., ch. iii., § 6.
[5] De Tocqueville, "De la Démocratie en Amérique," Vol. II., p. 88.

can be corrupted. It is unnecessary to buy all the electors; it is sufficient to buy the political wire-pullers, whom the electors follow like a flock of sheep.

The governments that proclaim the loudest the virtues of universal suffrage are foremost in corrupting it. Were they really convinced of the wisdom of the people, they would abstain from exercising the least pressure upon it, they would allow it to manifest its wishes freely. In practice, while exalting the discernment of the people, they treat it as if it were still under age, and endeavour to force their candidates upon it by promises, threats, and the abuse of influence. The poll, thus practised, is a mere electoral comedy.

When, after a *coup d'état*, a government invites universal suffrage to pronounce upon a constitution, the constitution is always accepted; the voting under these circumstances is a mere formality. In particular, what is to be thought of the sincerity of the votes recorded by an army under the eyes of its chiefs? Marshal Saint-Cyr, referring to the voting of the Constitution of the Year III., by the soldiers under arms, was right in remarking that "it was one of those political tricks with which the French are decoyed."

Governments purchase the votes of a district by the promise of aid or of public works; they purchase the votes of influential electors by promising them posts or decorations; they purchase the votes of functionaries by promising them promotion or threatening them with dismissal. Independent electors are warned that they need expect no favour or even justice from the administration. The churches of independent communes are not kept in repair, and their roads are kept up imperfectly. The constituencies that refuse to elect the official candidates have to suffer from the hostility of the government.

"Men," says La Bruyère, "are disposed to be the slaves of one man that in turn they may lord it over somebody else."[1] At the period at which he lived the great were content to be the slaves of the King's caprices in order to draw from their status at court the right of assuming haughty and domineering airs. At the present day men consumed by political ambition grovel before the people and the electoral committees, and seek in this abasement a means of raising themselves in the world.

"What a book to write—'The Manual of the Perfect Candidate'!" exclaims Maxime du Camp, recalling a definition of politics given him by a former ambassador: "A question of extorting hush-money, of trafficking and often of brigandage." The Manual is not lacking: it was elaborated long since, in a serious form that makes it all the more amusing, by Quintus, Cicero's brother, under the title, "The Candidate for the Consulship." This essay on candidature constitutes the manual of the perfect wire-puller. In it Quintus describes all the subterfuges a candidate

[1] La Bruyère, "De la Cour."

ought to employ and recommends their use to his brother.

The candidate, says Quintus, should, in the first place, be affable and prodigal of blandishments. He should attend the fairs and markets, and call each elector by his name, taking care to be accompanied for this purpose by a "nomenclator," who will adroitly prime him with the electors' names. "The inhabitants of towns and of the country think that they are our friends as soon as they are known to us by name."[1] Cicero followed this advice. He wrote to his brother that he was "as pliant as a hair." Plutarch informs us, moreover, that he imposed upon himself the painful obligation of learning the names of his electors: "He accustomed himself to be acquainted not only with the names of the men of some position, but as well with the part of the town in which they lived, the fine properties they had in the country, the friends they consorted with and the neighbours they visited."[2]

To show oneself to the electors, to talk with them and to shake hands with them, are most important points. "I conducted myself," says Cicero, "in such fashion that my fellow-citizens saw me every day: I was perpetually in the Forum."[3] Sketching the portrait of the candidate on his own account, Cicero said, in his speech in defence of Murena, that he should show himself

---
[1] Quintus Cicero, "The Candidate for the Consulship."
[2] Plutarch, "Life of Cicero."
[3] Cicero, "Pro Plancio," XXVII.

in the Forum and on the field of Mars, "with a confident and hopeful aspect and surrounded by a numerous retinue." The electors do not vote for the candidate who is not confident of success. "I shall vote for another," they say to themselves, "since he despairs of his own chance."[1]

In large towns the candidate should not be content with having himself accompanied by his friends; he will do well to have himself followed by paid partisans, who shall applaud him, make him ovations, and insult his adversaries.[2]

The candidate should be specially careful not to make enemies, and to abstain from denouncing abuses, or at least to await the termination of the electoral campaign before doing so. One of his friends having neglected this precaution, Cicero says to him: "You do not know how to stand for the consulship, Servius, as I have often repeated to you, and on the very occasions when I saw you acting and speaking energetically, it struck me that you were giving evidence of the courage of a senator rather than of the prudence of a candidate. . . . But is it, then, forbidden to denounce injustice? No, to do so is even a duty, but the moment when one is a candidate is not the moment at which to make accusations." (XXI.)

When a candidate it is above all necessary to show oneself compliant: this complacency, which is "improper and dishonourable in other circum-

[1] Cicero, "Pro Murena," XXI.
[2] Ibid., XXXII.

stances of life, is indispensable when one is a candidate," says Cicero's brother in turn; ". . . a candidate has no other choice, seeing that his looks, his expression, his words must adapt themselves to the ideas and tastes of all those with whom he comes into contact." (XI.)

The most important point is to make every class of society believe that one intends to serve its interests. Act in such a way that "the Senate shall hope to find in you a champion of its authority; the knights and the rich and law-abiding people, judging by all your actions, a friend of order and public tranquillity; the masses (but solely owing to the popular tone of your speeches . . .) a magistrate, who will not be hostile to their interests."

The influence of the nobles being still great, Quintus advises his brother to seek their support, by persuading them that, at heart, they are both friendly to the party of the great and far removed from that of the people, and that if their utterances have had a popular trend, the reason was solely the wish to conciliate Pompey. Most eclectic in his political connections, Cicero sought the support both of the great and of the people, of honest citizens and of the riff-raff. He curried favour with all parties: "I have not fallen in the esteem of honest citizens," he wrote to Atticus, "and I have risen high in that of the riff-raff."[1]

According to Cicero, a candidate should always be making promises; of what matter is it if he

[1] Letter to Atticus, No. 21

be afterwards unable to keep them? He exposes himself, it is true, to reproaches and expressions of discontent after the election, but this inconvenience is remote and of no great gravity, while his promises assure him a great number of votes. Candidates are no less prodigal of promises at the present day; to some they promise government posts and to others reforms they know to be impracticable. The election over, these promises are forgotten, and the people, annoyed at not obtaining what has been promised them, lend ear to the speeches of the demagogues, who make capital out of their deceptions and say to them: "Those who are badly off can only find a faithful champion in one who is badly off himself: poor and ruined citizens can have no confidence in the promises of rich and powerful persons. . . . The destitute need an audacious chief who is in a like plight to march at their head."[1]

In former times there were princes who were reduced to the *rôle* of adventurers, of *condottieri*, and who offered and sold themselves indifferently to all parties. Politics also have their *condottieri*, who sell their electoral influence to the highest bidder. They are veritable election contractors; the candidate does all he can to have them on his side, because when he has their support the electors follow like sheep. Wire-pullers of this sort were already in existence in Rome. Quintus urges his brother to solicit their good offices and to win them over to his cause "by any means

[1] Cicero, "Pro Murena," XXV.

whatever." Electoral agents were so numerous at Rome that they were divided into several categories; there were the *deductores*, the *divisores*, and the *sequestres;* the first concerned themselves with the purchase of votes, the second paid for them, and the third held the money promised the electors, who, become suspicious and trusting little to promises, used to insist on the money being paid over in advance to a sort of stakeholder. Cicero relates that Verres, to assure his election, caused ten baskets full of money to be taken to a senator for use in the *comitia*, and that a distributor had undertaken to guarantee the result in consideration of five hundred thousand sesterces, *deposited in advance*.[1]

At the present day it is still often the richest and most generous candidate who obtains the preference. A man with a large fortune picks out a poor constituency and gets himself elected by voters who had never heard of his name before the opening of the electoral campaign. A candidate recently elected in the South of France, on being asked whether it was true that his expenses had amounted to a million of francs, replied in an off-hand tone: "To scarcely a hundred thousand francs." When a candidate is in a position to spend a hundred thousand francs in a poor constituency his success is assured. The power of money in elections makes itself felt in England as well as in France. The matter aroused the serious attention of the

[1] Cicero, "First Speech against Verres," VIII.

English Parliament, which endeavoured to fix a limit to expenses by establishing a maximum. At Rome, Cato vainly endeavoured to put a stop to corruption. Having remarked that "persons went about bidding for and buying the votes of the people," he "bitterly rebuked the people for this base and shameful traffic," and brought an accusation against Murena, who had got himself appointed Consul by buying votes. Cicero, however, obtained the acquittal of Murena, and scoffed at the austerity of Cato and the Stoics.

In former times it was necessary to be either a soldier or a priest to arrive at power; "nowadays, thanks to the progress of rhetoric, it is sufficient to be able to speak well to become chief of the people."[1] This explains how it is that so many barristers are candidates. Quintus Cicero offers special advice to this class of candidates. Since a barrister is exposed to making enemies by pleading against the adversaries of his clients, Quintus advises him to present them his excuses by urging the necessities of his profession, and to promise them for the future great devotion to their interests and the aid of his eloquence.

A candidate must not content himself with being generous; when rendering a service the expression of his countenance should be eager and engaging, for electors "not only desire that one shall undertake to satisfy them, but that when giving the undertaking one shall make a show of zeal and of holding them in high esteem.

---

[1] Aristotle, "Politica," Bk. VIII., ch. iv., § 4.

.... People attach more importance to words and manners than to the service itself and to realities."

For country electors the year in which an election falls is a year of double harvests and free banquets. The candidates supply them with drink and often with food. This custom of banquets is very old; it existed in Athens and Rome.[1] In Aristophanes' comedy "The Knights" the following dialogue occurs between the people and the candidates. "'Take this drink,' says the first candidate. 'What delicious wine!' replies the people. 'Try this piece of rich cake,' retorts the second candidate. And who treats you the best, people, you and your belly?" The people are equally pleased with the wine and the cake and are perplexed how to choose between the good things offered them; they proceed to make a careful examination of the culinary merits of the two candidates, and leave them as long as possible in doubt so as to excite them to fresh liberalities.

There would be something to be thankful for if the candidates merely dealt out refreshing drinks to the people and nourished them with cake, but they also deal out sophisms and nourish them with

---

[1] Cicero approves of the repasts that a candidate gives in the interests of his election, and accuses Cato of excessive austerity because he blamed them (" Pro Murena," XXXV.). These corrupt customs contributed none the less to the fall of the Republic. The ambitious persons who wished to enslave the Roman people with a view to make themselves popular resorted to the practice "of often banqueting the public decennaries, taking the best means to circumvent this riff-raff, which is most impressed when the palate is tickled." (La Boétie.)

false promises; they appeal as much to the ear as to the belly.

Electoral corruption is often accompanied by fraud. The dead and the absent are made to vote; votes are inserted into the ballot-boxes before the poll has begun, voting papers prepared in advance are substituted for those in the ballot-box after care has been taken on some pretext or another to order the public out of the room. The constitution of the committee, a matter of great importance, is often proceeded with in a fraudulent manner; with the connivance of the mayor, the party in power causes some of its trusted adherents to pass the night in the room where the voting is to take place, or introduces them into the room before the town hall is opened, so as to assure the committee being composed of their partisans. In Provence there is a saying to the effect that he who controls the ballot-boxes controls the election, so easy is it for members of the committee to falsify the poll. All these different kinds of frauds have come under my notice in the course of my judicial experience; I have seen minorities assure themselves the majority by fraud and maintain themselves in power for several years.

From the moment that it is possible for candidates to get elected by fraud, flattery, and corruption there is little cause for astonishment that the moral and intellectual level of political assemblies has sunk so low and that statesmen are becoming of punier and punier calibre. A loud voice and an elastic conscience suffice of a sudden to enable men who represent neither labour nor intelligence nor honesty, to represent the people, to become famous, to attack Ministers, to treat in Parliament the gravest questions without understanding them, to upset legislation and to appoint or dismiss functionaries. This being the case, adventurers and persons of dubious status throw themselves into politics, with which modest and laborious men will have nothing more to do, and politicians are sure to come to the front of the type of Herennius, tribune of the people, whom Cicero styled "a starveling."[1] Demagogues wrest the power from the hands of wise men, and, like sailors who drive the pilot from the helm, they "seize upon the vessel, fall upon the provisions, drink and eat to excess, and steer the vessel as such persons might be expected to steer it."[2]

Discerning men are still met with in political assemblies, "but they are not listened to; pride, envy, and avarice are the three firebrands that have inflamed men's hearts."[3]

Aristotle was of opinion that in the majority of cases the crowd is a better judge than any individual whatever, and that it may be left the right of deliberating upon public affairs and of dispensing justice.[4] Montesquieu, too, has stated that the people choose their representatives with

---
[1] Letter to Atticus, No. 24.
[2] Plato, "Republic," Bk. VI.
[3] Dante, "Inferno," ch. vi.
[4] Aristotle, "Politica," Bk. III., ch. x., § 5; ch. vi., §§ 4-6.

admirable discernment.[1] Neither history nor the observation of facts seems to me to bear out this view. The Athenian democracy, which in reality was an intellectual aristocracy, often lacked discernment; the best citizens were persecuted, exiled, and condemned to death by it, and it loaded worthless men with honours. Socrates and Phocion were condemned to drink the hemlock, Aristides was banished, Miltiades thrown into prison, Themistocles died in exile, etc. The Athenian democracy was most jealous of men who distinguished themselves by their talent and uprightness; it ostracised such men. Montesquieu has affirmed that ostracism at Athens "was an admirable institution,"[2] and that it proved the mildness of the popular government that had recourse to it.[3] And yet a sentence of banishment for ten years was passed without the accused having an opportunity of defending himself.

The Athenian democracy often raised incapable and unworthy men to posts of honour. After Pericles, Athens was governed by Eucrates, a tow merchant, and by Lysides, a dealer in sheep. Hyperbolos, a lamp merchant, was most popular for a time. Aristophanes wittily pointed out this weakness of the people for incapable men who flatter them. In his comedy "The Knights," when the Generals Demosthenes and Nicias wish to get rid of the demagogue, "an out-and-out rascal,

---

[1] Montesquieu, "Esprit des Lois," Bk. II., ch. ii.; Bk. XI., ch. vi.
[2] Ibid., Bk. XXIX., ch vii.   [3] Ibid., Bk. XXVI., ch. xvii.

calumny personified, . . . who fawns like a dog, flatters (the people), caresses, blandishes and dupes them to the top of his bent," they offer the power to a pork-butcher, telling him: "To-day you are nothing, to-morrow you will be everything, the chief of happy Athens. . . ." The Pork-butcher: "Explain to me how a sausage-seller can become a great man." Demosthenes: "But that is precisely it; you will be great because you are a sorry, shameless rogue, a child of the markets."

Men are so constituted that they often experience a feeling of jealousy and aversion for those who are overwhelmingly their superiors. Mirabeau's talent brought him a number of enemies. The French Republicans who in recent times have been ostracised by their party have been so treated, not because they undertook the defence of liberty menaced by the Jacobin spirit, but because there was no pardoning them their superiority. Victorious generals have come under suspicion because they excited envy. At Athens as soon as a politician became popular on account of his uprightness and capacity, his adversaries denounced him to the people as aiming at a tyranny. Aristides was denounced by Themistocles. The hero of Salamis, having acquired great power, also excited jealousy and was banished in his turn. Cimon, one of the best of the Athenian generals, was falsely accused of peculation and ostracised. Pericles caused Thucydides to be banished, etc.

In the Athenian republics the people, when choosing their magistrates, often gave incapacity the preference over merit, and allotted posts to the unworthy. In our own time in France have we not seen the people prefer a schoolmaster to M. Ch. de Rémusat and M. Taine? During the French Revolution was not Marat the people's idol? The people have a liking for charlatans and scapegraces. The Kings who have been economical, pacific, and whose private lives have been without reproach, Louis XIII., Louis XVI., and Louis-Philippe, for example, have not been popular. On the contrary, opinion is in general indulgent towards the prodigal, the warlike, and the dissolute. To the man who counsels industry, thrift, and temperance, the people prefer the charlatan, who promises the impossible and keeps what is substantial for himself. The people are disposed to keep away from public affairs men of intellectual and moral superiority, of whom they are jealous, and prefer incapable men who resemble themselves. *Similis simili gaudet.* The following observation of Plutarch is still applicable to the people: "The people, . . who desired that all things should be entirely dependent upon them and their authority, were ill-pleased and grieved when some private person surpassed the others in good renown and good reputation."

In times of crisis the people forget their jealousies and appeal to the devotion of the men of talent of whom they stand in need, but in periods of calm they are none too capable of making a right selection unless they are guided. "There is nothing more deceptive than elections," says Cicero. "Who would have thought that Philippus, in spite of his talent, his services, his popularity, and his birth, would have been vanquished by Herennius? That Catullus, a model of gentleness, discernment, and integrity, should have been worsted by Mantius? Finally that Scaurus, a person of such importance, so distinguished a citizen, so courageous a senator, should not have got the better of Maximus?"[1] Who would have thought that at the elections of 1893 MM. Georges Picot, Paul Leroy-Beaulieu, de Mun, Piou, and Lamy would be beaten by their adversaries? Under the absolute monarchies of the past experienced statesmen were frequently removed from the conduct of affairs by court intrigues and the caprice of royal mistresses; for example, the two best Ministers of Louis XV., d'Argenson and Choiseul, owed their disgrace to Mdme. de Pompadour and Mdme. du Barry respectively. To-day they are kept out of office by the intrigues of the flatterers of the people and the ignorance of the masses.

The selections would be better if honest men of all parties could be brought to make common cause and displayed more activity, but in general they are indolent, apathetic, and indifferent from love of quiet and false prudence, "poor simpletons who believe they will still have their fish-ponds though the commonwealth cease to

[1] Cicero, "Pro Murena," XVII.

exist,"[1] and who imagine that politics will leave them alone if they do not concern themselves with politics. They ought to understand that the great danger run by society proceeds from the ignorance and incapacity of the people, who are none the less sovereign, and that it is the duty of good citizens to enlighten, love, and serve the people, to dissipate their prejudices, to foster their better feelings, and above all to unmask their flatterers. The people are only the prey of charlatans because they are insufficiently enlightened; to snatch them from the clutches of demagogues they must be educated. The education of the people is not the duty of the Government merely; it is the duty as well of all those who possess enlightenment, fortune, and leisure. The public affairs of a country ought to be the personal affairs of every citizen who loves his country.

Plato, convinced that politics are inimical to virtue, advised the wise man to keep aloof from the conduct of affairs. Epicurus made him the same recommendation if he would live happily. Neither seems to me to be in the right. The man who occupies himself with politics from a sense of duty need not demean himself, and in the feeling of the good he does and the evil he prevents he may find austere satisfactions to his conscience that are of greater worth than tranquillity.

Political indifference is a serious error, because it leaves the field open to the unworthy and the

---

[1] Cicero, "Letter to Atticus," No. 23.

incapable. Many people imagine that the very excess of evil may produce good,[1] and for this reason they do nothing to stop the evil. This conduct is neither estimable nor skilful: evil ought always to be prevented.

When Pompey endeavoured to keep Cato of Utica away from the Senate, Cato answered him that he "was not present to concern himself with the affairs of the commonwealth for the purpose of enriching himself, as was the case with some, nor to acquire reputation, . . . but having chosen participation in the government after mature deliberation as the proper occupation of a good man, he esteemed himself bound to attend thereto, and to give the matter even more careful thought than does the bee to the building of the waxen cells where it deposits its honey."[2] If honest men had, like Cato, a sense of their duty, they would be at pains to enter public life; instead of putting up with the democracy with disgust, they would do better to enlighten it, to give it their affection, and to direct it.

Absorbed by their business or their pleasures, the egoists, when they see the rising flood of barbarism that threatens to sweep away society, say with Louis XV.: "After me the deluge! After all, the present state of things will last as long as we shall." They forget that by leaving evil passions free to develop themselves the deluge may come quicker than they think.

[1] This false idea, which Mirabeau urged upon the Court, caused the Constituent Assembly to make grave mistakes.
[2] Plutarch, "Life of Cato."

Finally there are soured spirits who say with La Bruyère: "The only man I esteem more highly than a great statesman is he who refrains from becoming one, and who is ever strengthening himself in the conviction that the world does not deserve that one should occupy oneself with it."[1] La Bruyère, who was a Christian, should have remembered that the world always deserves that one should concern oneself with it, since it is the work of God, and contempt for humanity is not a Christian sentiment. Humanity, I allow, is not always engaging; it has its ugly aspects, but it has its noble aspects as well. Moreover, if it be often guilty, it is always unhappy, and its misfortunes, by inspiring compassion, should awaken at the same time the spirit of devotion. The Chancellor de l'Hopital, who lived at so gloomy a period, and who had himself undergone so many trials, spoke out against the discouragement that was overtaking good men, whom he advised to take part in public affairs, telling them: "After God, it is to our country that we owe the service of our devotion. When you have offered yourself to your country, persevere, suffer in its service, to the extreme limit of life, to the gates of the tomb, so long as it desires your aid."

[1] La Bruyère, "Des Jugements."

CHAPTER IX.

THE CORRUPTION OF LAW AND JUSTICE BY POLITICS.

The law as an instrument of injustice—English penal laws against Irish Catholics—Laws are made to favour the party in power—Exceptional laws are political laws—Lawyers find plausible reasons for bad laws—It is independent thinkers and not lawyers who improve law—Political assemblies often pass unjust laws—Laws are often passed under the influence of political passion—Characteristics of men in masses—In assemblies the violent often intimidate the moderate—Crude legislation and useful reforms—The corruption of justice by politics—Judicial murders—The calumniation of political opponents—Servility of judges to governments—Servility in the old English courts of justice—Juries and justice—French magistrates under the old régime—Governments dislike an independent magistracy—Independence of character essential to a good judge—Dangers of special commissions—The French Revolutionary Tribunal—Military men as judges—The police in politics—Judges should not be politicians.

The law has been transformed by politics into an instrument of proscription and spoliation. Barbarous peoples make use of arms to kill and rob; people who think themselves civilised make use of laws. The law is as murderous as firearms, as potent an instrument of destruction as the axe, and depredations go on under cover of it as highway robbery under cover of a forest. Murder and robbery have been made part and parcel of the law; proscription and spoliation have been given legal shape.

Legal proscription is more hateful than brutal violence, because upon iniquity it superimposes hypocrisy. The legists who lend persecution a legal guise are more depraved than those who butcher their fellow-men.

Politics have filled legislation with absurdities and hypocritical cruelties. Can anything be more monstrous, for example, than the English laws for the suppression of Catholicism in Ireland? The English legists devised a system of laws, of which Burke said that "it was the most cunning and powerful instrument of oppression that had ever been invented by the perverse genius of man to ruin, debase, and deprave a nation and to corrupt in it even the most unchangeable wellsprings of human nature." These atrocious laws, said Canning again, seem to be the outcome of all the most cruel researches against human nature, of all the most atrocious combinations against men. In order to keep the Catholics in a state of destitution and ignorance, the law had forbidden them the acquisition of landed property and the exercise of liberal professions. While not making Protestant instruction obligatory, the law banished the Catholic teachers; it did not forbid the Catholic form of worship, but it expelled the Catholic bishops and punished them with death in the event of their return, etc., etc.

These laws had for their object the despoilment of the Catholics as well as their persecution. "The English Parliament," says Walter Scott, "had arrogated to itself the right of making laws for Ireland, and exercised it in such a manner as to shackle the commerce of the kingdom as much as possible, to subordinate it to English commerce, and to keep it in a state of dependence." English legislation ruined the Irish wool manufacture. Ireland having protested against the law prohibiting the exportation of woollen goods, the House of Commons presented an address to the Queen complaining "that although the wool manufacture was a branch of English commerce, which the Legislature looked after with the utmost vigilance, yet Ireland, dependent upon and protected by England, not content with the liberty accorded it of having cotton manufactures, further claimed to devote its capital and credit to weaving woollens and manufacturing cloth to the detriment of England." Swift, indignant at English greed, urged the Irish in a pamphlet to make use of none but Irish products, and not to employ cloth stuffs imported from England. Criminal proceedings were instituted against the printer of the pamphlet.

I have cited the English laws against Ireland as an example of how persecution and spoliation are given hypocritically a legal shape. Analogous examples are to be found in the legislation of all peoples.

Politics, which are hostile to common law, tend

towards the creation of privileges; they have instituted privileged classes, orders, and castes which did not pay taxes, and obtained the most important public posts. Undoing the work of God, who gave the same rights to all men, they have created inequality in the matter of civil and political rights, they have altered the true mutual relations of men, and they have established inequality even in respect to justice.[1]

The law ought to aim at the protection of the liberty and property of all citizens, but politics have always obtained the passing of laws favourable to the interests of those in power. When the power is in the hands of an aristocracy, the laws are framed in the interests of that aristocracy, and in the interests of the democracy when it is a democracy that wields the power. Under the old régime commoners were excluded in a general way from public functions; in several Italian republics, on the contrary, this exclusion was visited upon the nobles.

Laws ought to be general and impartial: politics makes them biassed and frames laws of exception.

Legislation has been corrupted to such an extent by politics, that Sir Thomas More, who, as Lord Chancellor, was well versed in legal matters, could not refrain from exclaiming: "When I reflect upon the laws and governments of our world, may I die if I find therein even the merest shadow of justice or equity! Good God! what

[1] Under the old régime the nobleman guilty of a crime still enjoyed privileges. There were different penalties for the nobleman and the commoner.

equity, what justice is ours!"[1] The presence of unjust laws in the legislation of all peoples is to be attributed to political considerations. Laws of exception are always political laws, they are the arms to which parties have recourse to destroy their adversaries. In 1816 a Deputy cynically remarked in the Chamber: "Last year I voted measures of public safety, because they were to be employed against the opposite party; now that they may be employed against ourselves I will not hear of them."[2] When the law against the Emigrants was voted (it punished the crime of emigration with death) a speaker raised his voice in favour of the servants who had followed their masters abroad, but the Deputy who had charge of the Bill objected to him: "The law we propose is a law suggested by the circumstances; it is a weapon of offence; why occupy ourselves with any injustice it may involve?"[3]

When political passions have caused the voting of iniquitous laws, there may be found, not indeed a justification of these laws, but an explanation of them, and sometimes an extenuating circumstance in the passions of the legislators. What, however, is even more distressful than the voting of iniquitous laws, is their justification by legists who, considering them long after they were passed, do not share the political passions of the legislators. There is not an unjust law upon which the lawyers have not commented with approval.

[1] Sir Thomas More, "Utopia," Bk. II.
[2] Berenger, "De la Justice Criminelle," p. 12.
[3] Mortimer-Ternaux, op. cit., Vol. V., p. 164.

Grotius countenanced slavery, and Blackstone justified the assimilation of "papistry" to the crime of high treason.[1] Merlin, who was Procureur-Général at the Court of Appeal, "lent his great legal science and his marvellous skill as a lawyer to the framing of that masterpiece of insidious tyranny, the law of suspects."[2] The Chancellor Pasquier said of him: "I have never known a man less gifted with the sense of what is just and unjust. Everything appeared to him to be well and good, provided it was the consequence of a text."[3] On the occasion of the 18th Fructidor, the man whom Touillier called the prince of jurisconsults drew up in common with the Directors, who were the authors of this *coup d'état*, the Bill that ordained the transportation of a great number of the members of the Council of the Five Hundred, of the Council of the Ancients, and of two moderate Directors, Carnot and Barthélemy. Merlin, when Minister of Justice under the Directory, was consulted by a court-martial as to whether it ought to accord an emigrant a counsel as he had requested; his answer was, that the intention of the law had been to deprive the Emigrants of the services of counsel, a decision that was a reproduction of Robespierre's utterance: "Only patriots are allowed counsel." Cambacérès drew up the decrees organising the revolutionary tribunal. The future Minister of

[1] Blackstone, "The English Criminal Code."
[2] Albert Sorel, "L'Europe et la Révolution Française," Part 3, Bk. II., ch. iv.
[3] "Mémoires du Chancelier Pasquier," Vol. I., p. 268.

Justice of the Empire asked the Convention to nominate a revolutionary Ministry and to concentrate all authority in the same hands.[1] A great number of the jurisconsults have accepted the task of giving an appearance of legality to measures of exception and of justifying the violation of judicial procedure in political trials. The lawyers who sat in the Senate under the Second Empire voted the Law of General Safety, whereas a soldier, Marshal MacMahon, refused to vote it.

Legal science ought to be accompanied by a lofty intelligence and a philosophical spirit. In our time, Portalis, Troplong, Renouard, and F. Helie have possessed this philosophic spirit, but it too often happens that lawyers are slaves of the texts and do not comment on them in a critical spirit. In consequence it is philosophers and not lawyers who have brought about the most progress in legislation.

During the 18th century Voltaire and Beccaria contributed in a greater degree to the reform of criminal law than all the lawyers of the period.

Political assemblies have voted the most unjust laws with the utmost docility. The Roman Emperors, Henry VIII. of England, Robespierre, the Directory, Napoleon I., all despots in a word, have obtained the unreserved support of the political bodies for all the laws they have proposed. When Henry VIII. "wished to rid himself of his wives, Parliament lent him its aid; when he desired to put his Ministers to death, Parlia-

[1] Wallon, "Histoire du Tribunal Révolutionnaire," Vol. I., p. 52.

ment condemned them without judgment; finally, when the fancy took him to make laws of his own free will, Parliament gave him the authorisation.[1] When the first decree against the Emigrants was introduced not a single voice was raised against the injustice of the proposed measure. The Convention, which trembled before Robespierre, voted, without discussion, the 22 articles of the law of the 22nd Prairial, which hastened on a series of judicial murders, and then endeavoured to annul its vote. When the Directory laid the laws of proscription before the Five Hundred on the 18th Fructidor, nobody protested against their adoption. Later, after the explosion of the infernal machine, the Senate voted with the same docility the proscription of 130 democrats falsely accused by Fouché of this conspiracy and declared "that the resolution of the First Consul was a measure that safeguarded the Constitution."[2] In 1814 this same Senate which had shown itself so docile voted the deposition of the Emperor and prefaced its vote by an act of accusation against him. The constitutional scheme it adopted was voted unanimously; among those who voted it were regicides.[3]

[1] John Russell, "Essai sur l'Histoire du Gouvernement et de la Constitution Britanniques," p. 23.

[2] Fouché accused these 130 democrats, knowing them to be innocent, to save his situation. The First Consul learnt the truth later on, but evinced no regret: "he held that what had been done had been well done from every point of view; that he had been rid of what he termed the 'general staff' of the Jacobins." (Thiers, Bk. VIII.)

[3] The Senate forgot to insert in this constitutional scheme a clause relating to its pecuniary interests.

The passions that stir assemblies do not allow them to listen to reason when voting upon the laws submitted to them. In dispensing justice, as in passing laws, calm, self-possession, and impartiality are needed. Assemblies, however, are impassioned; fear, vanity, anger, and hatred assume extraordinary intensity in a gathering of men. Aristotle seems to me to be mistaken when he says that men assembled together are wiser than isolated men, and that the more numerous they are the wiser they are. "When an individual," he writes, "is the slave of anger or any other passion his judgment is necessarily warped. It would be exceedingly difficult, however, for the entire majority, in a like case, to lose its head and to blunder. . . . It may be admitted that the majority, each member of which, taken separately, is not a remarkable man, is yet superior to exceptional men, if not individually, at least taken as a whole, just as a meal of which the expenses are shared in common is more splendid than that for which a single person pays."[1] If the enlightenment of an assembly were in proportion to its number, as the magnificence of a dinner paid for in common is in proportion to the number of the guests, assemblies strong in number would be wiser and more enlightened and would vote better laws. In point of fact it is the contrary that occurs; the value of an assembly

[1] Aristotle, "Politica," Bk. III., ch. x., § 6; ch. vi., § 4. Spinoza also was of opinion "that it is almost impossible for the majority in a numerous assembly to agree upon what is absurd." ("Traité Th ologico-Politique," ch. xvi.)

does not increase with the number of the members composing it; on the contrary, the more numerous an assembly is, the less useful work it performs.[1]

Anticipating the observations made by contemporary psychologists upon the character of political assemblies,[2] Aristophanes, in opposition to the views of Aristotle, is of opinion that men when gathered together are inferior to isolated men, that their passions gather strength as their numbers increase, and that they are less reasonable when they form part of a crowd. When Cleon and the Pork-butcher are disputing the favours of the people, Cleon asks the people to convoke the assembly to decide which of the two has the most affection for it. Thereupon the Pork-butcher replies: "Yes, yes, decide, so long as it be not in the Pnyx (the place where the popular assemblies were held). *The People:* I cannot hold the assembly elsewhere. It is in the Pnyx that you must appear before me. *The Pork-butcher:* Ye Gods! I am undone. In his own home this old man is the most sensible of men, but as soon as he seats himself upon those accursed stone benches, he is then agape, as if he were hanging his pigs by the stalk."[3]

---

[1] Morality, also, does not increase with numbers. Men mutually influence each other for the bad. There is a rot peculiar to assemblies as to hospitals.

[2] Sighele, "La Foule Criminelle."

[3] Cato compared the Romans when they were gathered together in an assembly to a flock of sheep. Solon had made the same observation as Aristophanes upon the character of assemblies. He said to the Athenians: "Each of you in his private concerns is circumspect and cunning as a fox, but all together you are clowns and dull of understanding." (Plutarch, "Life of Solon.")

In numerous assemblies the violent intimidate the moderate and make use of them to get laws of proscription and spoliation voted. Did not the Girondins vote the death of Louis XVI., whom they wished to save, out of weakness and the fear of becoming unpopular, and vote, too, the creation of the revolutionary tribunal and of the Committee of Public Safety, both of them instruments of the most odious tyranny? Through fear the members of the "Plain" and of the "Marsh" became regicides and revolutionaries; they were the docile instruments of Robespierre, who protected them.[1] The violent would not succeed in getting laws of proscription and spoliation voted unless they had as auxiliaries moderate men, lacking force of character, to vote laws of which they inwardly disapprove.

Business discussions in a numerous assembly are always desultory and incoherent. Questions are studied to better purpose in committee than at public sittings. The real work is done in committees by men of ripe experience and by specialists. Fine speakers acquire too much influence

[1] Durand de Maillane, who belonged to the Right of the Convention, declared that Robespierre consistently protected the Deputies of the Right, "doubtless to make of them a rampart for himself in case of need." These Deputies long hesitated to make common cause with the adversaries of Robespierre so as to effect his overthrow. When Robespierre was attacked on the 9th Thermidor he turned to the Deputies of the Right and said to them: "Deputies of the Right, honourable men, virtuous men, give me the authorisation to speak which murderers refuse me." "He hoped," says Durand de Maillane, "for this reward for the protection he had afforded us, but our minds were made up." (Op. cit., p. 200.)

in a numerous gathering, whereas well-informed conscientious men do not occupy the place they deserve, because they speak without passion or any other concern than to arrive at truth and justice. When the leaders of the Catholic and Protestant parties assembled at Poissy, the Chancellor de l'Hopital begged the Queen to dissolve the gathering because it was too numerous and too passionate, and to replace it by five delegates from each party.

A numerous assembly is subject to the vagaries of a crowd; it has a weakness for voluble and sonorous discourses and for listening to orators who flatter its passions—to the well-informed man it often prefers the man who pleases. "Orators," said Rivarol, "are the passions of great assemblies." The gift of speech is not always accompanied by judgment, and fine speakers are at times more concerned with the effect produced than with the gist of the question under discussion. Napoleon I. said of them that "they lacked logic and were pitiable debaters." An orator experiences great pleasure in speaking and seeks agreeable emotions in an oratorical bout, just as a soldier delights in battle for the sake of the emotions it affords him. The pleasure of getting the better of a rival or of upsetting a ministry and taking its place are sweet to an orator, but the truth concerns him but little.

The parliamentary system has its good points, but it offers the disadvantage of favouring to too great an extent orators, barristers, and professors.[1] Men whose sphere is action or thought are eclipsed by men having the gift of speech. It is by speeches that great reputations are made. The right of speech in parliamentary assemblies is a guarantee of political liberty, and when it is exercised by such men as Royer-Collard, Martignac, de Serre, Guizot, Thiers, or Jules Simon, it conduces to the education of the country and enlightens opinion. Side by side, however, with these great orators, who combine solidity of thought and acquaintance with public affairs with the gift of speech, how numerous are the mere word-mills and the tinkling cymbals who have occupied the parliamentary arena. Of how many speeches may it be said: " *Verba et voces prætereaque nihil!*" How many vain and blundering speakers ask the Government, at a critical moment, for explanations that may give rise to grave difficulties! How many Deputies, afflicted with verbal incontinence, speak for the sake of speaking, and essay to be witty when the circumstances demand seriousness! "Since I have had the honour of belonging to the Senate," says a personage in Saint-Evremond's comedy, "Sir Politick," "I have observed that the desire to show off our wit and our conceit in our eloquence often make us wander from the subject under discussion to touch upon general topics which have nothing to do with the matter in hand." Mdme.

---

[1] In the Legislative Assembly 400 Deputies out of 745 were barristers who did not occupy the front rank at the Bar.

de Staël has remarked that the most inconceivable feature of the trial of Louis XVI. was the torrent of words poured forth by the Deputies in the course of so solemn a discussion: "To think that vanity should persist in connection with such a scene."[1]

What laws are to be hoped for from numerous assemblies, whose members have received no preparation for their *rôle* of legislators, and who are principally concerned with their electoral interests? They pile laws upon laws, incessantly making and unmaking them, according to the interest of the moment. Laws are no longer engraved upon marble or bronze, but are traced upon wax or sand, so short a time do they last. Their authority is affected by their mobility.

Laws are voted without having been studied, or without anterior laws being taken into consideration. It is pitiful to see inexperienced legislators, who are sometimes beardless, and whose orthography even is occasionally weak, play havoc with legislation, repealing useful laws, voting laws that are useless or harmful, after insulting each other in heated discussions, and supporting or combating Bills from purely political motives. Why should not Bills due to parliamentary initiative be referred to the Council of State? Why not have them examined by men who have made a special study of legislation? To make a pair of boots an apprenticeship is

[1] Mdme. de Staël, "Considérations sur la Révolution Française" Part III., ch. xii.

necessary, and it is equally needful to draw up the text of a Bill. If shoemakers made our clothes and tailors our boots, we should be badly shod and badly dressed.

Legislative instability is one of the dangers that attend democracy. The United States, where its working was long since pointed out by Hamilton, Jefferson, and Madison, suffer from it. What is more painful still, however, is the employment of fraudulent manœuvres to secure the passing of laws. The votes requisite to form the majority are sometimes obtained by corruption, fraud, and forgery.

While legislation is upset by useless or bad laws, necessary reforms are postponed. Why modify the law as to the sale of intoxicating drinks, politicians ask? The vendors of intoxicating drinks are excellent electoral agents! Why reform the law of elections in such a way as to allow of the representation of minorities? It is so agreeable to oppress our adversaries! Why do away with abuses by which we profit? On the eve of the Revolution, when it was proposed to effect reforms, a tax-farmer remarked, in like fashion: "Why change? We are so well off."

The Corruption of Justice by Politics.

"The Deputies who have recourse to bayonets are blunderers," said Camille Desmoulins. "The art of tyranny consists in attaining the same ends by means of judges." More, indeed, can be effected by political judges than by bayonets: the slaughtered adversaries can be slandered and dishonoured. The fury of the multitude and summary executions by arms are less horrible than judicial murders, which, accompanied as they always are by hypocrisy, lend a semblance of legality to violence.

The executioners pose as victims, and transform the victims into criminals, after the manner of the wolf rebuking the lamb for troubling the water. The Jews said to Pilate, when they led Jesus Christ before him: "We found this fellow perverting the nation."[1] Socrates was accused of corrupting the young. The Roman Emperors persecuted the Christians on the pretence that they disturbed the public peace. After the massacre of St. Bartholomew legal proceedings were begun against the victims; the Huguenots were accused of having contemplated massacring the Catholics. Henry VIII. calumniated his victims before putting them to death; he tried to dishonour Sir Thomas More by accusing him of corruption. Maurice of Nassau obtained the condemnation of Barneveldt by falsely accusing him of having intended to betray his country to Spain. Charles II. sent Sidney and Lord Russell to the scaffold by implicating them in a trumped-up conspiracy. When Colonel Hutchinson was arrested under Charles II., although a former adversary of Cromwell, he learned "that a ministerial despatch had enjoined upon the lieutenant

---

[1] St. Luke xxiii. 2.

of the county in which he resided to involve him in some conspiracy or other."[1] The Jacobins proscribed the Girondins—the truest defenders of the Republic—after accusing them of wishing to betray the Republic. At the time of the September massacres the imprisoned victims were accused of plotting against the Republic. At Bordeaux, during the Fronde, the "Ormée," anxious to commit its violent acts under the cloak of legality, also instituted a tribunal, in which an apothecary filled the post of Procureur-Général and the judges were artisans, shoemakers, and a confectioner.

Governments create exceptional tribunals to give an air of legality to proscriptions. As Commines says, they wreak their vengeance "under the shadow of justice, and have professional men ready to fall in with their wishes and to make out of a venial sin a mortal sin." It is well known how numerous political trials were under the Roman Emperors. "I have nothing else to write of," says Tacitus, "but barbarous orders, continuous accusations, . . . unjust condemnations, and trials that all terminate the same way."[2] Under the Roman Republic a law punished crimes that violated the dignity of the Roman people. "This law punished deeds, but left words unpunished. Augustus was the first to apply it to scandalous libels."[3] Tiberius extended it still further. Accusations of high

---

[1] A. Thierry, "Dix Ans d'Etudes Historiques," p. 91.
[2] Tacitus, "Annales," Bk. IV., § 33.
[3] Tacitus, "Annales," Bk. I., § 72.

treason became exceedingly numerous, and afforded informers a means of enriching themselves. "Tiberius always found judges ready to condemn as many persons as he could suspect."[1] It was his custom to be present at these trials. On one occasion, being highly incensed against a Pretor accused of having spoken of him in insulting terms, he declared that in this case he would himself give his opinion, aloud and on oath. A Senator, Cn. Piso, had the courage to say to him: "In what order will you give your opinion, Cæsar? If you speak first your opinion will be there for me to follow; if you speak after us all, I shall be afraid of differing from your opinion unwittingly."[2] Troubled by this speech, Tiberius abandoned his project and permitted the acquittal of the Pretor. The independence of Cn. Piso was not imitated by the other Senators, who vied with each other in servility. An historian was accused of having published a work in which he praised Brutus and termed Cassius the most ignoble of Romans: prosecuted by the creatures of Sejanus, he let himself die of starvation, and the Senate ordered that his books should be burned by the ediles. Under Nero, the Senators condemned the most virtuous citizens at a sign from the Emperor, on the plea that if they were not the enemies of the Emperor they were held to be. Trembling for their own safety, they sought security in servility. After the murder of Agrippina, they affected to believe that

---

[1] Montesquieu, "Grandeur et Décadence," ch. xiv.
[2] Tacitus, "Annales," Bk. I., § 73.

Nero had only ordered this crime to escape from a conspiracy, and they ordained prayers in all the temples and annual games to celebrate its discovery. Dressed in festive garments they came out to meet the parricide as he mounted the Capitol to render thanks to the gods. Every time that the Emperor ordered somebody to be exiled or assassinated, the Senators ordained a thanksgiving service.

Prior to the Revolution of 1688 the English courts were no less servile and cruel than the Roman Senate. Macaulay compared them to an unclean public slaughter-house, to which each party dragged its adversaries in turn, and where it found the same venal and ferocious butchers awaiting its custom.[1] After the massacres for which he was responsible in Ireland, Cromwell instituted a court, which continued to sentence the Catholics to death; it is known in history as the "court of carnage."

The jury showed itself more independent under Charles I. When Lord Strafford wished to make the county of Connaught an appanage of the King, he left no stone unturned to obtain a favourable verdict from the jury, but his efforts were unsuccessful. The jury also resisted Cromwell, who in his irritation at its independence re-established exceptional courts, and alleged that the institution of the jury was a hindrance to justice, since it subordinated the sacredness of verdicts to the whims of the ignorant and vulgar

[1] Macaulay, "Essays."

sort; that in this manner the most important points of law ceased to be decided in accordance with legal science, but were made to depend upon the whims and prejudices of a gathering got together at hazard and wanting in discernment, and sometimes in common sense. While not overlooking the justice of Cromwell's criticisms of the jury, criticisms identical with those formulated to-day by many criminalists, it must be added that the jury possesses in the highest measure one quality which makes its maintenance indispensable: it is independent. Politics cannot corrupt juries chosen by lot.[1] This independence is the surest guarantee of personal and political liberty. It was the jury that protected the Republicans against the vengeance of Cromwell, and that assured the safety of many incriminated Royalists. It was for this reason that Cromwell had no liking for the institution.

In the France of former times the jury did not exist, but the magistracy taken as a whole was upright and independent in spite of the pressure brought to bear upon it by the Government. "Nowhere at any period," says M. Cousin, "have men been afforded a like spectacle of a magistracy so imposing by reason of its independence, of its learning, of the severity of its morals, and of the austere life incumbent upon its members.[2] Royer-

---

[1] It is true that an effort is made to give politics a voice in the choice of jurymen by striking off the lists citizens who are not devoted to the Government.

[2] V. Cousin, "Madame de Longueville pendant la Fronde," p. 201.

Collard paid it the same compliment. "The disgraceful system," he wrote, "by which judicial posts were obtained by purchase was attended by the formation of an admirable magistracy that was the glory and strength of the last centuries of the monarchy." In the 16th and 17th centuries in particular, the magistracy counted in its ranks eminent men of lofty intelligence and noble character. When Henry of Guise, after driving Henry III. out of Paris, had an interview with the First President, Achille de Harlay, the courageous magistrate rebuked him so harshly for his ambition, that Guise, relating this interview later, could not refrain from saying: "I have been present at battles, at assaults, and at the most dangerous encounters in the world, but I have never been so taken aback as at my meeting with this eminent man." L'Hopital, by the loftiness of his intelligence and his greatness of character, is the type of the magistrate; a nobler character and a more balanced mind are not to be met with. De Retz eulogises the First President Molé in the following noteworthy terms: "Were it not a sort of blasphemy to declare that our century can show a more intrepid man than Gustavus the Great or Monsieur le Prince, I would say that M. Molé, the First President, was that man." Louis XVI. said of Lamoignon that he did not know of a more honourable man in his kingdom. Colbert, in spite of the odious manœuvres he employed, was unable to force the judges into condemning

---

[1] Royer-Collard, "Discours sur la Septennalité."

Fouquet to death; the judges resisted him. During the 18th century the magistracy, influenced by the prevailing corruption, abandoned its moral austerity, but preserved its integrity and independence. The errors historians lay to the door of the Parliament are to be ascribed to the confusion of its political and judicial attributions. When the Parliament was converted into a political assembly, it was invaded by the nobility, who altered its character.

Politicians look askance at and Governments have always complained of the independence of the magistracy. During the Restoration, the independent magistrates were treated as Liberals or Bonapartists, under Louis Philippe as Carlists, under Napoleon III. as Orleanists, and since 1870 as reactionaries and adherents of the clerical party. The fact that all parties when in power have accused the magistracy of sympathising with the fallen régimes is proof of its independence.

The frequent purifications of the magistracy effected by different Governments are the penalty of its independence. There have been cases of Attorney-Generals disgraced for having adopted an attitude in civil suits displeasing to politicians interested in the question before the court. In France, in the past, exile and even death was, on some occasions, the punishment meted out to magistrates for their independence. Under Henry II., for instance, some members of the Parliament having expressed the opinion that the

King ought to be implored to suspend the death edicts against heretics, the Sovereign visited the Parliament in person to intimidate the magistrates. Several of them defended their opinion in the presence of Henry II., who ordered their arrest. Among the number was Anne Dubourg, who was hanged and burned. On the 15th November, 1589, the Sixteen, displeased at an acquittal pronounced by the Parliament, caused the First President and two counsellors to be arrested and put to death, the accusation against them being that they were traitors and favourers of heresy. On several occasions the Parliament was exiled and counsellors were seized upon and imprisoned—even as late as the time of Louis XVI. —for having given a decision that did not fall in with the wishes of the Ministers. Richelieu banished several members of the Parliament whose independence was vexatious to him to a distance from Paris; he forced, too, a certain number of magistrates to wait upon him at the Louvre in the very chamber of the King, with a view to compel them to sentence the Duke d'Epernon to death.[1] He instituted irregular jurisdiction, and what is more, in order to have the judges deputed to try Marshal de Marillac in his power, he made them hold their sittings at Ruel, the seat of his summer residence. The Marshal claimed to be tried by the Parliament, and Mathieu Molé, at the time Procureur-Général, decided that such was his

[1] V. Cousin, "Madame de Longueville pendant la Fronde," p. 205.

right, but Richelieu had the decision annulled by a decree of the Council of State.

Mazarin, although less violent than Richelieu, occasionally rode roughshod over the magistracy; because he was displeased at his language, he caused Barillon, one of the Presidents of the Court of Appeal, to be imprisoned at Pignerol, where he died.

Napoleon I., imitating the example of Louis XIV. on the occasion of the trial of Fouquet, endeavoured to exert pressure upon the consciences of the judges of General Moreau. The Emperor, it is true, was sagacious enough to set his veto upon Moreau being tried by a court-martial specially constituted for the purpose. "It would be said," he remarked, "that I had wished to rid myself of Moreau by getting him legally murdered by my creatures." Still he was guilty of attempting to dictate their decision to the judges, who resisted his intervention energetically.

On the occasion of the trial of the Duke d'Enghien, Napoleon I. nominated the officers composing the court-martial that judged him. All the rules of judicial procedure were violated in the course of this trial. After the verdict the commissaries decided to write to the First Consul to acquaint him with the desire the Duke d'Enghien had expressed to be taken before him in person. As General Hulin was writing this letter, Savary entered the room where the court was sitting. He seized the General's pen, snatched it from him, and said: "Gentlemen, your labours are over. What remains to be done is my concern." Savary had had the grave dug several hours before the sentence was pronounced, so certain in his opinion was the verdict.[1] A similar incident is met with in Roman history. Nero had charged the tribune Vlianus Niger to put to death the tribune Flavius, who had said to him: "No soldier ever remained more faithful to you so long as you were deserving of affection; I began to loathe you when I saw you a parricide, the murderer of your wife, a coachman, a clown, and an incendiary." Vlianus, Tacitus relates, "had a grave dug in a neighbouring field, and Flavius, considering it to be neither broad nor deep enough, said to those around him: 'Even this matter is contrary to what is right.'"[2]

Yielding to political considerations, Napoleon I., copying the practices of the old régime, banished a number of men and women without a trial, and notably Mdme. de Staël, Mdme. de Chevreuse, and Mdme. Récamier.

Owing to the fact that Governments endeavour at times to influence the course of justice, firmness of character is the most important quality in magistrates. The most learned jurist is a bad magistrate if he is wanting in independence, and Bossuet was right in saying: "It is idle to hope to make a good magistrate unless you begin by making a good man. . . . A man needs to have acquired character before there should be

[1] "Mémoires du Chancelier Pasquier," Vol. I., pp. 190-192.
[2] Tacitus, "Annales," Bk. XVI., § 67.

any question of what rank is to be given him amongst other men."[1] A magistrate needs to have sufficient energy to resist the pressure politics will endeavour to exert upon his decisions. Pompey on one occasion "entered the court where justice was dispensed, intending to praise publicly Plancus," who was on his trial. Cato, however, who was one of the judges, stopped his ears with his hands, and did not hesitate to condemn the man whom Pompey protected.

Revolutionary tribunals, judicial commissions, military commissions, and mixed commissions are a mere parody of justice, for commissioners are not judges. Louis XI. used to entrust the judging of political trials to commissioners, to whom he distributed the property of the persons condemned. These commissioners, having an interest in pronouncing condemnations, implicated innocent persons, notably the Count du Perche, in false plots so as to obtain possession of their belongings.

The irregular tribunal guilty of the most atrocities was the revolutionary tribunal. The first revolutionary tribunal was instituted upon the motion of Robespierre to try the conspirators of the 10th of August, those, that is, who had opposed the insurrection. "Since the 10th August," said Robespierre, "the vengeance of the people is unsatisfied; . . it demands new judges created for the circumstance; . . . we demand that the guilty be tried sovereignly and without

[1] Bossuet, "Panégyrique de Saint Joseph."

appeal by commissioners chosen from each section." The first extraordinary tribunal, known as that of the 17th August, was suppressed on the 29th November, but on the 10th March following Danton procured the voting in the name of the safety of the people, and to try the anti-revolutionaries, of the most famous of the revolutionary tribunals. Couthon, who drew up the report, declared that all the rules of procedure ought to be violated in the public interest: "Whoever proposes to subordinate the public safety to the prejudices of the law courts, or the inventions of the lawyers, is a madman or a scoundrel, who aims at the legal destruction of the country and of humanity." Danton said that the revolutionary tribunal should "take the place of the supreme tribunal of the popular vengeance"; that is, that it should take the place of the September massacres. In point of fact the revolutionary tribunal was equivalent to legalised massacre.

Besides being more odious than brutal assassination, legal massacre sacrfices more victims. When a band of ruffians sets to work to slaughter, its fury soon cools down, or provokes a victorious counter-demonstration on the part of the public forces. When, however, a sanguinary tribunal is established it may exercise its functions for months in succession and send cart-loads of victims to the scaffold every day.

The judges and jurymen composing the revolutionary tribunal were appointed by the Convention. On the recommendation of Camille Desmoulins,

Robespierre gave the office of public accuser to Fouquier-Tinville, who wrote to Camille Desmoulins: "I am poor and burdened with children, and we are dying of hunger."[1] The principles of revolutionary politics preclude magistrates who are independent by their character and fortune being regarded with favour. To such are preferred docile magistrates, and in consequence men dying of starvation, like Fouquier-Tinville, are chosen. Fouquier-Tinville, like many other magistrates of the period, turned his office to pecuniary account, and made the lives and liberty of the accused a matter of barter.[2] More than one of the judges of the revolutionary tribunals resembles the portrait, sketched by the Deputy Albert, of a judge of Rheims, "upright in principle, but whom privation and lack of fortune had plunged into every excess, changing character according to circumstances so as to have a post, and in league with the wire-pullers so as to keep it."

These judges and jurymen, chosen by the Convention from among the fanatics, and fatly paid (18 francs a day), were merely the instruments of the Jacobins. Herman, the President of the revolutionary tribunal, was, like Fouquier-Tinville, a creature of Robespierre. The cabinet-maker Duplay, with whom Robespierre lodged, was one of the jurymen. Other members of this tribunal were working-men or labourers. To deprive the juries of all independence they were

[1] Michelet, op. cit., Vol. VII., p. 64.
[2] "Mémoires de Morellet," Vol. II., p. 22. "Mémoires de Mallet Dupan," Vol. II., p. 495.

made to deliberate aloud in the presence of the judges. During the trial of Danton the members of the Committee of Public Safety surrounded the judges and the jury, even while they were deliberating. Prieur has left it on record that he had frequent interviews with the presidents of the revolutionary tribunal, and that through them he exercised great influence over the tribunal.[1] Collot d'Herbois issued orders to the revolutionary tribunal. One of the judges having informed him that he found nothing suspicious in the conduct of a young man he had ordered him to cross-examine, Collot retorted: "I ordered you to punish the man, and I desire that he shall die before the end of the day. If the innocent were spared too many guilty would escape. Go about your business."[2] By the terms of the 10th clause of the decree of March 10th, 1793, a commission of six members of the Convention was charged with drawing up the acts of accusation, with supervising the preliminary inquiries, and with keeping up a regular correspondence with the public accuser and the judges. When the judges acquitted prisoners, the tribunal was "purified," and the persons acquitted were tried over again. Prieur and Lebon imprisoned judges who abstained from invariably passing death sentences. Barras and Frénon had the public accuser and the president of the Marseilles revolutionary tribunal arrested and brought to Paris because out of 528 prisoners

---

[1] Taine, Vol. III., p. 218.
[2] Ibid., p. 284.

they had only guillotined 162. (Taine, Vol. III., p. 285.)

The task accomplished by these judges was so repellent that one of them admitted that to overcome his repugnance he was in the habit of swallowing a large glass of spirits to give him strength to attend the sittings.[1] Fouquier-Tinville declared: "I should prefer digging the ground to being public accuser. Were it possible I should hand in my resignation."[2]

Although less ferocious than the Convention, the Directory was no more respectful of the independence of the magistracy. The electoral assemblies of Paris having elected moderate judges, the new authority annulled the elections. In 1797, under the Directory, the Minister of Justice decided that the civilians implicated in an unimportant Royalist conspiracy should be tried by court-martial. The accused carried their case to the Court of Appeal, which decided in their favour. The Minister, however, ordered the court-matial to take no account of the decision of the Court of Appeal, and did his utmost to induce the military judges to pass sentence of death, but they stopped short at imprisonment. To punish the Court of Appeal for its independence, the Directory renewed it in part.

To satisfy the requirements of politics justice must be expeditious. No importance is attached to the danger of judicial errors, the right of appeal

---

[1] Taine, Vol. III., p. 325.
[2] Wallon, "Histoire du Tribunal Révolutionnaire," Vol. IV., p. 129.

is suppressed, and it is desired that decisions be executed without delay. By the terms of clause 13 of the decree of the 10th March, 1793, constituting the revolutionary tribunal, the sentences were to be carried out without recourse to the Court of Appeal. There was no right of appeal against the decisions of the military commissions set to judge the Emigrants accused of having borne arms against their country, and the sentences were to be carried out within twenty-four hours.

On various occasions, under the First and Second Empires, special courts and mixed commissions were instituted, composed in part of magistrates and in part of officers of the army. In defiance of the promise contained in the Charter that no more extraordinary tribunals should be created, courts of high commission, in which officers were associated with magistrates, were instituted under the Restoration. Special tribunals thus composed are open to grave objection. The habit of mind of officers, though tending to endow them with the qualities proper to their profession, scarcely fits them to judge political or criminal cases.

Politics spoil whatever they meddle with. I have pointed out how they attempt to tamper with the composition of juries. During the past few years they have been modifying the elections for the boards of arbitration between working-men and their employers. The central electoral and watch committee of the Paris working-men delegates imposes upon candidates a programme, whose first clause runs as follows: "Every candidate for the post of working-man delegate to the board of arbitration, shall declare that his object is the entire suppression of employers of labour and of wages. To attain this result he shall declare himself a partisan of the struggle between the classes." In this way a candidate for judicial functions, whose duty it would be to undertake to examine in a spirit of equity the disputed questions submitted to him, binds himself, on the contrary, to approach them in a spirit of prejudice and of hatred against employers.

Under the influence of politics the police has often developed into a veritable inquisition. "A Chief of the Police," said Talleyrand, "is a man who occupies himself in the first place with what concerns him, and in the second place with what does not concern him." To the political police is due the invention of the *agent provocateur*. Robespierre, in order to furnish the revolutionary tribunal with victims, introduced police spies into the Paris prisons.

A magistrate ought not to belong to a political party, because party spirit is narrow, partial, impassioned, and exacting. The examples of Cardinal de Retz, of Talleyrand, a bishop, of the Oratorian Fouché, of the Capucine Chabot, show what becomes of priests when they meddle with politics. In the same way, by the examples of Dumouriez, Pichegru, Moreau, Bazaine, and Boulanger, we learn what happens to generals who mix themselves up in political intrigues. Politics are no less prejudicial to magistrates, for what Fénelon said of the profession of courtier may be said of that of politician: "This profession spoils all others." One would be better off in a land of savages than in a civilised country in which justice is subjected to the influence of politics. The poisoned arrow of the savage, the tooth of the lion, and the poison of the viper are less to be dreaded than the servility of a Jeffreys, a Laubardemont, or a Fouquier-Tinville. A wild beast merely kills a man; a political magistrate may take away at once his life and his honour.

CHAPTER X.

THE CORRUPTION OF PUBLIC MORALS BY POLITICS.

The character of the government affects the character of the nation—Evil results of frequent changes of government—Politicians of the Talleyrand and Fouché type—Fortunes made in politics—Political upstarts—Political ambition—Place hunters—Bureaucracies in democracy—Aristocracy in the nineteenth century—The two ruling passions among men are the desire for honour and wealth—Thiers on political corruption—The administrative services in France—The relation between moral and political corruption—Bentham on the French character—Comparison between France and Rome—A nation must not always be judged by the character of its politicians.

The character of a nation is always modelled upon the character of its Government. A licentious Court inculcates licentiousness; a cruel Government renders the people cruel; corrupt representatives of the people promote corruption among the electors; a venal administration propagates venality. Bad Governments have for their consequence a low level of popular morality. Men improve morally when they are well governed. Good examples set by those in authority incite to honesty and uprightness. A just Government inspires the sentiment of justice. A Government which practises fraud and deceit inculcates double dealing and hypocrisy. If the Government be high-handed and oppressive it makes the country apprehensive, lethargic, suspicious, and servile.

The Venetian Inquisition corrupted the people by its system of terror, spies, and informers; its secret agents were everywhere, and bronze receptacles at the street corners awaited the deposition of denunciations. Politics, by inviting treacherous accusations, degrade men's characters. There was formerly a law in England that offered a reward to the person who denounced a Catholic bishop. In virtue of various edicts of the Kings of Spain, the children of heretics were disqualified from occupying any public function unless they had denounced their father. Who will believe that these laws and many others of a like nature did not pervert the public conscience by offering the informer a reward?

How can the people be taught the respect of what is right and the love of justice if those in authority violate right and set the example of injustice? Is it possible for the ambitious men, who overthrow the constitutions they have sworn to defend, to teach respect for legality and the pledged word? A nation is educated by following the example of the great. It adopts the ideas, the maxims, and the habits it sees put in practice.

Bad political morals spread to the people; they accustom it to deceit, cruelty, and injustice, and they diminish its loathing for evil. The immorality of those who govern infects, sooner or later, those who are governed.

Luxurious and debauched Courts have spread the taste for luxury and pleasure and communicated their vices to the country. The shifty policy of the petty Italian princes has favoured the development of duplicity among the compatriots of Machiavelli.

Do not the Governments that multiply decorations foster vanity? Do not politics promote alcoholism by favouring the sellers of intoxicating drinks, who are influential electoral agents?

Why are the French lacking in initiative and for ever having recourse to the State? The practice of allowing the central authority undisputed control of public affairs has certainly had for consequence the weakening of the will. Had the French been put in possession of political liberty at an earlier date, their spirit of initiation would have been more developed.

The Tuscan character, which was violent and crafty at the time of Machiavelli, became milder afterwards with the establishment of a paternal Government; it was possible to abolish the death penalty in the country without danger to the public tranquillity.

It was the cruel and grasping policy of the Genoese in Corsica that modified the character of the inhabitants of the island, who in ancient times, as Diodorus Siculus avers, were reputed to be the mildest and most pacific of peoples and the most faithful observers of justice. After the cession of the island to Genoa by Pisa, the Corsicans were so oppressed and pillaged by their new masters that they rose in revolt to secure their independence. The rebellion having been repressed with implacable cruelty, the oppressed race was animated by an ardent desire for vengeance. Moreover, as all the Government posts were given by the conquerors to ruined Genoese nobles, who administered the country without equity, the Corsicans were unable to obtain justice and adopted the custom of the *vendetta*.

The English nation, for a long time so restless, has become tranquil, staid, and circumspect since it has enjoyed a good Government.

By attracting the nobles to the Court and transforming them into courtiers, Louis XIV. deprived them of all loftiness of character. He rendered petty those who were styled the great. On their estates they were proud and independent; at Court they became vain, frivolous, and grasping, and contracted luxurious tastes and idle habits.

Louis XIV. contributed to make opinion indulgent for adultery by legitimising the children who were born to him outside wedlock.

The Terror rendered cruel even those who fought against it, and it left its mark upon the youth of the richer classes. Thanks to its teaching, moderate men learnt violence.

Frequent changes of government develop scepticism and the revolutionary spirit. In a country where everything is possible and nothing lasts, where a man of the stamp of Malesherbes is guillotined, and the regicide Fouché becomes the Duke of Otranto under the Empire and Minister under the Restoration, people cease to believe in anything, and are prepared for everything; and when a nation no longer believes in anything, it believes in force and money.

Insurrections and *coups d'état* have been so frequent for the past hundred years in France, that they have demoralised the country. The triumph of might makes people lose confidence in right and destroys their faith in justice: it encourages the ambitious and those who have lost caste.

France has passed from Louis XIV. to the Girondins, from the Girondins to Danton and Robespierre, from the men of the Terror to the men of the Directory, from Barras to Bonaparte, from Napoleon to the Bourbons, from the elder to the younger branch, from the Orleans to the Republic, from the Republic to the Empire, from the Empire to the Republic. Incessantly bandied about from one régime to another, perpetually changing its constitution and its principles, torn by the parties disputing power, France resembles "a sick person who is unable to find rest upon his couch, and who endeavours to quiet his pains by changing his position." Dante's[1] lines upon Florence may be applied to it: "How often, during the time you can call to mind, have you changed

---

[1] Dante, "Purgatory," ch. vi.

laws, coinage, magistracy, and habits, and renewed the chiefs of the city!"

Amid these frequent changes of government, what becomes of the dignity of the functionaries, who serve the régime they combated and combat the régime they served? In a Court of Appeal of the South of France, the Procureur-Général of the Empire, having received the decrees of the Senate of the 3rd and 4th April, 1814, pronouncing the deposition of Napoleon I. and calling Louis XVIII. to the throne, addressed a circular to the courts of his jurisdiction, inviting them in the following terms to recognise these decrees: "In doing so you will follow the example of the whole of France, and you will experience, I have no doubt, a very agreeable satisfaction in giving expression to sentiments which were already in your heart." When Napoleon returned from the Isle of Elba, the former Procureur-Général of the Empire, become a zealous Procureur-Général of the Restoration, wrote on 25th March, 1815, a fresh circular, in which he advised fidelity to the legitimate sovereign. "The enemy of the world's peace," he said, "has penetrated into the heart of France, the torch of discord in his hand, with the very evident intention of leading its inhabitants astray and of stirring up civil war. . . . Let the rallying cry of all be 'The King, the Constitutional Charter, the Fatherland,' and the scourge of France and Europe will return into nothingness. It is not given to all to hasten to the field of honour, arms in hand, to repulse and destroy the common enemy; but . . . the magistrates as well have laurels to gather. . . . The misfortunes that would threaten us were audacity to triumph over royal kindliness, were crime to prevail over virtue, offer you a magnificent opportunity of proving your attachment to King and country. . . . The enemy marches to his tomb, though he believes himself to be marching to the capital of the kingdom." The enemy having made himself master of Paris and France, the zealous Procureur-Général of the Restoration again became the not less zealous Procureur-Général of the Empire, and addressed two circulars, dated 18th and 22nd April, 1813, to the courts in his jurisdiction, acquainting them with the intentions of the Emperor. All the magistrates appointed by Louis XVIII. were only allowed to continue their functions after the Emperor had ratified their appointments. In consequence, all the heads of jurisdictions were invited to furnish information as to their political conduct. They were also ordered to convoke the tribunals with a view to the taking of the oath of obedience to the Imperial institutions and of fidelity to the Emperor.

Frequent changes of government call into being a class of men always ready to range themselves on the side of the strongest party and to insult the vanquished party which they have been serving. In view of a political change they take care to have connections among all parties, and they always suit their opinions to circumstances.

There are even men, Talleyrand and Fouché for example, who, as soon as the régime they have been serving has fallen, boast that they aided in its overthrow by secret intrigues and culpable manœuvres. In order that their newly-fledged devotion to the new order of things may not be doubted, they insult the fallen régime with the same baseness with which they flattered it when it was in power. It is precisely those who enjoyed to the fullest extent the favours of the fallen régime that are the first to abandon it, and to turn towards the rising sun. The new Governments, while despising such men, accept their services, because they know them to be docile, while they keep independent men at a distance. "The truth is," says Bossuet, "that the unjust man can espouse all designs, hit upon all expedients, espouse all interests. To what use can be put the upright man, whose talk is always of his duty? He is the incarnation of unswerving principles and of inflexibility, and there are so many practices to which he cannot lend himself that in the end he is looked upon as a man who is good for nothing and entirely useless."[1]

The public conscience is demoralised by the spectacle of the variations of politicians, the courtiers of each and every régime, yesterday the passionate lovers of liberty, to-day the servants of a dictator; now Radicals, now the champions of authority;

---

[1] Bossuet, "Sermon sur l'Ambition."

formerly defenders of the throne and altar, at present flatterers of the people and insulters of the clergy.

Again, the spectacle of fortunes rapidly acquired by the aid of politics demoralises the laborious portion of the community. Politicians are seen to pass suddenly from poverty to fortune; yesterday they were loaded with debts, to-day they possess "gardens, to create which the entire surface of the ground is transformed, fountains, statues, boundless parks, and houses the keeping up of which entails an outlay that surpasses the income derived from the estate on which they stand. What is the origin of these possessions?"[1]

Revolutions, turning society topsy-turvy, humble those who were of high station and exalt those of low rank. It has been said of a sovereign:

"To-day upon the throne, to-morrow in chains."

A deputy of the Opposition in prison to-day is in power to-morrow. If it suffice, to become Deputy or Minister, to have undergone imprisonment, how great is the temptation for those who are low down in the world, and who have their fortune to make, to endeavour to upset the established order of things, and to get themselves thrown into prison! Has not the spectacle been offered of a schoolmaster, Buchot, being appointed Minister of Foreign Affairs by the Committee of Public

[1] Fénelon, "Direction pour la Conscience d'un Roi."

Safety,[1] of petty college professors becoming Ministers of Public Instruction, of mediocre barristers becoming Ministers of Justice, Ministers of Agriculture, Ministers of Commerce, Ministers of Public Works? So many undistinguished men rise to high situations, so many high functionaries and Ministers grow up like mushrooms in the space of a few hours on the political dungheap, that a wild ambition turns all heads and induces fortune-seekers to throw themselves into the political fray.

In the 17th century Bourdaloue, in his admirable sermon on ambition, upbraided those who rose without preparation to the higher dignities of the State, on the pretext of hereditary rights. At the present day the ambition of politicians is the source to the State of the same dangers as the ambition of the great; the scandal of political appointments has succeeded to the scandalous transmission of posts by heredity. Swift and Beaumarchais have satirised "this shameful manner of obtaining high office by rope-dancing." To-day it is by dancing upon the political tightrope that high posts are secured, and it may still be said: "A man of figures was wanted for this post and a political mountebank obtained it."

In 1793 the majority of the members of the

[1] This person, says Taine, was "a stupid member of the clubs, an inveterate billiard player and haunter of cafés, scarcely capable of reading the documents that were brought to him to sign at the café where he passed his life." ("La Révolution," Vol. III., p 64.) When he left the Ministry, Buchot asked his successor to give him a place as clerk, and, this being refused him, a situation as office porter.

Paris Commune were working-men. Business men of shady reputation, bailiffs and other dismissed law officers, got themselves appointed members of the revolutionary committees by pretending to be Jacobins and patriots. At the present day they profess to be Socialists and Radicals in order to get themselves elected Municipal Councillors, General Councillors, and Deputies. Even waiters, cobblers, and commissionaires, by dint of proclaiming their revolutionary opinions, are seen to obtain access to the Municipal Councils of large towns, to become directors of hospitals and of charity boards, a post that allows them to distribute to themselves the sums intended for the poor.

Fortunes acquired through politics are made so rapidly that people are not content to climb the rungs of the social ladder, but wish to reach the top at one bound. Every citizen wishes to be a politician, all politicians desire to be Deputies; all Deputies would be Ministers or at least Under-Secretaries of State; all Ministers wish to be Presidents of the Council, all Presidents of the Council to be Presidents of the Republic. Ambition is legitimate when it aims at the public good, when it is moderate and served by talent and honourable means. There are noble ambitions; the desire to lead one's country towards justice and liberty, to reform abuses, to redress injustice, to enlighten the people, such are praiseworthy ambitions and even duties. The absence of ambition among honourable men is

ever a public misfortune, for it hands over the
power to the unworthy. If those who are worthy
of electoral mandates do not seek them, they will
be seized upon by the undeserving. In consequence, a moderate ambition, which sets itself
a lofty goal, is useful to society. In the case of
nations endowed with a parliamentary régime, it
is necessary to the proper working of the government. "In our country," an Englishman has
said, "men of talent, intelligence, and energy are
divided into two classes: that which is in possession of the Ministry, and that which is striving
to secure it."[1] It is imperative, however, that the
struggle to arrive at power should be conducted
on honourable lines, and with the object of serving the country and improving its institutions
and laws. A boundless, precocious, and egoistical political ambition merely results in disorder
and agitation, is the source of intrigues, cabals,
and rivalries. What becomes of the public interest when politicians strive to obtain office and
allot themselves places in the Cabinet, not in
consideration of their experience and their special
acquirements, but according to the importance of
this or that group and other secondary considerations of parliamentary tactics? What can be
thought of the spectacle of men of disappointed
ambition, who, fallen from power, cannot console
themselves with being again mere private persons,
but set to work to form immoral coalitions with

[1] Sallust says of Catiline: "Vastus animus immoderata, incredibilia, nimis alta semper cupiebat." (V.)

their former adversaries, and attack what they have just been defending and defend what they have been attacking?

It is not Ministers only who say: "*Quo non ascendam?*" The unclassed, the incapable, the ambitious, the petty functionary, throw themselves into the political fray, and the quicker to make their way they adopt the most advanced opinions.

Schoolmasters and beardless young professors, entirely lacking in judgment, forsake their classes to blossom into leaders of revolutionary parties, and aspire to represent the country when all they represent is vanity and presumption; inexperienced barristers, who are ignorant of the law, set themselves up as legislators; doctors, incapable of healing their patients, undertake to heal the diseases, which they have never studied, of the body politic. Everybody turns his back on his profession; nobody keeps his place. The cobbler declines to stick to his last, the cook to his kitchen—

> Everyone buzzes around in the sphere of politics,
> Everyone wishes to meddle therewith.[1]

It would seem as if politics relieved those who aspire to public functions of the necessity of study. Nobody is acquainted with his own capacities, and nobody makes his merit a measure of his ambition. Shoemakers are still to be found who make shoes, bakers who knead, tailors who make clothes, millers who grind flour, blacksmiths who shoe horses, and grocers who sell

[1] Barbier, "Les Iambes."

groceries, but how numerous are the artisans who in their workshop or shop, at their kneading trough or their ovens, cherish the dream of ceasing to knead, to work up leather, to shoe horses, to cook or to sell groceries! Their dream is not chimerical: they obtain important posts when they are in a position to render electoral services. Power is looked upon as a cake of which everyone demands his share; public functions are booty of which everybody attempts to possess himself, without considering whether he is competent. Already, under the Convention, the spectacle was afforded of working-men being appointed judges, and invoking their patriotism or their hatred of aristocrats as entitling them to these important functions. In 1793 there were butchers, shoemakers, and petty shopkeepers who were persons of importance, disposing of the life and liberty of their fellow-citizens. Cicero, after citing the example of a clerk of the court who had become a quæstor, and of other obscure citizens who had risen to the highest rank, added: "It is but too certain that in the presence of such examples of fortune, civil wars will not be wanting."[1]

Politics corrupt the country when they reward electoral zeal by appointments it is hard to justify. One of the principal missions of a Government is to place authority in good hands, to seek out merit and to reward industry. When electoral agents are given the preference over good functionaries, not only do the latter suffer, but the

[1] Cicero, "De Officiis," Bk. II., § 8.

State is deprived of their services. When public functions are no longer allotted to men of intellectual and moral value they cease to be useful and may become harmful.

In former times the beginning of each reign was marked by a rush for posts and pensions. At the opening of the reign of Henry II., for example, the Montmorencys and the Guises seized upon all posts. "There did not escape them," says a contemporary, "any more than flies escape the swallows, a situation, dignity, bishopric, abbey, office, or other tit-bit, but it was immediately snapped up."[1] The numerous changes of government and Ministry have still further multiplied the place-hunting and whetted the appetites of those who practise it. "The Ministries," it was already remarked by Montesquieu, "follow each other and destroy each other here like the seasons."[2] Ministerial instability has still further progressed since the time of Montesquieu; it occasionally happens that a single season sees several Ministries. Each Minister on arriving at power has his relations, his friends, and his electors to provide for; he is too good a relative, too good a friend, too good a compatriot to refuse them anything; he has his re-election too much at heart not to prefer election agents to the most

---

[1] At the death of Henry II., postulants crowded to Fontainebleau in such numbers that Cardinal Lorraine had a gallows erected at the gate of the palace, and ordered them to take their departure within twenty-four hours, under pain of being hanged. (Villemain, "Vie de L'Hopital.")

[2] "Lettres Persanes," Letter No. 38.

capable functionaries. The Ministers' offices have become registry offices for election agents.

The Abbé Siéyès remarked in his "Essai sur les Privilèges," that intrigue and mendacity had become the special occupation of the privileged class; they have become the occupation of politicians. Citizens have ceased to rely upon their own efforts to improve their position; they await the favours of the Government, they count upon political recommendations. Everywhere the spectacle is on view of outstretched hands and opened mouths. In consequence, it is incorrect to affirm, as has been done,[1] that the plague of functionaries is peculiar to monarchies: it is an evil from which all régimes suffer, and democratic régimes to a greater extent than the others. A democracy multiplies functions so as to reward electoral services, it resorts to dismissals in order to create vacancies. Under the monarchies, the nobility rushed to the Court to solicit posts and pensions, and the assassination of the Duke d'Enghien did not damp the ardour with which it served Napoleon. The defenders of the throne and altar, who had incited the Vendéens to resistance, were even seen to bow before the "usurper" and to range themselves among his courtiers. Under a Republic there may be no places such as Chamberlain, Lord High Equerry, or the like, but there are an infinite number of administrative situations, and the number is always augmenting. In 1793 the Jacobins

Barni, "La Morale dans la Démocratie."

installed themselves in every post, although they were in general incapable of filling them. "They were entirely unacquainted with administrative matters," says Michelet. "Certain of them scarcely knew how to write."[1] Almost all of them became functionaries; they invaded the staffs of the various Ministries and created a great number of new posts. When Danton entered upon office he found situations for all his creatures.

General Foy, in the course of a speech he made under the Restoration, was interrupted by one of his colleagues, who asked him to define the word "aristocracy." "The aristocracy of the 19th century," he answered, "is the league, the coalition of those who wish to consume without producing, to live without working, to occupy all posts without being qualified to fill them, to appropriate all honours without deserving them."[2] As politics are practised at the present day, what difference is there between the democracy and the aristocracy? Politics still bring into being aristocrats, privileged persons, who desire to live without working, and to occupy all posts without being in a position to fill them.

Prior to 1789 the nobles considered themselves entitled to pensions, and Fénelon himself was grieved when he saw them languishing in the ante-chambers at Versailles without reaping an advantage. At the present day politicians consider they have a right to pensions, and the

[1] Michelet, op. cit., Vol. VII., p. 62.
[2] "Discours du Général Foy," Vol. II., p. 34.

Deputies are grieved when they see their electors languishing in the ante-chamber of a Minister without obtaining a pension in the shape of a sinecure. At the assembly of the States-General held at Paris in 1615, the third estate implored the King to suppress the pensions he was paying a number of the gentry. Taxpayers might still make the same demand in respect to a number of pensions paid to politicians.

Political parties cannot bring themselves to practise equality before the law and to admit everyone to posts in the gift of the Government. There always exists a category of citizens placed outside the law or held in suspicion. Previous to 1789 this was the case of Protestants and Jews, during the Revolution of nobles and priests, under the Restoration of Liberals. At the latter period the persons favoured were those of good birth and religious principles. At the present day matters are reversed: the persons who cannot boast birth, and who lack religious principle, have the preference.

From political considerations incapable men are often installed in public functions with a view to their being made use of as docile instruments.[1]

[1] It was on the recommendation of Robespierre that the schoolmaster Buchot was appointed Minister of Foreign Affairs, and that Henriot, previously a petty clerk, was appointed to the command of all the troops in Paris. The couple were docile instruments in the hands of the Jacobins. Ronsin had Rossignol appointed commander-in-chief with the intention of using him as a screen and keeping the power in his own hands. "You are making a mistake," said Rossignol himself, "I am utterly incapable of commanding an army." However, he exercised the command, say what he would. (Michelet, op. cit., Vol. VIII., p. 26.)

Politics bring the administration into discredit by causing public functions to be assigned to electioneering agents. Where public functions cease to be the reward of industry and merit, they lose much of the esteem in which they ought to be held. The functionaries themselves, placed under the supervision of politicians who have power to appoint, promote, and dismiss them in accordance with their electoral interests, cease to have the authority they would possess if they were the stable and independent representatives of the Government.

It is a great misfortune for a country when its public functions cease to be a sign of intellectual and moral superiority, and when, in consequence, they are the less esteemed and sought after. To counterbalance the influence of money, which is perpetually on the increase, it is needful that side by side with the careers that bring wealth to those that follow them there should be other careers that ensure esteem to those that pursue them and that are valued for the honours they involve. The two chief motives that influence men are honour and money. The desire to be esteemed is a curb upon the passion for wealth; if, however, the esteem that ought to attach to public functions is on the decrease, the result is that the sentiment of honour itself diminishes in the country, and the power of money augments. And "there was never a more revolting spectacle," says Cicero, "than that of a city in which superiority is dependent upon fortune."

Politics, by developing favouritism,[1] created habits which are intolerable amongst a free people; mendacity is promoted, intrigue fostered, and idleness encouraged. Citizens who are always on the look-out for a Government situation, who are always in search of a post, acquire craft and cunning but lose in dignity. Besides, the multiplication to an undue extent of functionaries renders the sincerity of elections impossible. The functionaries are so numerous, and the pressure they exert so strong, that they prevent the wishes of the country being freely manifested.

When politics admit of the purchase of votes, and of their being paid for in posts, how is it possible that the moral sense of the country should not be contaminated by the spectacle of this trafficking? Trafficking in connection with elections teaches a nation to sacrifice the general interest to personal and local interests. The electors do as they see others do; they cease to consider the general interest and are desirous of having a representative in their service who shall occupy himself with their local interests, their petty concerns, who shall bring their demands to the notice of the different Ministers and execute their commissions. They elect not a representative of the country, but a sort of commission agent.

In a speech delivered in 1846, M. Thiers, after having recalled the disadvantages of absolute

[1] Formerly, prior to 1789, the State had only a very small number of posts in its gift; the number of such posts at the present day is considerable.

Governments, pointed out the shortcomings of popular Governments and the moral corruption that elections spread through the country. "The master," he said, "is not above, he is below; the lower ranks have got to be flattered; . . . . the work of carrying on deplorable intrigues has got to be proceeded with down to the uttermost strata of society, with the result that liberty, whose outcome should be to extend participation in public affairs, often only extends corruption, like those poisons which, introduced into the blood, carry death wherever the blood carries life." The political virus penetrates everywhere and vitiates all the organs of society. The quest of popularity corrupts at once candidates and electors; only flatterers are left. The Deputies flatter the electors, the Ministers flatter the Deputies. The habits of flattery become general, develop into a recognised institution, and destroy authority everywhere; professors flatter their pupils, parents flatter their children. Those who ought to command, obey, and those who ought to obey, command. What has become of the authority of the executive power in the State, of the authority of parents in the family? Every description of authority has fallen into discredit. Astonishment is expressed at the progress of anarchy, but anarchy is everywhere; it is in the air, in ideas, in literature, in the family, in the public service, in the Government.

Anarchy reigns in the administrative services; the fate of the functionaries no longer depends upon their superiors in rank. The departments, the communes, are in a state of anarchy; the authority of the Prefects is annihilated by the influence of Deputies and Senators, who substitute the harmful action of local tyranny for the beneficent action of impartial administration. At various periods the provinces have been under the yoke of petty village tyrants. "The years 1815 and 1816," says M. Guizot, "will be disagreeably remembered, more particularly on account of the tyranny rampant in small towns, of the overbearing attitude of village potentates, of the crowd of obscure country squires that suddenly came to the fore throughout France, making the country the object of their threats and vexations, spreading anxiety in these districts and humiliating their neighbours." At the present day the petty local tyrants have ceased to be country squires, but they still impose upon the inhabitants the heaviest and most humiliating yoke. This social disorganisation is the outcome of the weakness of the executive power and the omnipotence of the Deputies. A nation suffers when the executive power is too weak as well as when it is too strong. Bossuet was entirely justified in saying: "What you desire should be weak that it may not oppress you, becomes powerless to protect you." The power of the Deputies must not be confounded with the Parliamentary régime; government by Deputies is mere anarchy. That order should reign it is necessary that each branch of authority should exercise its normal attributes, that the Government should govern and that the Assembly should supervise. A sovereign or an assembly that is all-powerful abuses its authority; all authority needs to be limited that it may not become tyrannical. At the present day politicians encroach upon the administrative sphere to such a degree that Deputies and Senators have been seen to meddle in the Assembly or at public meetings with the revision of criminal trials, to proclaim the innocence of accused persons whom a jury had pronounced guilty, and to throw suspicion upon the innocent.

The political corruption of Athens and Rome was a consequence of moral corruption, but the moral corruption was increased in turn by the conflicts of ambitious politicians, who depraved the people the better to obtain the mastery over them and to make them instruments in their hands. At the present day corruption is spreading from private to public life. Can it be expected that electoral and parliamentary morals should be good when morals in general are bad? Why should politicians be models of unselfishness and austerity when covetousness and sensuality are the two characteristic features of contemporary morals? When so many writers are seen to prostitute their pens, is it astonishing that politicians should prostitute their influence and their votes? In turn, however, their malpractices pervert the moral sense of the country which is witness of them. Who has not heard electors exclaim: "I should like to be Minister of Finance for twenty-four hours!" They are not indignant at the conduct of Ministers who take advantage of their term of office to enrich themselves; they envy them and confess that in their place they would act in the same way.

Corrupt political morals have changed the French national character, which was upright and generous and marked by indifference to money and a keen appreciation of honour. At the beginning of this century, Bentham wrote: "An Englishman cannot enter France without observing how the sentiment of honour and contempt for money descend, so to speak, to the lower social ranks to a far greater degree in France than in England." It is not the sentiment of honour and contempt for money that descend to-day from the political sphere to the lower classes. The country has been so demoralised by the examples of political corruption it has had before it, that it is but moderately incensed by scandals which at another period would have moved it to the highest pitch of indignation.[1]

The fact that the contemptuous attitude of the public has ceased to find expression in revolutions is assuredly no cause for complaint; we have had revolutions enough, and if indignation still overthrew Governments, we should change

[1] The mayor of a rural commune remarked to me recently: "I know that our Deputy is a man of shady character, but even if he had been sentenced to eight years' penal servitude I should vote for him because he renders me services."

them too frequently. Still, indifference with respect to the dishonesty of politicians is a grave symptom. It constitutes a danger for political liberty, of whose existence morality is an essential condition. Corruption leads to despotism, and social decomposition paves the way for a dictatorship.

However afflicting may be the spectacle of parliamentary morals in France, Italy,[1] America, and other countries, it must not be thought that the advent of the decadence of these peoples is inevitable and irresistible. God has made nations curable, and France more curable than any other nation, because of the mobility of its character. If its virtues are fragile, its vices are ephemeral. It passes from one passion to another with extreme rapidity. In 1789 it was all aglow for liberty; a few years afterwards it had tired of liberty and was solely concerned with pleasure, which it neglected in turn for military glory. At the present day it is enamoured of luxury and material comfort; to-morrow it will be stirred by nobler passions, concern for the poor, the spirit of sacrifice, the desire for social reforms. England, like France, has traversed periods of political corruption, and has not succumbed to them.

In the case of other peoples, of Athens and Rome in particular, moral and political corruption has carried in its wake, it is true, the loss of liberty

[1] According to an Italian criminalist, G. Ferrero, political corruption is even more rampant in Italy than in France. ("Panama et Panamino.")

and national greatness, and the morals of these peoples offer alarming similarities to those of France. Still, how many differences there are that are to the advantage of France! How many moral forces, how many reasons for hope that the Romans lacked! France has an army whose patriotism and abnegation are admirable, that is sound to the core, and that does not concern itself with politics. The Roman army, on the contrary, of the period of Sylla, Pompey, and Cæsar, was corrupted by the lavish gifts of its generals, by the plunder of the provinces, by habits of debauch and drunkenness. It was the army that overthrew the Republic and established the Dictatorship.

The backsliding of a small number of French politicians cannot be compared with the more widespread venality of the Romans.

In spite of the increasing number of social parasites, an increase wrought by politics, the morals of the French people cannot be assimilated to those of the mob that haunted the Forum, *plebs sordida, et circo ac theatris sueta*, as Tacitus called it, to those of that "back of the treasury"[1] which was always begging and never satisfied.

In the shape of a moral support the Romans had nothing but the Pagan religion, which, moreover, had degenerated during the last years of the Republic, and had lost all moral efficacy. Contemporary society, on the contrary, possesses

[1] Cicero's " Letters to Atticus," No. 21.

a firm moral basis in the Christian religion. Spiritual beliefs are beginning to regain their hold upon cultivated minds. Great efforts are being made to make the people understand that it is atheism and not Christianity that is its real enemy, and that liberty, equality, and fraternity are better assured by putting in practice the precepts of the Gospel than by scepticism and materialism. Signs of a moral reawakening are apparent.

Bossuet made a profoundly wise utterance when he said: "A man should not be allowed to completely despise himself." This advice is applicable to nations as well as to individuals; to despise oneself is very dangerous; a nation ought not to exaggerate its moral wretchedness, nor to parade its social sores. Still, it is well to treat them with the red-hot iron of justice; this ought to have been done with less delay and greater decision in the Panama affair, so as to have avoided the coming into play of the time limit, and so that every rotten spot might have been reached. Justice, like fire, purifies everything.

Moreover, it is not right to judge a nation solely by its political class, to which it is often superior. The fanatics of the Terror, the corrupt men of the Directory, Napoleon's courtiers, the Deputies of the "unfindable" Chamber, etc., do not represent the true France. It is only a small minority that has been involved in the crimes and corruption of the various Governments. The mass of the people has always been honest, laborious, and thrifty, and the friend of order and liberty; it was less fanatical, less cruel, less corrupt, less servile and less intolerant than the parties in power. It is not absolutely correct to say that a people always has the government it deserves. The policy of the Terror, the policy of corruption, the policy of the Dictatorship, the policy of religious intolerance, the policy of irreligious intolerance, have been successively imposed upon France, but without representing its true aspirations. France desires a Government that persecutes nobody, that protects the rights of everybody, that assures peace and upholds the necessary liberties, political liberty, religious liberty, educational liberty, that substitutes in a word a broad national spirit for the spirit of party.[1] It desires, too, a Government that shall govern, that shall put an end to vexatious local tyrannies, to the illegitimate pressure exerted by politicians, and to their meddling with the administration. It desires, above all, that political and business matters shall be kept apart.

[1] "A government incapable of putting a curb upon its party, and that allows its party to lead it, is contemptible." (Thiers, "La Monarchie de 1830.")

CHAPTER XI.

CONCLUSION.

Politics are not above the moral law—Machiavelli's doctrines are immoral rather than profound—An immoral policy is unworthy of modern society—The moral standard of politicians is determined by public opinion—Moral beliefs are the only remedy for political corruption—Modern society is suffering from moral disease—The principles of international politics—The true field of international rivalry—International arbitration—Politics without morality mean the ruin of society.

Politics have become discredited by the employment of culpable expedients and the adoption of immoral maxims; for their reputation to be retrieved they must be brought into accord with morality. After having resorted for so long to cunning and falsehood, to intrigue and violence, politics, were it only for the novelty of the thing, should try the effect of fair dealing, tolerance, and justice. To-day, more than at any period, novelty is liked. And what greater novelty could there be than politics conducted on moral lines? It is possible that people will end by recognising that in public as in private life honesty is the most effective and the most skilful policy. Not only should Machiavelism be loathed by honourable people, but it should be regarded as fatal to the true interests of nations. A great policy cannot be immoral. Craft and violence may score ephemeral successes, but they do not assure the greatness and prosperity of a country. The successes achieved by an immoral policy are not lasting; sooner or later nations, like individuals, politicians, just as private persons, are punished for the evil or rewarded for the good they do. Political crimes are punished more often than is supposed. Those who put their adversaries to death by poison or upon the scaffold often undergo a like fate; those who send others into exile are exiled in their turn.

There is more immorality than profoundness in Machiavelism. It was not a shifty and violent policy that was pursued by Saint Louis, L'Hopital, Henry IV., Sully, Turgot, Franklin, or Washington. Their example shows that it is possible to be a great King, a great Minister, a great citizen, and at the same time an honest man. On the other hand, mighty geniuses have been the ruin of the peoples they have governed, because they despised justice and pursued a Machiavelian policy. Napoleon I., who was solely guided by reasons of State, lost his senses in the end and embarked upon the war in Spain and the Russian campaign. Danton and Robespierre, who did not lack talent, brought the Republic to ruin through trying to save it by the Terror. Liberty is not to be imposed by the guillotine; fraternity is not established by the extermination of its adversaries; the reign of justice and equality is not founded by popular or judicial massacres.

The disciples of Machiavelli declare that politicians should resort to violence and even to crime, if to do so be necessary for the safety of the people, but what they call the safety of the people is often nothing more than the safety of their rule. The authors of the 18th Fructidor, who carried out that *coup d'état* under pretext of saving the Republic, violated the law solely with a view to escaping a personal danger; and far from saving the Republic, by demanding the intervention of a general they created a precedent for the 18th Brumaire. The public safety is an excuse for all violence and every iniquity. Moreover, when a political crime is really committed to assure the safety of the people, there is no proof that the crime is necessary, or that the people might not have been saved by other means. The safety of the people lies rather in respect for legality than in its violation. A people that does its duty can await the future with confidence; if it suffers for the moment in the cause of justice it is rare that the day of reparation does not dawn, for in the case of nations, as in that of individuals, it is virtues that elevate them and vices that debase them.

A Machiavelian policy is not a great policy; to practise it a great genius is not necessary. It is easier to govern by expedients than by principles. What is more, there has ceased to be any necessity for a policy of this sort in modern societies. It is comprehensible that Machiavelli's prince, that is to say, an absolute sovereign, should find it to his interest to sow division among his subjects in order to rule them; on the other hand, the maxim, "Promote division in order to reign," is out of place in a free Government that is supported by opinion and whose interest it is to unite and not to divide the community. Terror may be an instrument of government for a popular or military dictator, but it becomes inapplicable under a government of opinion. This being the case, instead of saying, as under the old system of politics, "Cunning, still cunning, and always cunning; audacity, again audacity, and always audacity," the watchword ought to be under the modern system of politics, "Straightforwardness, still straightforwardness, and always straightforwardness; justice, still justice, and always justice."

Diplomatic dissimulation becomes more difficult with the publication of parliamentary debates. This publicity, which has its inconveniences, offers the advantage that it is profitable to morality. It is impossible for a Minister to confess in a public discussion that he harbours unjust projects. Moreover, as public opinion becomes more enlightened, and acquires greater weight, its sound common sense takes the place of the finessing of the diplomatists. A crafty policy is not always the most skilful. Henry IV. did not have recourse to craft.[1] A diplomatist who is in

---

[1] When he was still merely the King of Navarre, he declared with justifiable pride in a proclamation: "Who can reproach the King of Navarre with having ever broken his word?"

the habit of resorting to falsehood ceases to inspire confidence and at once loses the greater part of his authority.

A policy based upon immorality is antiquated and unworthy of modern society; it pre-supposes contempt for humanity, and an antagonism that ought not to exist between those who govern and those who are governed. The policy of free peoples ought not to resemble the policy of absolute sovereigns; it is founded upon the respect of legality.

Whatever the sceptics may say, craft and violence are not necessities of politics. As society becomes more enlightened, politics may attain to greater perfection. Corruption is not an indispensable method of government; liberty can exist without license. It is allowable to hope for a state of things in which the administration will be impartial, the legislation equitable, the elections sincere, and in which industry and merit will be rewarded. The European Governments show better faith in respect to their financial engagements at the present day than in the past; they are conscious that it is to their interest not to tamper with their coinage, and not to go bankrupt, and for the reason that public confidence in their credit is their principal force. Why should they not arrive at understanding that they ought to have the same respect for liberty and human life as for the public debt?

The progress of public reasonableness is most of all to be counted upon to render politics more straightforward and more in accordance with equity. Politicians, assemblies, and sovereigns, knowing that they will be called upon to give an exact account of their conduct before the tribunal of public opinion, will become more circumspect in the employment of expedients of a kind to arouse public indignation. Politics should serve an educational purpose as well as maintain order and protect material interests. Men are governed by ideas and sentiments as well as by appeals to their interests and to force. A lofty sentiment does not spoil politics. The great advances made in the sphere of politics have been advances of a philosophical order and have been due to an application of Christian philosophy. Unprincipled politics are Pagan politics, and their result is not the progress of society. The true policy consists in an application of reason to the affairs of the State.

Scepticism has brought into existence at the present day a generation of politicians who set more store upon palpable realities than upon principles. A policy of expedients and of vulgar satisfactions is the outcome of scepticism. The change that has taken place in our political morals has deep and remote causes. A people that used to be chivalrous, that despised money, that was fired with ardour for noble causes, now for political liberty, now for military glory, does not become positively sceptical, indifferent to principles, and attached to material interests in a day. This change of character is the result of the numerous deceptions it has experienced, of the frequent revolutions it has undergone, but also of the weakening of spiritual beliefs.

"When a republic is corrupt," says Montesquieu, "none of the evils that crop up can be remedied, except by removing the corruption and reinstating principles; any other corrective is useless or a fresh evil."[1] The suppression of the parliamentary régime would not be a remedy, the establishment of a dictatorship would be a fresh evil and a worse evil. The true remedy consists in a return to principles. Politics, like human life, need to be spiritualised unless they are to fall into the mire and to remain there. To change the persons composing the political world would be insufficient, unless a moral reform be effected at the same time. Clearly if the new politicians were as devoid of principles as the old, all that would have been done would have been to exchange fat for lean kine, who in turn would wish to wax fat. Between fatted sceptics and lean sceptics the difference is but slight, or if there be any difference it is rather in favour of the former. Obviously satiated sceptics are less dangerous than sceptics whose appetites are keen, because it may be hoped that, having looked after their own interests, they will at last look after those of the country. This, according to Saint Simon, was the cynical remark made by Maison when the direction of the finances was taken from him. "They are making a mistake,"

---

[1] "Esprit des Lois," Bk. VIII., ch. xii.

he exclaimed, "for I had looked after my own interests and was going to look after theirs."

A return to principles and moral beliefs and the substitution of ideas for appetites are, in consequence, the true remedies for that hideous malady political corruption. It is only in the power of great passions to drive petty passions from the field. As long as noble sentiments, love of country and of liberty and purifying beliefs, are not revived in a country the parliamentary atmosphere will remain vitiated.

Doubtless to exercise authority it is not sufficient to be above reproach; a clear intellect, tact, and experience are necessary. Talent, however, without morality is insufficient, and mere intelligence is no preservative against moral backslidings. Nobody would entrust his daughters or his fortune to the care of a clever but dissolute and extravagant man. Why then confide the country and the public fortune to the care of men of pleasure, who easily develop into men whose sole concern is money? When a money- and pleasure-loving man declares himself a friend of the people, who can believe in his sincerity? Affection is not proved by words, but by acts. The true sentiments of politicians are not to be judged by their professions of faith or their humanitarian speeches, but by their character and their habitual conduct. The probity expected of the head of a Government involves not only his own personal integrity, but the choice on his part of men of integrity for his Ministers. "If we would pass for men of integrity," says Cicero, "we should not only display probity ourselves, but exact it of those about us."[1]

Statesmen would avoid many political errors if they were more respectful of justice; their political errors are often moral errors; their good sense and their skilfulness suffer in proportion as they swerve from the dictates of equity; they abandon themselves to passions that cloud their intelligence. Just ideas and wise resolutions are inspired by an upright conscience, whose qualities influence the intelligence. To be a man of good sense it is sufficient to be an honest man.

By again becoming moral, politics would be brought back into unison with common-sense, and would be cured of two serious diseases called the Socialist madness and the Anarchist madness that are the result of the sophisms by which we are inundated, and of the letting loose of evil passions. We lack reasonableness at the present day; our brains are disordered; our good sense, a quality that used to be particularly distinctive of the French, has been affected by innumerable philosophical, economical, and political sophisms that reach us from Germany, Italy, England, the East, and even from India. Good sense has ceased to guide our thoughts and actions since we have adopted German pessimism and socialism, English evolutionism, Italian scepticism, Russian Nihilism, and Asiatic Buddhism. Let us become Frenchmen again and Christians,

---

[1] "Second Speech against Verres," Bk. II., § 10.

let us return to the school of good sense and morality.

The malady from which contemporary society suffers is a moral disease rather than a political or economical disease. It is doubtless useful to improve institutions and to reform abuses, but how much more necessary it is to reform morals and to give tone to men's minds by healthy ideas and moral beliefs. If society is to be saved from the corruption by which it is invaded, and from the revolutionary barbarism by which it is threatened, spiritualist teachings must be restored to the place they formerly occupied in men's minds and in politics; this is the only way to save them from the clutches of envy and hatred.

The sentiment of duty and of personal responsibility must be re-established in the public mind and in the education of the young. It is necessary to fight against the sophisms which lead to the absorption of the individual by the State, and to the conversion of every citizen into a part of a colossal machine that produces wealth and distributes it according to each man's needs. The true remedy for the crises we are traversing is a return to the old morality, which teaches that working-men in common with their employers are intended to do their duty, and to labour, and have their responsibilities. What other doctrine will teach the rich the spirit of sacrifice, and the voluntary renunciation of what is superfluous, and the poor the obligation of personal effort, the merit of patience, and respect for legality?

It is not by encouraging atheism and materialism that a Government effects an improvement in morals, that it stills passions and relieves wretchedness. Hostility to religion is contrary to sound politics. Merely from the utilitarian point of view the blindness and perversity are incomparable of those incredulous fanatics who would rob their fellows of the beliefs in which they find consolation. Who can deny that the religious sentiment conduces to morality? The more religious citizens there are in a State, the fewer are the restless spirits, the Socialists and the Anarchists. In a period of scepticism, materialism, positivism, evolutionism, and nihilism, who can dream of denying the immense services rendered by Christianity in inculcating the dignity of human nature and the obligatory character of duty, and in opposing the worship of an ideal to the worship of the golden calf? In a society in which there is talk of nothing else but of the struggle for life, of the rights conferred by might, of the elimination of the weak, of the disgrace of poverty, of the all-powerfulness of wealth, religion teaches self-sacrifice, respect, and love for the poor, and responsibility before God and before the conscience. At a period in which Socialism, grown more and more threatening, demands that the State should be omnipotent, Christianity again performs a useful work in standing out for the rights of the human being and the rights of the conscience, and in setting limits to the action of the State. If spiritual beliefs were not regaining their hold over men's minds one would be forced to tremble for the future of society, for "there comes a day when truths that have been scorned announce themselves by thunder-claps."[1]

Nations, too, in their mutual relations, have every interest not to separate politics from morality. A sound policy, no less than morality, dictates to them justice and charitableness, which are alone capable of preserving peace and with it the benefits it carries in its train. The policy that teaches nations that they should envy, hate, and injure each other, that their conduct should be solely guided by their interests, and that the difficulties that crop up between them should be settled by force alone, such a policy is criminal and mistaken. The statesmen who counsel this narrow and egoistical, this envious and malevolent policy, are shortsighted, they are merely alive to the interests of the moment that are a source of division, but they are blind to the interests which the peoples have in common, and above all to the disastrous consequences of antagonism and war; they do not keep in view the benefits of peace and the horrors of war.

How far preferable to an envious and ambitious policy that divides nations would be a just, friendly, and moderate policy that would bring them together! How far happier the nations would be if they would cease to lend themselves to a revengeful and high-handed policy! What a pitch of prosperity Europe would have reached if,

[1] E. Augier, "La Contagion," Act IV., scene iv.

realising the project of Henry IV., it had applied to politics the rules of good sense and Christian morality. The aspect of the world would be changed if the nations, considering themselves members of the same family, would banish violence and craft from their councils. The policy of Christian peoples is still Pagan: it must become Christian if the world is to enjoy peace.

Carried away by his somewhat excessive enthusiasm for military glory, M. Thiers has remarked: "What purpose would the strength of nations serve if it were not expended in attempts to gain the mastery over each other?" It seems to me, however, that the strength of nations might be more usefully employed than in realising dreams of conquest, which are so dearly paid for in money and blood, and which end in disasters and catastrophes. Every time that a nation has sought to conquer other nations, it has caused torrents of blood to flow without profit to itself. All those who have entertained dreams of conquest have met with failure. To establish their supremacy Charles V. and Napoleon I. caused millions of men to perish, and they were unable to attain their goal: the former died in a convent, the latter on the rocks of Saint Helena; Spain and France were ruined by their ambitious policy. To how many conquerors may not these words of the Bible be applied: "The hammer that shattered the nations of the universe has itself been broken in pieces."

A policy that aims at international equilibrium

is better than a policy of conquest.[1] Empires that are too vast cannot last; they succumb, sooner or later, to a coalition between the other nations. That one nation should rule over another is always a danger to the common liberty, for a nation that is too powerful, like a too powerful sovereign, has a difficulty in keeping within the limits of a wise moderation. If the desire for domination be of value as a motive force in politics, why should not moral domination achieved through science, literature, and institutions be made the object of the activity of nations?

Sceptics are disposed to smile when they hear moralists express the hope that international wars will cease, and that arbitration will take the place of recourse to force. Lord Salisbury, however, who at one time considered this hope a dream, is now of opinion that it is realisable. "Civilisation," he has said, "has substituted law court decisions for duels between private persons and conflicts between the great. International wars are destined in the same way to give place to the courts of arbitration of a more advanced civilisation."[2] In 1883 Switzerland and the

[1] "I have persistently shown myself to be hostile to conquest; I was not even willing, at the time of our greatest military prosperity, that we should make the Rhine the limit of our territory." ("Exposé de la Conduite Politique de M. Carnot," p. 50.)

[2] Speech delivered at Hastings, May 18, 1892. I borrow this quotation from a very interesting paper by M. Arthur Desjardins ("Académie des Sciences Morales et Politiques," July, 1892). Henry IV., who was in no way a dreamer, had considered possible the substitution of arbitration for the employment of force, and the constitution of a European confederation.

United States pledged themselves to submit to a court of arbitration all difficulties arising between them during a period of thirty years. In 1888 France contracted a similar engagement with the Equatorial Republic. In 1890 the plenipotentiaries of seventeen American Republics, assembled at Washington, admitted the principle of permanent arbitration.

It may be hoped, in consequence, that war will become rarer and rarer in proportion to the progress of civilisation and of the moral and economical solidarity existing between different nations. The new engines of war, the destructive force of which augments every day, also contribute to the maintenance of peace, because peoples and sovereigns recoil in terror from the frightful consequences of a war waged with such formidable engines of destruction. The tendency of public opinion is more and more to compel Governments to maintain peace. It may be hoped in consequence that war, which is already more civilised, will become of rarer occurrence.

Sully, whom this idea had caused to smile in the first instance, ended by esteeming it possible. "I remember," he says, "that the first time I heard the King discuss a political system by which all Europe might be divided and governed like a family, I scarcely listened to the Prince. Thinking that he only spoke in this way to amuse himself, or perhaps to have the honour of having profounder and more acute opinions upon politics than ordinary men, my answer assumed partly a jesting tone, partly a tone of compliment. . . . I was convinced at the finish that, however disproportioned the means might seem to the end, a series of years during which every act, whether in connection with negotiations, finances, or the remaining necessary matters, should constantly be made to bear upon the object in view, would smooth away many difficulties."

Still, as peoples and sovereigns have a tendency to become intoxicated by success, historians and moralists ought to unite their efforts to combat their unruly impulses. Historians, who habitually admire success, too often forget, when narrating wars, to inquire into their morality and utility; they almost always exalt the conquerors, and in this way corrupt public opinion, by accustoming it to allow itself to be dazzled by success. They should keep a little of the admiration they lavish upon conquerors for the upright men who have given evidence of their love of humanity and of their respect for human life.

As to the moralists, it is necessary that they should unceasingly combat the sophisms of immoral politics by declaring that reasons of State are the negation of reason; that the object of government is not to divide but to unite; that the lesser morality does not destroy the higher morality, because there are not two moralities; that public safety lies in justice alone; that the end does not justify the means; that illegitimate means result in the end being unattained; that right is superior to might; that justice is the supreme law; that the maxim that right is on the side of the strongest is a maxim good enough for wolves but not for men.

Science without conscience, Rabelais has said, is the ruin of the soul. Politics without morality are the ruin of society.

THE END.

D. APPLETON AND COMPANY'S PUBLICATIONS.

THE CRIMINOLOGY SERIES.
Edited by W. Douglas Morrison.

CRIMINAL SOCIOLOGY. By Professor E. Ferri. 12mo. Cloth, $1.50.

"A most valuable book. It is suggestive of reforms and remedies, it is reasonable and temperate, and it contains a world of information and well-arranged facts for those interested in or merely observant of one of the great questions of the day."—*Philadelphia Public Ledger.*

"The scientist, the humanitarian, and the student will find much to indorse and to adopt, while the layman will wonder why such a book was not written years ago."—*Newark Advertiser.*

THE FEMALE OFFENDER. By Professor Lombroso. Illustrated. 12mo. Cloth, $1.50.

"'The Female Offender' must be considered as a very valuable addition to scientific literature. . . . It is not alone to the scientist that the work will recommend itself. The humanitarian, anxious for the reform of the habitual criminal, will find in its pages many valuable suggestions."—*Philadelphia Item.*

"This work will undoubtedly be a valuable addition to the works on criminology, and may also prove of inestimable help in the prevention of crime."—*Detroit Free Press.*

"The book is a very valuable one, and admirably adapted for general reading."—*Boston Home Journal.*

"This book will probably constitute one of the most valuable contributions in aid of a nineteenth century sign of advanced civilization known as prison reform."—*Cincinnati Times-Star.*

"There is no book of recent issue that bears such important relation to the great subject of criminology as this book."—*New Haven Leader.*

OUR JUVENILE OFFENDERS. By W. Douglas Morrison, author of "Jews under the Romans," etc. 12mo. Cloth, $1.50.

"An admirable work on one of the most vital questions of the day. . . . By scientists, as well as by all others who are interested in the welfare of humanity, it will be welcomed as a most valuable and a most timely contribution to the all-important science of criminology."—*New York Herald.*

"Of real value to scientific literature. In its pages humanitarians will find much to arrest their attention and direct their energies in the interest of those of the young who have gone astray."—*Boston Daily Globe.*

IN PREPARATION.

CRIME A SOCIAL STUDY. By Professor Joly.

CRIMINAL ANTHROPOLOGY. By Dr. J. Dallemagne.

D. APPLETON AND COMPANY, NEW YORK.

D. APPLETON AND COMPANY'S PUBLICATIONS.

***D**EGENERATION.* By Professor MAX NORDAU. Translated from the second edition of the German work. 8vo. Cloth, $3.50.

"A powerful, trenchant, savage attack on all the leading literary and artistic idols of the time by a man of great intellectual power, immense range of knowledge, and the possessor of a lucid style rare among German writers, and becoming rarer everywhere, owing to the very influences which Nordau attacks with such unsparing energy, such eager hatred."—*London Chronicle.*

"The wit and learning, the literary skill and the scientific method, the righteous indignation, and the ungoverned prejudice displayed in Herr Max Nordau's treatise on 'Degeneration,' attracted to it, on its first appearance in Germany, an attention that was partly admiring and partly astonished."—*London Standard.*

"Let us say at once that the English-reading public should be grateful for an English rendering of Max Nordau's polemic. It will provide society with a subject that may last as long as the present Government. . . . We read the pages without finding one dull, sometimes in reluctant agreement, sometimes with amused content, sometimes with angry indignation."—*London Saturday Review.*

"Herr Nordau's book fills a void, not merely in the systems of Lombroso, as he says, but in all existing systems of English and American criticism with which we are acquainted. It is not literary criticism, pure and simple, though it is not lacking in literary qualities of a high order, but it is something which has long been needed. . . . A great book, which every thoughtful lover of art and literature and every serious student of sociology and morality should read carefully and ponder slowly and wisely."—*Richard Henry Stoddard, in the Mail and Express.*

"The book is one of more than ordinary interest. Nothing just like it has ever been written. Agree or disagree with its conclusions, wholly or in part, no one can fail to recognize the force of its argument and the timeliness of its injunctions."—*Chicago Evening Post.*

***G**ENIUS AND DEGENERATION.* A Study in Psychology. By Dr. WILLIAM HIRSCH. Translated from the second edition of the German work. Uniform with "Degeneration." Large 8vo. Cloth, $3.50.

"The first intelligent, rational, and scientific study of a great subject. . . . In the development of his argument Dr. Hirsch frequently finds it necessary to attack the positions assumed by Nordau and Lombroso, his two leading adversaries. . . . Only calm and sober reason endure. Dr. Hirsch possesses that calmness and sobriety. His work will find a permanent place among the authorities of science."—*N. Y. Herald.*

"Dr. Hirsch's researches are intended to bring the reader to the conviction that 'no psychological meaning can be attached to the word genius.' . . . While all men of genius have common traits, they are not traits characteristic of genius; they are such as are possessed by other men, and more or less by all men. . . . Dr. Hirsch believes that most of the great men, both of art and of science, were misunderstood by their contemporaries, and were only appreciated after they were dead."—*Miss J. L. Gilder, in the Sunday World.*

"'Genius and Degeneration' ought to be read by every man and woman who professes to keep in touch with modern thought. It is deeply interesting, and so full of information that by intellectual readers it will be seized upon with avidity."—*Buffalo Commercial.*

D. APPLETON AND COMPANY, NEW YORK.

D. APPLETON & CO.'S PUBLICATIONS.

NEW EDITION OF PROF. HUXLEY'S ESSAYS.

COLLECTED ESSAYS. By THOMAS H. HUXLEY. New complete edition, with revisions, the Essays being grouped according to general subject. In nine volumes, a new Introduction accompanying each volume. 12mo. Cloth, $1.25 per volume.

VOL. I.—METHOD AND RESULTS.
VOL. II.—DARWINIANA.
VOL. III.—SCIENCE AND EDUCATION.
VOL. IV.—SCIENCE AND HEBREW TRADITION.
VOL. V.—SCIENCE AND CHRISTIAN TRADITION.
VOL. VI.—HUME.
VOL. VII.—MAN'S PLACE IN NATURE.
VOL. VIII.—DISCOURSES, BIOLOGICAL AND GEOLOGICAL.
VOL. IX.—EVOLUTION AND ETHICS, AND OTHER ESSAYS.

"Mr. Huxley has covered a vast variety of topics during the last quarter of a century. It gives one an agreeable surprise to look over the tables of contents and note the immense territory which he has explored. To read these books carefully and studiously is to become thoroughly acquainted with the most advanced thought on a large number of topics."—*New York Herald.*

"The series will be a welcome one. There are few writings on the more abstruse problems of science better adapted to reading by the general public, and in this form the books will be well in the reach of the investigator. . . . The revisions are the last expected to be made by the author, and his introductions are none of earlier date than a few months ago [1893], so they may be considered his final and most authoritative utterances."—*Chicago Times.*

"It was inevitable that his essays should be called for in a completed form, and they will be a source of delight and profit to all who read them. He has always commanded a hearing, and as a master of the literary style in writing scientific essays he is worthy of a place among the great English essayists of the day. This edition of his essays will be widely read, and gives his scientific work a permanent form."—*Boston Herald.*

"A man whose brilliancy is so constant as that of Prof. Huxley will always command readers; and the utterances which are here collected are not the least in weight and luminous beauty of those with which the author has long delighted the reading world."—*Philadelphia Press.*

"The connected arrangement of the essays which their reissue permits brings into fuller relief Mr Huxley's masterly powers of exposition. Sweeping the subject-matter clear of all logomachies, he lets the light of common day fall upon it. He shows that the place of hypothesis in science, as the starting point of verification of the phenomena to be explained, is but an extension of the assumptions which underlie actions in every-day affairs; and that the method of scientific investigation is only the method which rules the ordinary business of life."—*London Chronicle.*

New York: D. APPLETON & CO., 72 Fifth Avenue.

D. APPLETON AND COMPANY'S PUBLICATIONS.

MISCELLANEOUS WORKS OF HERBERT SPENCER.

SOCIAL STATICS. New and revised edition, including "The Man *versus* The State." A series of essays on political tendencies heretofore published separately. 12mo. 420 pages. Cloth, $2.00.

"Mr. Spencer has thoroughly studied the issues which are behind the social and political life of our own time, not exactly those issues which are discussed in Parliament or in Congress, but the principles of all modern government, which are slowly changing in response to the broader industrial and general development of human experience. One will obtain no suggestions out of his book for guiding a political party or carrying a point in economics, but he will find the principles of sociology, as they pertain to the whole of life, better stated in these pages than he can find them expressed anywhere else It is in this sense that this work is important and fresh and vitalizing. It goes constantly to the foundation of things."—*Boston Herald.*

VARIOUS FRAGMENTS. 12mo. Cloth, $1.25.

Along with a considerable variety of other matter, these "Fragments" include a number of replies to criticisms, among which will be found some of the best specimens of Mr. Spencer's controversial writings, notably his letter to the London *Athenæum* on Professor Huxley's famous address on Evolutionary Ethics. His views on copyright, national and international, "Social Evolution and Social Duty," and "Anglo-American Arbitration," also form a part of the contents.

EDUCATION: Intellectual, Moral, and Physical. 12mo. Paper, 50 cents; cloth, $1.25.

CONTENTS: What Knowledge is of most Worth? Intellectual Education. Moral Education. Physical Education.

THE STUDY OF SOCIOLOGY. The fifth volume in the International Scientific Series. 12mo. Cloth, $1.50.

CONTENTS: Our need of it. Is there a Social Science? Nature of the Social Science. Difficulties of the Social Science. Objective Difficulties. Subjective Difficulties, Intellectual. Subjective Difficulties, Emotional. The Educational Bias. The Bias of Patriotism. The Class Bias. The Political Bias. The Theological Bias. Discipline. Preparation in Biology. Preparation in Psychology. Conclusion.

THE INADEQUACY OF "NATURAL SELECTION." 12mo. Paper, 30 cents.

This essay, in which Professor Weismann's theories are criticised, is reprinted from the *Contemporary Review*, and comprises a forcible presentation of Mr. Spencer's views upon the general subject indicated in the title.

D. APPLETON AND COMPANY, NEW YORK.

D. APPLETON & CO.'S PUBLICATIONS.

HYPNOTISM, MESMERISM, AND THE NEW WITCHCRAFT. By ERNEST HART, formerly Surgeon to the West London Hospital, and Ophthalmic Surgeon to St. Mary's Hospital, London. New edition, enlarged and revised. With new chapters on "The Eternal Gullible" and "The Hypnotism of Trilby." 12mo. Cloth, $1.50.

"Mr. Hart holds it as proved beyond all reasonable doubt that the hypnotic condition is an admitted clinical fact, and declares that the practice of hypnotism, except by skilled physicians, should be forbidden. He affirms its therapeutic uselessness, and condemns the practice because of the possibilities of social mischiefs. . . . His personal experiences in the 'New Witchcraft' enable him to exercise a critical check on the wild theories and unsupported assertions of others."—*Philadelphia Ledger.*

MESMERISM, SPIRITUALISM, ETC., HISTORICALLY AND SCIENTIFICALLY CONSIDERED. By WILLIAM B. CARPENTER, M. D., F. R. S. 12mo. Cloth, $1.25.

"The reader of these lectures will see that my whole aim is to discover, on the generally accepted principles of testimony, what *are* facts; and to discriminate between facts and the inferences drawn from them. I have no other 'theory' to support than that of the constancy of the well-ascertained laws of Nature."—*From the Preface.*

PRINCIPLES OF MENTAL PHYSIOLOGY. With their Application to the Training and Discipline of the Mind, and the Study of its Morbid Conditions. By WILLIAM B. CARPENTER, M. D., F. R. S. 12mo. Cloth, $3.00.

"Among the numerous eminent writers this country has produced none are more deserving of praise for having attempted to apply the results of physiological research to the explanation of the mutual relations of the mind and body than Dr. Carpenter."—*London Lancet.*

NATURE AND MAN: Essays, Scientific and Philosophical. By WILLIAM B. CARPENTER, M. D., F. R. S. With an Introductory Memoir by J. ESTLIN CARPENTER, M. A., and a Portrait. 12mo. Cloth, $2.25.

"Few works could be mentioned that give a better general view of the change that has been wrought in men's conceptions of life and Nature. For this, if for nothing else the collection would be valuable. But it will be welcomed also as a kind of biography of its author, for the essays and the memoir support one another and are mutually illuminative."—*Scotsman.*

"Mr. Estlin Carpenter's memoir of his father is just what such a memoir should be—a simple record of a life uneventful in itself, whose interest for us lies mainly in the nature of the intellectual task so early undertaken, so strenuously carried on, so amply and nobly accomplished, to which it was devoted."—*London Spectator.*

New York: D. APPLETON & CO., 72 Fifth Avenue.

D. APPLETON AND COMPANY'S PUBLICATIONS.

JAMES SULLY'S WORKS.

STUDIES OF CHILDHOOD. 8vo. Cloth, $2.50.

An ideal popular scientific book. These studies proceed on sound scientific lines in accounting for the mental manifestations of children, yet they require the reader to follow no laborious train of reasoning; and the reader who is in search of entertainment merely will find it in the quaint sayings and doings with which the volume abounds.

CHILDREN'S WAYS. Being Selections from the Author's "Studies of Childhood," and some additional matter. 12mo. Cloth, $1.50.

This work is mainly a condensation of the author's previous book, "Studies of Childhood," but considerable new matter is added. The material that Mr. Sully supplies is the most valuable of recent contributions on the psychological phases of child study.

TEACHER'S HAND-BOOK OF PSYCHOLOGY. On the Basis of "Outlines of Psychology." Abridged by the Author for the use of Teachers, Schools, Reading Circles, and Students generally. Fourth edition, rewritten and enlarged. 12mo. Cloth, $1.50.

"The present edition has been carefully revised throughout, largely rewritten, and enlarged by about fifty pages. While seeking to preserve the original character of the book as an *introduction*, I have felt it necessary, in view of the fact that our best training colleges for secondary teachers are now making a serious study of psychology, to amplify somewhat and bring up to date the exposition of scientific principles. I have also touched upon those recent developments of experimental psychology which have concerned themselves with the measurement of the simpler mental processes, and which promise to have important educational results by supplying accurate tests of children's abilities."—*From the Author's Preface.*

OUTLINES OF PSYCHOLOGY, with Special Reference to the Theory of Education. A Text-Book for Colleges. Crown 8vo. Cloth, $3.00.

ILLUSIONS. A Psychological Study. 12mo, 372 pages. Cloth, $1.50.

PESSIMISM. A History and a Criticism. Second edition. 8vo, 470 pages and Index. Cloth, $4.00.

THE HUMAN MIND. A Text-Book of Psychology. Two volumes. 8vo. Cloth, $5.00.

D. APPLETON AND COMPANY, NEW YORK.

www.ingramcontent.com/pod-product-compliance
Lightning Source LLC
Chambersburg PA
CBHW030357230426
43664CB00007BB/632